D1400211

Unfinished Work

Unfinished Work

THE STRUGGLE TO BUILD AN AGING AMERICAN WORKFORCE

JOSEPH COLEMAN

OXFORD
UNIVERSITY PRESS

OXFORD
UNIVERSITY PRESS

Oxford University Press is a department of the University of
Oxford. It furthers the University's objective of excellence in research,
scholarship, and education by publishing worldwide.

Oxford   New York
Auckland   Cape Town   Dar es Salaam   Hong Kong   Karachi
Kuala Lumpur   Madrid   Melbourne   Mexico City   Nairobi
New Delhi   Shanghai   Taipei   Toronto

With offices in
Argentina   Austria   Brazil   Chile   Czech Republic   France   Greece
Guatemala   Hungary   Italy   Japan   Poland   Portugal   Singapore
South Korea   Switzerland   Thailand   Turkey   Ukraine   Vietnam

Oxford is a registered trademark of Oxford University Press
in the UK and certain other countries.

Published in the United States of America by
Oxford University Press
198 Madison Avenue, New York, NY 10016

Library of Congress Cataloging-in-Publication Data
Coleman, Joseph, 1963–
Unfinished work : the struggle to build an aging American workforce / Joseph Coleman.
pages cm
Includes bibliographical references and index.
ISBN 978–0–19–997445–0 (hardback)
1. Older people—Employment—United States.   2. Older people—Employment.   3. Population
aging—United States.   4. Population aging.   5. Manpower planning—United
States.   6. Manpower planning.   I. Title.
HD6280.C555 2015
331.3'980973—dc23
2014024998

9 8 7 6 5 4 3 2 1
Printed in the United States of America
on acid-free paper

For Rose,
who raised me with her labor

Contents

Acknowledgments

Writing a book is at once the loneliest of tasks and one of the most social. This one would not have been conceived, reported, or written without the help of many. So many, in fact, that my greatest regret is that I will fail to name them all. Any errors are my own.

My first thanks go to the people who opened their workplaces, their thinking, and their lives to me for no better reason than to help a journalist attempting to write his first book. These are the people who populate these pages.

In Japan, this includes the people at Yamashita Kogyosho, Kato Kogyosho, Sanyo Tekko, Koreisha, Tokyo Job Center, Irodori, and the many people I spoke to on Okikamuro island. Special thanks to Tsuneko Hariki, Tomoji Yokoishi, Hiroyuki Fujii, Atsushi Seike, Tomoyo Takagi, Tetsuro Kawauchi, Tatsuto Yamashita, Kiyoto Yamashita, Jiro Kunimura, Hirohisa Matsumoto, Shouji Matsumoto, Kumiko Watanabe, Takashi Suzuki, Makiko Miyoshi, Keiji Kato, Florian Coulmas and Susumu Okada. Chiaki Kitada was a patient and resourceful assistant for my work in Japan.

In France, I thank everyone at Danh Tourisme, Aveva, and BiTWiiN. Special thanks to Michel Wattree, who taught me the attractions of Route 66. I also thank Josette Duede, Anne-Marie Guillemard, Serge Volkoff, Annie Jolivet, Philippe Thurat, Benedicte Gendron, Gerard Cornilleau, Bertrand Favre, and Michel Bocquet. I owe Bastien Inzaurralde for his invaluable assistance tracking down older workers and the companies that employ them.

In Sweden: everyone at TRR, Pensionärspoolen, and Arbetsförmedlingen were extremely helpful. My appreciation goes to Kjell-Åke Ericsson, Ann-Sofi Sjöberg, Louise Lagerling, Tord Strannefors, Seppo Rytkönen, Håkan Gustavsson, Ingemar Eriksson, Eskil Wadensjö, Anders Östebo, Roland Kadefors, Sabina Dubrowska, Patrik Magneby, Kenneth Kjörnsberg, Morgan Svensson, Linda Norman, and Claes-Göran Olaussson, to whom I offer a special thanks for believing for a few hours that I was indeed an incredibly youthful 63-year-old, rather than someone who'd been born in 1963. Jenny Soffel was supremely organized in her research assistance.

In the United States: Ron and Sue Dziuda, David Bachtel, Kelly Lapetino, Mary Gajcak, John Heinz, Kathy Auriemma, Sara Rix, Masa Higo, Laura Leonti, Tim Dutton, Paul Anderson, Bob Carter, Tom Esselman, Nancy Schlossburg, Kathy Black, James House, Ken Fougerousse, Glenn Glass, Jamie Burns, Lorraine Pagni-Kiefer, Kenn Curzon, Lisa Ohmstede, Chris Van Gorder, Veronica Zaman, and Vic Buzachero. Thanks as well to the folks at Mature Services in Akron: Rita Hall, Laurie Sibila, Chris Walker, Paul Mangus, Don Zirkle, David DeShon, Sue Dukeman, and Vanessa Claxton. A special thanks to Julie Cotton, who not only told me about her own life, but also was exceedingly generous with her address book as I attempted to wrap my head around Sarasota.

I've had valuable financial and logistical support from Japan's Center for Global Partnership and the New York-based Social Science Research Council. Abe Fellowships in 2009 and 2011–12 paid for the extensive travel involved in this book. I also enlisted the invaluable help of Mary McDonnell, Nicole Restrick-Levit, Takuya Toda-Ozaki, Fernando Rojas, and Frank Baldwin. Without the Abe, this book would not have been possible. For this support I am forever grateful.

My colleagues at Indiana University have also provided strong backing for this project. I'd like to thank Lesa Hatley-Major, Bonnie Brownlee, and Michael Evans for helping me make some room among my duties to complete this project, and friends among the faculty who have been generous with words of encouragement and advice. A special thanks to Brad Hamm for bringing me to Indiana in the first place, a move that was instrumental in translating this book from a vague idea in my head into printed words on the page.

I appreciate the kind attention of Terry Vaughn at Oxford University Press for taking on this project initially. Oxford editors Scott Parris and Cathryn Vaulman have been supportive, generous, and patient throughout the process. Thanks to my agent, Jessica Papin, of Dystel & Goderich Literary Management, who saw the possibilities in this project in its beginning stages, and helped coax it ahead from proposal to completion. I am grateful for the efforts of Augustine Leo and Jerry Altobelli to turn a manuscript into a book.

My admired friend and colleague Tom French has helped me from the very beginning with every kind of support imaginable, always with great generosity, imagination, and energy. Philip Taylor of Australia's Monash University was kind enough to point this stranger in the direction of some of the leading experts in this field around the world. Many thanks to Harvey Sterns of the University of Akron, who adopted me for a few days in Akron and allowed me to roam his extensive library. Former AP colleague Charles Hanley was, as always, unwavering in his encouragement.

Finally, I thank my family, Kyoko, Ema, and Sean, for inspiring and delighting me, and for putting up with my absences and obsessions.

Author's Note

This is a work of nonfiction journalism, based on reporting in the United States, Japan, France, and Sweden conducted between 2010 and 2014. Additional material was collected in Japan in 2005. All the names and details describing the people in this book are real. The events described here include scenes that I witnessed directly and those reconstructed from interviews with participants and examination of government documents, archival materials, and/or news footage. I have attempted to make clear throughout by context or footnotes whether I was present at certain events or not. Descriptions of subjects' thoughts are based on what they told me in interviews.

Unfinished Work

Introduction

The aging of the workforce in the advanced economies of North America, Europe, and East Asia has begun in earnest and will accelerate in coming decades. The transition so far has been messy: elderly poverty is growing and companies are struggling to adjust to the changing capabilities and needs of their workers. Older employees and job-seekers increasingly feel that their age is being held against them. Trained, energetic would-be older workers are frustrated by a job market that fails to take full advantage of their talents. Governments in the advanced industrial economies stretching from East Asia across North America to central Europe have in large part acknowledged that the "older worker issue" needs attention, and all are raising retirement ages. But their management of this shift varies widely: some governments are heavily invested in retraining older citizens and finding them work, while others are leaving the transition to the supply and demand of labor. All have faced mixed results.

The premise of this book is that we can do better. Preparing for and smoothing the path of the aging workforce of the future should be one of our leading priorities. Now we have the chance to put in place the policies and funding that will help retrain mid- and late-career workers so they can extend their viability and value as workers. We can encourage companies to reorganize their workplaces to adjust to older employees. We can redesign our outdated and threadbare retirement system—not to penalize workers for retiring early, but to make it easier, more profitable, and more comfortable to do what increasing numbers of people already do: work later in life.

Later retirement has become a necessity for many Americans. Scant savings, the decline of the company pension, and the overall failure of the 401 (k) system to replace it mean many of us won't have the money to retire. For some, working later in life is a choice. Growing numbers of people, still vital and ambitious into their 60s and later, will want to keep working as an outlet for their energy and talent. Still others will be drawn into longer worklives because they have skills and knowledge that are in growing demand in the labor market, and companies will make it worth their while to stick around. All but the wealthiest of us will be hemmed in by the declining ability of governments to finance retirement and health care.

There are several factors driving this transformation. Let's start with the most obvious: aging. The numbers are indisputable. In 1950, a little more than 200 million people in the world were aged 60 or over. That had increased to nearly 810 million by 2012, and was projected to skyrocket to 2 billion by mid-century. Demographers have forecast the aging of the planet's population for decades, and if any mistakes have been made, they have underestimated the acceleration of the graying. Societal aging ranks with climate change and energy, economic instability and the spread of nuclear weapons, as the planet's chief challenges for the coming century.

Two powerful engines are behind the aging trend. One is the unprecedented extension of lifetimes in the 20th century, abetted by the dramatic reduction in infant mortality, particularly in the industrialized countries of Europe, North America, and East Asia. Between 1970 and 2010, global male life expectancy soared from 56.4 years to 67.5 years, a gain of more than 11 years, according to the Global Burden of Disease Study 2010, published in *The Lancet*, a leading medical journal. Women gained even more, increasing from 61.2 to 73.3 in the same time frame. Lifetimes in industrialized countries far outstrip those global averages, reaching their pinnacle in Japan, where women live until they're 86, men until they're 80.

What that means, simply, is more old people. And this is a great achievement; as never before, the average citizen in wealthy nations—and even not-so-wealthy nations—can expect to live to an age our recent ancestors would only have dreamed of. We enjoy more birthdays, more graduation and wedding parties of our grandchildren—and great-grandchildren—and more years with beloved partners and family members than any generation before us.

And yet, it also means... well, more old people. More people taking retirement and pension benefits, more people requiring treatment for illnesses like heart disease, cancer, and Alzheimer's. More people needing astronomically expensive end-of-life care. More people depending on the young and middle-aged to work and generate the economic wealth needed to pay the bills to keep their elders fed, sheltered, and healthy.

If only there were all those young people to pay for it. Over the past half-century, the wealthy world has discovered a difficult truth: people in rich industrialized countries make fewer babies. Science has given us birth control. Growing gender equality—and the needs of the capitalist economy—have allowed women to study and work rather than marry and have families at a young age. Housing and educating children are expensive, particularly in cities. Incentives have changed: Children generate income on the farm, but they consume it in the city. So our urbanized societies have fewer of them. Demographers say the fertility rate—the number of babies per woman—needs to be at least 2.1 to keep a population steady. Rise above that, and the population will increase; drop below it, and the population will decrease. In East Asia and parts of Europe, fertility rates have been below 2.1 for many years, dipping as low as 1.2 or 1.3 at times in Germany, Italy, and Japan. Global fertility has dropped 14 percent since 1995, from 2.8 to 2.4, according to the U.S. Census Bureau. Population growth has more or less stalled in Japan, and the government expects a steep decline in the number of Japanese over the next century. What all this means, simply, is that the older population is growing more quickly than the working population, particularly in developed countries. Japan currently is the only country where people aged 60 or over make up 30 percent of the population. By mid-century, such countries are forecast to number 64.

Now, all of this might be more manageable, if only it hadn't happened so quickly, in just a few short decades after World War II.

And if it weren't for the boomers.

After the wholesale slaughter and destruction of 1939–45, soldiers came home across Europe and North America and Japan and focused on what young people do when they're not busy killing each other or cowering in air raid shelters: they had kids. In astounding numbers. The population boom that accompanied the economic expansion of the postwar years remade the world. Boomers brought us rock music and women's liberation and a consumer culture that shocked and outraged their elders. They also constituted a massive demographic bubble. In the United States alone, there are more than 70 million baby boomers. This population expansion worked well enough in the first few decades after the war: plenty of kids in the 1950s and 1960s to buy records and go to movies and flood universities, plenty of adults in the 1970s and 1980s and 1990s to buy cars and houses, and power factories and Wall Street and technological change. They had the best of conditions—they were more numerous than the old people they had to take care of, and they didn't have too many children to put through college. All the while, they consumed unprecedented amounts of education and training, and developed the technical skills and knowledge at the core of the workforce.

But now they are getting older, and the rest of us face a quandary. What happens if they all empty out of the economy, taking their skills, education, knowledge—and tax revenues—with them? Persistently high unemployment rates in North America and Europe suggest there are not enough jobs and too many job-seekers, but studies have shown we may also be suffering from a mismatch in the labor market. The economy needs *more* highly educated workers than we are producing, not fewer. The McKinsey Global Institute published a report in June 2012 forecasting a shortage of up to 18 million college-educated workers in advanced nations by 2020. It appears the last thing we want to do is hussle boomers with bachelor's and master's degrees out the door into retirement.

The other question is: who will pay for the ever-increasing years out of the workforce? Social Security is estimated to be flush enough to pay full benefits for the next 20 years without reform, but then payouts are expected to drop to 75 percent, as the growth of beneficiaries outpaces the growth of contributors and the Social Security trust fund runs dry. Some have estimated that the single step of raising the minimum retirement age to 70 would yield about $30 billion in savings over the next 20 years. Medicare, the government-run health care system for the elderly, faces much starker financial challenges as the boomer generation moves into old age. Certainly there are more ways to reform Social Security to ensure its survival: raising the cap on income subject to Social Security tax, say, or cutting benefits to wealthier retirees. Economists say more years on the job, even just a few, could buoy these systems by allowing workers to postpone the drawdown of benefits while paying into the system for a longer time, and many governments, including that of the United States, are making their citizens wait longer to get their state pensions.

But Social Security is only part of the picture. It's no secret that the retirement-to-grave company pension has become a thing of the past. In 1975, more than half—58 percent—of private sector workers with company retirement plans had traditional, defined-benefit pensions—the kind that you get from your company more or less for free, with guaranteed payments until you die, sometimes with reduced benefits for surviving spouses. Real security. Not for everybody, but for most private sector workers, many of them in the middle class. By 2005, the proportion of those with traditional pensions had fallen to 33 percent, according to the National Institute on Retirement Security. And it kept falling. The 2012 National Study of Employers showed that portion had fallen to 22 percent. Now it's clear we're eliminating this pension system without an adequate replacement. So-called defined contribution plans—that is, the 401 (k) and similar vehicles—have solved the problems of corporations by foisting the responsibility for retirement largely on the individual. But they haven't been so great for individuals themselves. Employees preoccupied with paying today's bills have not focused on distant retirement: enrollment is lacking, participants don't put enough money into the accounts, and they don't invest as wisely as pension-account managers. And then, of course, something like the Great Recession can come along and wipe out investments just as participants are about to embark on retirement.

But this book is not only about finances. And it's not a call to balance our budgets on the backs of older workers. At the center of our discussion is a question contained within the more prosaic concerns of labor markets or entitlement programs: what are we to do with the extra years that science has given us? Can we create greater meaning for our lives in those additional years? How can we go about doing that? As we'll see in these pages, for many of us, the answer can be found in the same activity that has given shape to our lives thus far: our work.

It's already happening.

Over the past decade or so, people across the industrialized world have begun working later in life at an increasing pace. In 2002, 13.2 percent of Americans aged 65 and older were in the labor force. By 2012, that percentage had increased by more than a third to 18.5, and is forecast to surge further to 23 percent by 2022. This trend and the flexibility of the more freewheeling labor market in the United

States have made our country one of the world leaders in elderly employment. Similar trends among older workers are found in the developed countries of East Asia and some parts of Europe. And even more people would work or job-search if there were more opportunities. This book illustrates the diversity of experience among these older workers: from unemployment, poverty, and frustrations of part-time jobs to the strains and satisfactions of fast-paced, demanding workplaces. Our older workers are poor or rich or somewhere in between. They work in hospitals and factories and classrooms and rice fields. But they all face similar questions: Should I work or should I retire? Can I continue to work if I need or want to? Will I have a useful, fulfilling role in the workplace? Or will I face what sociologist Richard Sennett calls the "specter of uselessness?"

The implications go far beyond the countries or regions discussed in this book. In a generation—or perhaps less than a generation—the burgeoning economies of China and India will face their own quandaries of aging and work. Thanks largely to its one-child policy, China risks becoming the first major economy in modern times to become old before it becomes rich, with potential consequences for the global economy. Solutions that today's wealthy countries formulate could help guide the aging countries of tomorrow.

This book is filled with the stories of older workers, and these narratives pose their own questions. How should we manage this transition to an older workforce? Can we manage it? The choice is no longer whether we should have an older workforce. The older workforce is a fact that grows every day. The choice is whether we acknowledge this fact and encourage steps—in policy, in company boardrooms, and in individual lives—to lead our aging population to a more comfortable, profitable, and fulfilling final decade of work. The alternatives are grim: ever-increasing elderly poverty as we push older people out of the workplace while cutting retirement benefits; the continued waste of talent and energy as people are shunted aside in their 50s and 60s; deepening social and economic isolation for millions of older Americans. What should we do with our extra years of life? It would be tragic if the best answer our civilization could come up with is nothing.

While the backdrop to this book is global, its focus is on individuals. Over the past three years, I've traveled more than 50,000 miles—to various points in Japan, France, and Sweden, and across the United States, from Akron to San Diego, from Sarasota to Plainfield, Illinois—in search of a vision of the aged workforce of the future. I've interviewed dozens of workers, economists, business owners, and managers. I've spend days with elderly farmers, aging factory workers, wrinkled handymen, desperate elderly job-seekers, frustrated salesmen. The narratives captured here illuminate several important aspects of the story of the evolution of the aging global workforce. Together, they map out the problem we confront, show us some avenues forward, and illustrate for us the dangers of inaction. Perhaps above all, they reveal how adjusting to the aging of the workforce can usher in reforms and improvements that benefit workers across the spectrum of age. It turns out that conditions that are good for older workers are good for all of us. Because older workers *are* us.

Here are the corners of the aging global workforce we will explore:

- Tsuneko Hariki toils on the frontier of aging and work. In her early 90s, she works for an agricultural cooperative created 25 years ago to save a dying village in southwestern Japan. Hariki and others like her are members of the fastest growing demographic in the workforce of the developed world: the aged. What can we learn from their experience and the companies that employ them?
- In Plainfield, Illinois, Ron Dziuda, too, is on a frontier of sorts: the 21st-century economy. The view from here isn't rosy. This descendant of Polish immigrants had achieved the middle-class American dream. A house in a tidy subdivision, a solid marriage, four kids headed to college. Then he was downsized in his mid-50s in the bitter aftermath of the Great Recession, cut adrift in an America that can be no country for older workers.
- At 62, Rita Hall is following rules set for the working poor who want a job. Every day, this laid-off hospital worker who takes lunch at the Salvation Army makes hundreds of phone calls in Akron, Ohio, in the service of the largest public job training program for older Americans. She's prayed hard, put her faith in God. Never missed a day of work. Now she has a shot at a real job and $2 an hour more than minimum wage. Will her years of training finally pay off?
- Jamie Burns concentrates on two activities: training new employees at San Diego's largest health care provider, and playing music with her retired schoolteacher husband. At Scripps Health, the 57-year-old doesn't have to choose between the two. The non-profit's staged retirement program allows her to work part-time, keep full-time benefits, and spend the rest of the week gigging in southern California. The program is one of the reasons Scripps is a leading American innovator in retaining older worker in the labor force.
- Like Rita Hall and Ron Dziuda, Kjell-Åke Ericsson lost his job. But he had something sturdy to fall back on: one of Sweden's biggest job councils. Now the 51-year-old jewelry salesman meets with a job counselor who commands a budget that could send him back to school for training to meet the needs of today's job market. The councils are one instructive reason why Sweden has one of the world's best records for keeping older workers employed until full retirement age.
- In 2007, Tatsuto Yamashita felt blessed. The artisans at the center of his company in southwestern Japan were unique, perhaps the only people in the world who could fashion the nose cones of high-speed trains with hammers. But he also had a problem: they were about to retire. So he lured them with reduced hours and turned them into teachers and promoters dedicated to raising the

next generation of hammer men. The story of Yamashita Kogyosho illustrates the power of older artisans as mentors.

- American Julie Cotton has always made her career on her own terms, and she's not about to stop at 65. On the East Coast, she helped doctors balance their work and their families. On the West Coast, she coached executives looking to reenergize. Now in Sarasota, the land of the retired, she champions the skills of older workers while developing her latest skill, memoir-writing. Cotton belongs to a new breed of 60-somethings: educated, energetic, and determined to make a difference.

- For decades, Michel Wattree plied the highways of Europe, hauling whatever needed hauling from France to Italy, from Yugoslavia to Poland. Now he's in his mid-60s, but he's not ready to give up work—and that makes him something of a revolutionary in France. Leaders here once believed early retirement would create jobs for the young. But that policy failed, and now France is finding the habit of quitting before 60 is hard to break. Wattree and the bus company he works for illustrate how things are changing slowly even in the world's most vacation-loving societies—and how far there still is to go.

We will end our journey close to where we started, on Japan's Okikamuro Island, one of the oldest corners of our aging world. The old people here—and just about everyone on the island is old—have worked all their lives, as farmers, fishermen, and shopkeepers. Their work, even if it has dwindled with age to hoeing tiny plots of vegetables, has remained an enduring symbol of their independence, and their reason for living.

Before we go any further, I urge the reader to consider an important caveat. I am not advocating one set of policies over another, nor am I attempting to illustrate how free markets are superior to state-led solutions, or vice versa. It is not my intention to show how one country has solved this policy question while other are floundering. None of the countries I've visited has answered fully the demands of older citizens for meaningful work. They all, however, are finding measures of success and failure in interesting, instructive ways that are similar in some aspects and very unique in others. If I'm arguing anything, it is that at the very least, government should have a coherent, clear-eyed, and humane policy toward older workers, one that encourages companies to capitalize on older workers' value and allows the workers themselves greater freedom to exercise their talents and capabilities. Societies themselves will have to figure out ways of doing that based on local circumstances and needs. This book is a sampler of some of the policy tools at work today.

Finally, the workers profiled here should not be seen as representatives of their respective countries, but rather as members of a growing global class of people: the older workers of the developed world.

Our journey starts in Tsuneko Hariki's workshed.

Haruko Takao, 68, shows some of the plants she grows to produce seasonal garnishes as a member of the Irodori cooperative in Kamikatsu, Japan, in July 2012.

1

Tsuneko Hariki and the Rich World's Coming of Age

KAMIKATSU, *Japan*

Tsuneko Hariki ambles around slowly in an apron and wooden slippers in a work-shed behind her house. The shed is simple: the floor is bare cement, the windows are sheets of corrugated plastic held in place with plywood boards. In a typhoon, the place doesn't look like it would last ten minutes. Tsuneko is equally unadorned. Her legs bowed with age, she supports herself when she moves around the shed with a hand on a tabletop, or by holding onto a shelf as she passes it. In her early 90s, she's well past much fuss about her appearance. Dirt is crusted under the horned nails of her knotted fingers. A white cap covers a head of hair dyed black, her one nod to vanity. Under a crisp white apron, she wears a blue plaid workshirt. When she laughs, her face breaks into a hundred wrinkles. And she laughs a lot—a dry, raspy laugh, like feet shuffling through gravel.

Tsuneko's work, too, is clear and simple. In the morning, her fax machine grinds out a scroll of orders of leaves for the day—nandina, holly, sakura. Dwarf bamboo. She fires up a computer, using a square keyboard and an oversized mouse designed for her aging hands, and checks the day's leaf prices, which fluctuate with changing demand. This helps her decide which orders are worth filling. If cherry blossoms are in higher demand than usual, then she goes with them; if sassafras is priced high, she picks that. When I visited her last, it was early July, and the hills behind her work-shed were lush with Japanese maple leaves, deep green after the monsoon season in June.

After checking prices, she and her daughter-in-law, Shigemi Hariki, who at 63 seems like a girlish kid sister, step out into their fields to clip sprigs and branches from the trees. Right behind the house is a vegetable garden. Scattered over her land, among the rice fields and plots of cucumbers, eggplant, tomatoes, and corn, are 100 varieties of trees.

A steady rain is falling on the day I visit Tsuneko. I wander through the back of her house calling her name. The raindrops beat an even rhythm on the roof of her empty shed. I walk back into the street, take out a cell phone, and call one of her relatives, who assures me Tsuneko is home. I trudge to the shed again and there she is, squating on a stool, as if she'd been there the whole time. "Ah," she says, looking up at me in vague recognition. "I was inside doing the laundry." Then she bends to her task: sorting through piles of leaves, arranging them in groups of 20, clipping dried bits, and gently putting them in plastic foam trays and cardboard boxes.

I ask her the same question whenever I see her: Why are you still doing this?

"I really like work," she says as she plows steadily through the pile of momiji on the short table in front of her. "If I sit around doing nothing, it's just a waste of time."

"Besides," she adds with a sandpaper laugh. "I like to make money."

That she does. The 190 members of Irodori, the agricultural cooperative that Tsuneko belongs to, can make as much as $10,000 or $20,000 in a single month. That would be a significant sum anywhere, but it goes an especially long way in her hometown of Kamikatsu-cho, a hamlet of barely 2,000 people tucked in the mountains of Shikoku, the smallest of Japan's four main islands. Some months are far more lucrative than others, and general earnings are falling in hard economic times. But Tsuneko has managed to do quite well—well enough, in fact, to plunk down a total of 10 million yen, about $100,000, in down payments on homes for two of her grandsons.

Tsuneko doesn't boast about this, and only speaks of the down payments if someone else brings them up. But her role in the family is clear.

"If I just keep all the money and die, then no one will say 'thank you'," she says, arranging the leaves on plastic foam trays she then wraps in cellophane. "I'm all by myself and I don't need money for kimono or nice clothes. They'd just say 'My grandma made tons of money and didn't tell anyone about it!'"

Tsuneko's humility, her work and surroundings, the way she talks about her achievement, her dirt-caked fingernails; these are all a bit deceptive. In fact, she is at the center of one of Japan's—and the world's—most intriguing experiments in elderly employment. The Irodori project has managed to combine profits with older workers, hard-nosed business sense with deep-rooted Japanese traditions, aesthetics with demographics, and topography with plain old luck, in a unique and enduring way.

There still are many young people in Japan, and the costliest dangers of a super-aged society—damaging labor shortages, social welfare systems tapped out by legions of old people—are many years from becoming a threat. Working in the present to avoid such a fate requires a vision of the future. We begin our search for that vision with Tsuneko Hariki because Japan is the tip of the spear, the most elderly corner of the rapidly aging industrialized world.

Kamikatsu seems an unlikely place for a vision of the future. If anything, this tiny village is well insulated from many of the social forces buffeting modern, highly urbanized, media-saturated Japan. The hamlet is tucked among vertiginously sloped mountains 330 miles from Tokyo. The provincial capital, Tokushima, is a mere 25 miles away, but it's really another world, with gleaming department stores and Starbucks and bored-looking teens sporting tinted hair and jeans with beltlines slipping to their thighs. The bus journey from Tokushima station can take nearly two hours to wind through the hills before arriving in Kamikatsu, and by then the mind of the traveler has fallen decades back in time. The hills—and the hills are everywhere, upright and sharply sloping—are heavily forested with cedar and red pine and chinquapin oak. Kamikatsu has been a foresting center since feudal days and the loggers are still at it, mowing down chunks of hillsides, the freshly cut quarry stacked in neat pyramids by the sides of the roads.

The dramatic hills are what give Kamikatsu one of its comparative advantages: a dynamic landscape that soars from only 100 meters (300 feet) above sea level to 1,500 meters (4,500 feet). To the west stands Mt. Takamura, the source of the Katsuura River, which winds through the town. So, depending on elevation and wind patterns, Kamikatsu enjoys a proliferation of micro-climates. This means that the area nurtures a wide variety of flora, including the many leaves and blossoms that Tsuneko Hariki plucks every morning from her garden.

Kamikatsu's other comparative advantage is less obvious. Old people.

In the mid-1980s, a young Kamikatsu agricultural cooperative extension official named Tomoji Yokoishi was flummoxed. He was working in a dead-end town that had nothing going for it. A killer snowstorm and frost in the early 1980s had wiped out the seedless mandarin "mikan" orchards the village relied on for a large chunk of its livelihood. Nearly half the town's residents were age 60 or older. The place was going nowhere in a hurry, like thousands of rural towns all over Japan. In fact, Kamikatsu was something of a leader in the wholesale abandonment of the Japanese countryside. In remote Shikoku, far from the bright lights, universities, and employment centers of Osaka and Tokyo, the young people of Kamikatsu had little reason to stick around, even before the frost clobbered local mikan growers. The industrial boom of the 1960s and 1970s had already siphoned off younger labor from the farms and small towns around the country. As Japan urbanized, the city had a powerful cultural pull as well. In contrast to places like Kamikatsu, where life had changed little in decades, by the 1980s major Japanese cities felt like the center of the world. Japan was rising to the top of the global economy. Traders and real estate speculators in Tokyo were sprinkling gold flakes on their chocolate mousse; the young could giddily slide from a carefree life at college into plentiful, well-paying jobs at the world's wealthiest companies. Later in the decade, Japanese corporations would buy up trophies like Rockefeller Center and

Columbia Pictures. Historian Paul Kennedy's *The Rise and Fall of the Great Powers* pointed to Japan as a leader of the evolving global system.

Fewer and fewer young people saw any benefit to sticking around growing rice or sawing down trees in the mountains of Kamikatsu. They left in droves for Tokushima, or Osaka, or Tokyo, leaving behind a population of aging farmers. The story has played out in villages and small towns all over Japan—and is still going on today. Whole towns have literally disappeared as their aging populations have dwindled and vanished. While the world focused on the financial and industrial might concentrated in Tokyo and Osaka, places like Kamikatsu were gradually sliding into oblivion. From a population of nearly 6,500 in 1950, the town had less than 3,000 people left by the time Yokoishi was casting about for some way to keep the place alive.

Yokoishi found his answer on a trip to the city. In Osaka, a relentlessly urban concrete jungle of nearly 3 million on the main island of Honshu, he sat in a sushi restaurant when he noticed a group of young women looking admiringly at their plates. It wasn't the food they were enamored with—it was the garnishes, sprigs of whatever leaves and blossoms that nicer restaurants decorate their offerings with. The art of the garnish is advanced in Japan. The country made the transformation from rural to urban only in the decades since World War II, and food in Japan is still largely governed by the seasons. This is no longer a matter of necessity—modern refrigeration and greenhouses have made any vegetable or fish available any time of the year. But Japanese culinary aesthetics still hold that foods should be eaten in season: skipjack tuna and asparagus in spring, eel and eggplants in the summer, and so on. Garnishes follow similar patterns: cherry blossoms in spring, red maple in autumn.

Yet at the time Yokoishi noticed the women gazing at their lunch plates, he believed there was no real business in Japan for supplying garnishes. Restaurants informally collected their ginko leaves and plum blossoms, relying on personal gardens or those of friends or associates. Cheaper eateries and takeout joints depended on thin plastics to mimic the seasonal flavor of the well-appointed garnish. However, at the sushi restaurant in Osaka, the garnishes were authentic. The women picked the sprigs up, gazed at them, and then did something that changed Yokoishi's life and the lives of many of his elderly neighbors in Kamikatsu: the women carefully folded the leaves in spotless pink handkerchiefs and secreted them into their purses for safekeeping. Yokoishi had one thought: *Garnishes are a precious thing.* Nearly as precious, it turned out, as the food on the plate.

Had he found something his town could sell for profit? If ever there were a business custom-made for Kamikatsu, this was it. There in Osaka, Yokoishi thought of the wooded slopes of Kamikatsu and their thousands of flowering trees. The place was a veritable garnish factory, with leaves and blossoms growing wild on every hillside. And what could be a more perfect livelihood for a population of old people, many of them with dozens if not hundreds of trees on their own properties?

No machinery was needed. No heavy lifting. All the old folks had to do was wander out into their gardens and pick some leaves or flowers. The most they'd need would be a lightweight tree pruner to get at the high branches. The idea took root in his mind.

The men of Kamikatsu just laughed when Yokoishi came home with his plan. Leaves were going to save the town? No way. The old days were best, they said—citrus groves galore, lots of young people to tend to them, and men in the woods mowing down trees for the Japanese miracle economy of the 1960s and 1970s. Rice terraces on the hillsides. Compared to those glory days, leaves were just a joke. They were everywhere, like weeds and dirt—and who would pay for dirt? And that was just the resistance among his would-be suppliers. Yokoishi also faced demand-side obstacles. He worked in agricultural extension, and he knew little about the restaurant business other than what he found out during his sushi bar epiphany. Aside from that, it wasn't easy to convince restaurant owners to pay for something that they'd always just taken care of on the side for free.

But Yokoishi says he saw no other way out of the town's demographic crunch. If nothing was done, he envisioned a dire future for the village—more young people leaving; the old folks falling into inactivity, lethargy, and earlier sicknesses and depression; and soaring nursing home and health costs. The town would go bankrupt in just a few years, he reasoned, unless he could find some way to get the elderly energized, engaged, and making some hard cash.

"If there's no work, there's no money," he told me in his office. "As long as they can work, then I think we can do something. If they sit in a room in a nursing home and do nothing, then that will cost a lot of money."

Then Yokoishi discovered a curious thing: some of the town's aging women, women like Tsuneko Hariki, then in her 60s, didn't turn up their noses at the thought of picking leaves for a living. Instead, they embraced his idea. Japanese women of her generation often pride themselves on their practicality and financial sense, and they typically rule inside the confines of the home. Men often hand over their paychecks to their wives and subsist on an allowance, knowing little or nothing about the financial workings of the home. So while Yokoishi's idea of turning to leaf production had little allure for men enamored of a rosy view of a quickly departing past, the women found the prospect of making some cash with a minimum of heavy labor very appealing. Tsuneko has fond memories of what Yokoishi was trying to do for the town. "He thought we didn't have any good work or any way to make a living, so he looked for a way for us," she said. The Irodori Project, a cooperative headquartered at Kamikatsu town hall, was founded in 1986.

The first years were rough. Initial sales were just 1.2 million yen, or about $7,400 at the exchange rate at the time. Yokoshi ended up spending a chunk of his own pay haunting pricey restaurants in Tokushima, Osaka, and Kyoto, learning the business and making contacts. He even took some of his elderly co-op members to a high-class restaurant in the city so they could see with their own eyes what they had to do and the standards they had to meet. Yokoishi still has a photograph of the women, kneeling in a line on the tatami-floored dining room, sipping miso soup straight from the bowl.

The research paid off: Yokoishi eventually learned how to cater his products for the market, bolstered quality control in the fields and work-sheds of Kamikatsu, and fine-tuned his marketing and distribution network. In 10 years, annual sales soared to 170 million yen—about $1.5 million at 1996 exchange rates, according to one study of the cooperative. By 2005, some members were making so much money that these country folk could barely come up with ways to use it.

It was around this time that Irodori first popped up on my radar screen in Tokyo. As part of a string of stories I was doing for the Associated Press on Japan's aging society, I went down to Kamikatsu for a visit and got my first look at what Tsuneko and others in the village were doing to extend their productive lives well into their 80s. Irodori was still housed in the Kamikatsu town hall, but it was making a countrywide impact through national broadcaster NHK and other media reports.

When I came for my first visit in 2006, Tsuneko, back then a youthful 84, waddled into her living room, got down on her knees on the tatami mat floor, and turned on her Logitec computer. By then, the cooperative had become quite sophisticated. Irodori had a webpage that posted the market prices for each of the dozens of types of leaves and blossoms cultivated in the area. So folks like Tsuneko would get up in the morning and check the market, looking for rising prices when determining what to pick for the day. The cooperative office would send out faxes to each member with orders as they came in, and the members would call the main office to get a lock on an order they wanted to fill.

Life hadn't been particularly gentle on Hariki. Born in 1921, she married into a conservative family—so conservative that she and her husband dined separately: her husband took the dining room while Hariki ate with servants in the kitchen. He died at 82 in 2003. "He didn't like fat on his meat, he didn't like curry," Hariki snorted. "He complained a lot."

She, on the other hand, prided herself in being able to eat anything—and do any kind of work. Up until 20 years ago, Hariki says she could hoist a 70-pound sack of rice onto her back and carry it through the neighborhood.

"I couldn't do that today, no way," she says laughing. "That's heavy. In the old days, I did some pretty heavy work." By the old days, she means when she was in her late 60s. These days, she doesn't go out into her rice fields to stoop and plant, but she still prepares the stalks for the thrasher and helps dry out the grains.

Engaging in meaningful activity has given Hariki and other Irodori members a feeling of vigor and satisfaction. But it has also boosted their social standing and their roles inside their own families. They're not dependents; they're breadwinners. And we find more and more people like Hariki all over the world these days.

The fax machine rang and started spitting out a message: an order of 20 lotus leaves, at 500 yen apiece.

"Quick! Give me the phone," barked Tomoe Tamura. It was summer 2010, and the white-haired 72-year-old had suffered a stroke three years earlier, paralyzing her left side. Her brown wooden cane leaned up in a corner behind her chair. But her right side was still fine, and when her husband Riichi proffered her the receiver, she grabbed it and thumbed in the number to Irodori's main office. "Yes, it's Tamura. We'll take the order."

The Tamuras had been Irodori members for 13 years. Riichi Tamura, now 80, used to be an eel fisherman and cook. He'd catch the slimy critters, considered essential summer fare in Japan, grill them slathered in a sweet brown sauce, and sell them in his own shop. But sales were on a long decline, and the couple needed something else to do. Like so many in this town, they found their answer in the trees that grew all around them.

"This work is light," Riichi said, lifting up a plastic foam box to illustrate his point. "I thought it would be easy and make us some money. But it's tough. Of course, we're old, and farming is not a 100 percent successful business."

Old they may be, but the Tamuras still have plenty of fire in the belly—just the kind of attitude Yokoishi wanted to engender among the gray-haired populace of Kamikatsu. Over the years he has woven competitive elements into the business. Orders are filled by the first member who calls the main office, so getting up late or slipping into a lengthy nap can cost members the chance to make more money. Then the cooperative posted monthly earnings leaders, so participants had added incentive—bragging rights in a small, tight-knit community—to put in the extra effort.

The Tamuras certainly have put in the effort. They quickly cottoned onto the concept of supply and demand. Waiting until particular leaves and flowers were in full bloom—and therefore plentiful—could mean missing the height of their value as garnishes. The larger the harvest, the lower the price. The best prices could be obtained right before the season and sometimes in the off-season, when certain leaves were rare but might still be needed. So they built a small greenhouse to get a jump on the weather and hit the beginning of the season with mature produce. Tomoe said green Japanese maple leaves, momiji, sell for 180 yen a batch in summer—but 300 yen a batch in winter.

By the same token, when prices are low, the Tamuras don't flood the market with even more leaves. "I decide for myself how much I put out," Riichi, a garrulous man with a blue vest over a white T-shirt, bellowed in his workroom, owl-like large-lens glasses perched low on his nose. "If we put out too much, then the price will collapse!"

Supply and demand play a leading role in the success of elderly employment schemes anywhere. Money is a key motivator—and one of the reasons why such projects in Japan sometimes work, and sometimes don't. When older people need money, because of low pensions or other reasons, common sense dictates they are more eager to stay on the job. The reverse is also true: retirees who have access to more generous pensions—employees of big-name companies or government agencies, for instance—have less incentive to keep trudging to work every day. In country towns like Kamikatsu, far from the reaches of mega-companies like Toyota or Sony or Mitsubishi, many workers are dependent on the national pension system, which pays base benefits of about $700 a month. So the elderly here want to supplement their income.

"It's fine for those bureaucrats to retire and live off their pensions," Riichi said. "I get a pension too, but I can't live off that. I have to work!" He continued: "If you go to a big company, you're guaranteed a job until you're 60, and then you get a good pension. But not around here," he said, banging his fingers on the table.

In addition to shoring up their finances, the money has also bolstered the Tamuras' sense of usefulness in the family. Like Tsuneko Hariki, they have helped relatives with home purchases, always an extremely costly investment in Japan. Not only are land and building materials more expensive than most other places, the quirks of the housing market make home-buying even more difficult. Japanese homes are not typically built to last more than 30 years, and people rarely will buy an existing house. More often, families buy land, knock down any buildings on it, and start from scratch. A used home is worth only the land it sits on—a worthy investment in the days of soaring land prices in Japan, but not now. Land prices have stagnated and even dropped in some places over the past 20 years. So homeowners can rarely expected to recoup their money by selling their home; in most cases, they have to face the fact that the money is lost and they can never move.

In the Tamuras' case, they're helping a son pay off his mortgage—winning Riichi bragging rights he had no hesitation to deploy.

"I'm the one paying off his loan!" Riichi thundered. Then he softened his tone. "He's got to pay to send his kids to school. Living these days is expensive for four people," he said. "He was saying, 'Oh, I have this loan,' and so I said, 'I'll take care of it.'"

One listens to these conversations, these elderly proud of their enduring financial muscle and the help they were able to offer their children and grandchildren, with mixed feelings. On one hand, it's wonderful and a benefit to society for the aging to retain their usefulness in society, to be able to participate more fully in community, business, and family life. And if one believes in the lines by Welsh poet Dylan Thomas that we should "rage, rage against the dying of the light," then one can only cheer on these 80-year-olds who are plowing on decades past their prime, waking up in the morning, busying their hands with work, and sharing the fruits with their descendants.

And yet, it also struck me as sad how in some cases, these grandparents and great-grandparents felt their value to their families came down to the money they made. Riichi, as an unvarnished realist and businessman, stated this in the boldest way. "Maybe if I didn't have money, my son wouldn't bring his kids up to see us," he said. The comment may have been said half in jest, but only half. What other conclusion could these people come to, in a society that sees itself as baldly materialistic? And has it ever been any different? Over the centuries, what folklore has built up around the cat-and-mouse game played between the generations over wills and inheritances? The Tamuras are playing an ancient game, and Irodori has given them, for the time being, a strong enough hand to keep a place at the table.

Money aside, the work has brought one unalloyed benefit to Tomoe Tamura: rehabilitation.

She had been one of the most active Irodori workers. She figured in many of the group's promotional items, such as books and DVDs. An expert flower arranger, Tomoe designed an extensive garden city hall planted at the entrance to a tunnel that led to the town. A photo of the garden hangs on the wall of the workroom she shares with Riichi. Then she suffered a stroke. Her companions from Irodori sent her gifts and a poster made from a photo of her garden as she struggled through eight months of rehabilitation in the hospital. They all had the same message for her: "You have to come back to work with us when you're ready."

So she did.

"I'd done this work for more than 10 years, so my body remembered all the moves, though I can only use my right hand," she said.

Indeed, despite the left hand lying motionless in her lap, Tomoe is a hard-driving worker. She jumped on the order that curled out of the fax while I was there and then commandeered her team: husband Riichi and a neighbor, Yoshihiro Fukuta, 74, a retired taxi driver who came by to help assemble the leaves and take them to be delivered.

Fukuta credited Tomoe with getting him started in the business. "She taught me everything," he said. He and Riichi went out to the Tamuras' greenhouse and garden, coming back with armfuls of lotus, dazzling green Japanese maple, and stalks of bamboo leaves. For about an hour, they put together the orders, slicing off the dried bits of leaves, shaking out stems and other debris. Tomoe arranged the sprigs neatly on plastic foam trays fed by Riichi. At the end, Riichi opened up an invoice book and put it before Tomoe, holding down the pages as she scrawled in the order.

"I make her write it," he said. "It's rehabilitation."

Tomoe looked up as her husband tore the invoice from the book. "I'll do this as long as I'm alive," she said. "As long as I can get to this chair from the bed, I'll keep going."

People like the Tamuras and Hariki have achieved remarkable things with the help of Irodori, crafting livelihoods during a time of life that much of modern society has considered little more than a postscript. At the same time, Kamikatsu's keen eye for publicity has put it on the national media map, where it is known both for aging "leaf ladies" and a much-ballyhooed campaign to turn it into a zero-waste town. Websites abound, the town is mentioned abundantly in the domestic and foreign press, and some co-op members, including Hariki, have become minor media stars.

Yet Tomoe's comments pointed indirectly to a sober truth: grim as it is to contemplate, one day she won't be able to make that journey from her bed to the workroom chair. Indeed, while the business model in Kamikatsu has found a way to make the most of villagers' twilight years, it has not conquered the inevitable, final decline. True, Irodori is growing stronger, with nearly 200 members now, the oldest, as of 2012, a stunning 98. But many members have already hit the stage at which they can work no longer. I saw the process at work firsthand. In 2006, Makiko Shobu was a spry, energetic woman, scrolling up and down a computer screen and crowing about her earnings. "I have a real feeling of abundance," she said, squinting through her eyeglasses in her workroom. "If I'm doing a fun job, then I won't get sick." Yet when I visited the town again four years later, she was no longer working. "It's too bad," said Hariki, shaking her head and speaking solemnly. "I hear she's not doing very well."

Yokoishi also does not seem interested in adapting his business model to other villages. The area's topography, the variety of temperatures and climates in a concentrated area, is too rare in Japan, he said. "There are hardly any places with mountains like this," he said.

There is one thing, however, that he's very interested in—keeping Kamikatsu alive. So Irodori is branching out into a new demographic: young people. "We're looking at the next generation, people aged 23 to 57," said Yokoishi. "We're teaching them about the area, the leaf business, and other work as well."

To draw that demographic, Irodori has set up a series of seminars to educate outsiders about the town and about the cooperative project. At one seminar, about 15 students—three of them women—gathered in a conference room for a presentation on Kamikatsu and the challenges it faces. The instructor, Yoshikiho Fukuda, plodded methodically through the town's situation, the falling population, the health care and hospital arrangements, education. Like in many towns in Japan, Kamikatsu's schools are closing at an alarming rate. In the 1960s there were five elementary schools here; by 2010, there was only one left. There are only 10 or 12 children in each grade and students have to move to Tokushima City and live in a dormitory when they get to high school.

During a break, Fukuda said the town was eager to draw more newcomers as the elder generation quickly fades away. He shook his head. "I wonder how many more people will die this year."

Yokoishi is banking on several trends in Japan in his quest to revitalize Kamikatsu and prepare for the coming decades. One is the shaky economy and youth joblessness and underemployment, which, as is common in industrial economies, runs higher than the overall rate. Jobless young people in the city might find employment in the countryside appealing. Accompanying that is a growing dissatisfaction among Japanese youth with the assumptions of older generations: that men must dedicate their lives to their jobs and companies; that happiness and success are measured by material goods and status within a company; and that the good life is to be had in the centers of the large cities rather than in rural hamlets like Kamikatsu. This town, like many in the countryside, has seen a trickle of urban refugees coming back from the cities.

In a nation that only in the last 70 years or so has transformed itself from an overwhelmingly agrarian country into the relentlessly urban powerhouse of today, a return to rural roots is heavily romanticized. Such moves are celebrated in countless TV dramas and movies, casting the move back to the country as a return to essential Japanese values of family and purity.

Naoya Murata was one of the urban refugees looking for a fresh start. He grew up in the prefecture in a farming family, then, like so many others, he took off for the city as soon as he could. He went to university in Tokyo, then worked in the sales department for an electronics company. Six months before we spoke in 2010, he was laid off and came back to his parents' home. Murata, a gentle, soft-spoken man who posts photos of his cat on the Internet, said his main goal was to bolster his family's vegetable farming business by using some of the methods of Irodori, such as using the Internet for PR. In the meantime, he was weighing the benefits of a permanent move to the country.

"It was tough at first," he said. "I thought the countryside was kind of boring, and even on my days off I'd have to work at farming. But then I met some people and talked to them and I realized that there were a lot of interesting people here. There's not much entertainment, not so much shopping, but it's the people who are interesting."

While Irodori has until now been a model based on the revival of a village by capitalizing on the energies and imagination of its elderly population, demographics are once again turning its focus in another direction. For Murata, the innovative business methods of Irodori could point out the way toward a different way of life for people like himself.

"I've been back for six months, and now, instead of returning to the city, I think I might be able to have a comfortable life in the countryside," he said.

Tsuneko Hariki fingered the leaves absentmindedly as she talked, telling me about her impressive extended family: eight grandchildren, 10 great-grandchildren. It was the summer of 2010, and she was 89 years old. In her rambling farmhouse, she lived with six other family members spanning four generations.

"I'm so happy they're with me. When you're old, who knows, there's a lot to worry about," she said. "But I'm happy."

I gazed at her hands as they worked the leaves, sorting them into groups. Then, in the middle of a sentence, she grabbed a pair of scissors with out-sized handles for her old hands to grasp. In one fluid motion, she sliced the slightly browned edge of one of the leaves, put the scissors back, and continued gathering the maple stems. She never missed a word in the conversation. The move was so quick and smooth I would have missed it if I hadn't been looking at her hands at the right moment.

I turned my attention back to her words as she sat, back bowed, jaw to her chest, fingers in constant motion.

"I think I want to work until I'm 90. After that, I'll depend on heaven," she said. "If I live until 100, I don't know, people that age just sleep all the time. It makes no sense."

She paused a minute and looked up at me.

"There's a woman who was my age, now she's in a nursing home and she sleeps all day. Poor thing," she said, shaking her head. "She doesn't even recognize her own family."

The opportunity to work has the power to fundamentally alter the arc of these individuals' economic and personal power over the course of their lives. Despite the romantic view that people at one time respected the elderly, old age has always been a time of cruel decline and often of neglect. The difference these days is that the period of decline lasts longer. The parents who shouldered the burdens of work and child care and education through midlife gradually shed their authority as they age. Work ends and retirement begins, bringing life on a fixed income. Children have long since left the nest and now are at the peak of their powers, with their energies focused on work and their own children. Gradually, the relationship is inverted—parents slowly become the dependents, and children the caretakers.

But in this tiny town in the Japanese mountains, Irodori has tinkered with that pattern. Through economically meaningful work, physical and mental activity, and their ability to earn money, these older cooperative members have found a way to keep a foothold in the family—to bolster their social position and maintain a role in the family as caretakers. Kamikatsu is no paradise—the work would bore those looking for challenging employment, and not many people are going to stay sharp or agile enough to work until they're 90. But this place shows there is a way for us to remained relevant and stave off Sennett's specter of uselessness—at least for a little while.

The journey to Kamikatsu, like many of the journeys chronicled in this book, is a long one. We may never really get there. It is a very unique place. More importantly, powerful forces are arrayed against those who would venture forth—illness and dementia, bodily decline after a life of punishing labor, an economic system too poorly organized to provide work even for the fittest and most capable, let alone those who are older. For more than a half-century, our political and industrial elite have had abundant access to evidence that work opportunities for older Americans are needed, possible, and profitable. And yet, many of us in our 50s and 60s remain frustrated—and in some cases, impoverished—by the lack of sufficient progress.

Our journey toward some possible answers moves now to America, where success and accomplishment sit side-by-side with failure and despair. Here, some workers with the right skills, education, or employers can practice their professions well into old age, while others less skilled, educated, and advantaged—or less lucky—can be pushed from the workplace in late middle age, and have to battle their way back into what a U.S. senator once described as "the mainstream of life."

This chapter is based on material gathered from three visits to Kamikatsu: April 2006, July 2010, and July 2012. All figures related to Irodori are attributable to cooperative records unless otherwise noted.

Kenn Curzon, 90, sits in his parking management office at Scripps Memorial Hospital La Jolla; La Jolla, California, in November 2012.

2

Embracing the Aging American Workforce

LA JOLLA, *California*

Jamie Burns doesn't need to work. At 57, this energetic veteran Scripps Health employee doesn't need to stand up in front of dozens of colleagues in a window-less room at a hospital in La Jolla, California, and guide them through a "Learning Management System." She doesn't need to make sure they all have usernames and passwords. And she doesn't need to train them on how to keep payroll or timesheets.

After all, compared to the unemployed older workers we'll meet in later chapters, Burns is one of the lucky ones. Her husband is retired on a California state public schoolteacher's pension. They lived well within their means over the years, and now they can enjoy the fruits: savings and investments to back them up in retirement. And Burns has plenty of other things to do besides work. She plays the hammered dulcimer and does regular gigs with her guitar-playing husband around the San Diego area. She's on a full-bore campaign to learn the harp. When she's not playing music, she's busy packing in a daily schedule of running and kay-aking. Yoga on Fridays and Mondays. Theater on Sunday nights.

"I could quit tomorrow," she told me during a break between classes at Scripps Memorial Hospital in November 2012, her auburn hair curling to just above gold earrings. "I have music! I can volunteer, I can walk, I can run, I can go down to the beach and paddle."

"So I'm not going to have a problem not working," she said. "I have plenty to do, and there's a bucket list of things I haven't done."

Indeed, if this were the 1980s, when many American companies were intent on flushing 50-something workers out of the system to save money and make room for younger hires, Burns would be a prime candidate for early retirement. She has her health, and her retired husband is plenty young enough—63—to enjoy every-thing she can enjoy. And they live in a part of the world that, with its beaches, swaying palm trees, and constant sunshine, is about as elder-friendly as any major city in the United States.

So why is she still on the job?

Scripps made her an offer she couldn't refuse.

At the Intensive Care Unit, 53-year-old nursing mentor Lorraine Pagni-Kiefer wasn't thinking about early retirement. She was thinking about cardiac arrest.

A woman had been rushed to Scripps Memorial's ICU with a wildly erractic heartbeat just as Lorraine arrived at 6:30 a.m. for a 12-hour shift. Lorraine and the nurses she mentors jumped right to work: they gave the patient CPR and shocked her heart with a bolt of electricity to get it beating regularly again.

It worked—for the time being.

"That's how we started our day," Lorraine said.

Now it was mid-morning and Lorraine wanted to check up on how the woman and the nurses caring for her were doing. The prognosis wasn't overly optimistic—in the harsh lingo of the ICU, the patient was "circling the drain"—so it was important to keep an eye on her and the nurses on the case. Lorraine pulled back the curtain and had just enough time to inquire about the patient when an alarm went off.

Beep-beep! Beep-beep!

She pulled the ringing pager out of the holster on her hip.

"We're going."

She grabbed a rapid response bag filled with medicine and equipment and dashed out the swinging doors toward the elevator. "Sometimes we go days without getting a rapid response," she said as she hurried down the hall. "This is exciting!"

Down on the first floor, the conference room was packed and the theme was British.

Scripps Health employees milled around circular tables decked with red and blue tablecloths decorated with tiny Union Jacks and topped with three-tier-high tea trays loaded with cookies, cakes, and little pastries. A display near the window featured a photo of the unsuspecting birthday boy: a smiling man in a pith helmet.

Suddenly, the crowd hushed. The time was near. Some chuckled with anticipation. "He thinks it's another construction meeting," one woman exclaimed, giggling. Somewhere, a video camera chimed to life.

Finally, the door clicked opened and the cause of all the fuss stepped in on a silver aluminum cane.

"Oh God," he gasped.

The room erupted into cheers, clapping, and whooping. The celebrants broke into a rendition of the World War I music hall tune "It's a Long Way to Tipperary." Kenn Curzon, a tall, British-born man with a modest combover of bright white hair, prominent jowls, and a red, white, and blue ribbon pinned to his lapel, circled the room, shaking the hands of the men, embracing the women.

"Thank you! Thank you for your service!" shouted one man.

Curzon shot back: "I've got to go back to work now!"

The joke wasn't lost on the crowd as he posed for photos and laughed with his colleagues.

On this day, Curzon, the manager of Scripps's parking service, was at a surprise party for his 90th birthday. He'd been working in some shape or form since the 1930s—well before nearly all his colleagues were born. He'd stormed the beaches at Normandy on D-Day. He'd pampered Mercedes customers on the West Coast of America. He'd even played Smokey the Bear for a few years for the U.S. Forest Service.

But he wasn't ready to get all sentimental about it just yet.

"You've touched so many lives, Kenn, more than you'll know," Curzon's boss, Robert Bullock, said in a short speech, his voice breaking with emotion. "Happy birthday, from all of us."

"Oh," Curzon said bashfully, his British accent still strong after six decades in America. "Don't be crying."

The silver labor force is at work across the spectrum of the American economy. Older workers process our insurance claims, run machines in our factories, and pour our coffee. They program our computers, command our armies, and design our policies. They raise our cattle on the farm, grind the beef at the butcher, and flip our burgers in the kitchen. They develop and produce our medicines, and they stock the shelves at CVS. And, yes, they greet shoppers on the way in at Walmart and Lowe's, and ring up their bills on the way out.

Later in this book we will meet older Americans who are struggling to gain a toehold in the workforce. We'll see how governments and employment agencies in America, Europe, and Japan are adjusting policies to help older people to work and encourage companies to hire them. We've already seen one example—Irodori in Japan—of a small outfit trying to capitalize on the skills of seniors to turn a profit. We will see more examples later. But in this chapter, we will look at how companies motivated to keep aging workers on the job are developing strategies—some tried and true, others innovative—to keep skilled and energetic people like Jamie Burns, Lorraine Pagni-Kiefer, and Kenn Curzon from retiring.

For such companies, the decision to hold onto older workers is not always a question of choice—it's a matter of survival. Boomers who were educated and trained in the decades when the United States became the world's preeminent industrial, financial, and technological power hold the knowledge and skills that keep whole sectors of the economy running. Downsizing and restrictions on new hiring in the Great Recession and earlier have slowed the influx of fresh talent into certain key industries, and many fear the en-masse retirement of highly trained older workers could leave these companies critically wounded in the battle to compete internationally.

Despite these needs, certain factors have sapped American corporate enthusiasm for hiring and retaining aging workers. First, damaging stereotypes about older employees abound. Aside from that, the Great Recession has focused companies' attention on survival. The popular response to that is cutting costs through layoffs, encouraging attrition (read: retirement), and elimination of training budgets. Nurturing workers so they can be productive later in life is often considered a luxury that only the most profitable can afford. Steps to retain these workers are seen as more of an additional cost rather than as a long-term benefit.

But companies that reject such tactics and embrace the aging worker are getting new attention. How do they do it? A closer look at organizations that have had success in keeping older workers on the job reveals a common set of characteristics. Many have innovative personnel management systems. Instead of rigid, one-size-fits-all personnel hierarchies, such companies allow themselves the flexibility to toy with job descriptions, scheduling, and workflow to account for individual workers' needs, capabilities, and preferences. Such flexibility, of course, doesn't only benefit older workers, and companies often have implemented these changes as a way to draw the best employees across all ages.

Another method companies have used to accommodate older workers is playing with the process of retirement itself. In the heyday of corporate America, work and retirement were considered mutually exclusive—you were either fully retired or fully employed. Companies now are finding they can hold onto valuable older workers by staging their retirement, allowing employees to downshift to part-time work, keeping their brains on the job while giving them more slack to do all the things people in their late 50s and 60s might do, such as care for an elderly parent, pursue long-neglected hobbies, or just catch up on spending time with a spouse.

Finally, training is getting a closer look. In the old days, many larger companies took their in-house training functions for granted. But over the years, as the labor market evolved and companies tightened their belts, hirers increasingly wanted their new employees to be ready to hit the ground running. American companies have essentially outsourced their training to universities, vocational centers, and other companies, dismantling their training structures and thereby narrowing the length of any one individual's term of employability. Young workers face a familiar Catch-22: everyone wants them to be experienced, but no one will hire them to provide that experience. For older workers, it means that once their skills are outdated—a common problem in an age of rapid technological change— they must rely on their own initiative and bank accounts to retrain or face being squeezed out of their jobs by executives looking to cut costs.

The companies that we're looking at in this chapter say they have found they can extend the productive years of employees—and their utility to the company—by expanding training opportunities. They've also found it's cheaper in the long run to train a 55-year-old employee or fund additional education than it is to push her into early retirement and hire someone else.

Scripps Health is widely recognized as a leader among such companies. Over the past decade, Scripps has appeared regularly on AARP's list of top employers for those over 50, and won the top honors in 2011. AARP cited Scripps for implementing a staged retirement program; guiding employees as they transition from work to retirement; maintaining an alumni network that keeps retirees engaged and finds them work, sometimes back with Scripps; and participating in a health insurance savings plan that can be used for premiums in retirement, among other policies.

The moves at Scripps also underscore the emergence of the health and education professions—widely considered among the bright spots of the future on the U.S. economic horizon—as the leaders in employment strategies for older American workers. Scripps vies for AARP recognition with health providers such as the National Institutes of Health and Mercy Health System of Janesville, Wisconsin, as well as educators such as Cornell University and Brevard Public Schools in Florida. The health profession gives us perhaps our fullest picture of an industry that is not only accommodating the aging of its workforce but, driven by business imperatives, is putting in place policies and structures to nurture workers and extend their economic value as employees as they move into their 50s and 60s.

It's a complex picture, for it's not just a single policy that has kept older workers like Jamie Burns, Lorraine Pagni-Kiefer, and Kenn Curzon on the job. And policy does not operate in a vacuum. Targeted, progressive practices have helped make these workers' decisions to stay at work easier, but those employment choices are driven by an array of other factors—loyalty to the company, individual circumstance, spouse relations, working conditions. Some of these factors the company can influence, intentionally or not. Other factors are beyond its reach.

For Jamie Burns, the decision to stick with Scripps grew largely out of two pieces of cartilage and skin so essential, so taken for granted, that most of us never give them a second thought.

Ears.

Jamie Burns likes to see her life as intertwined with Scripps Health.

The company got its start when philanthropist Ellen Browning Scripps—whose brothers built the newspaper chain of the same name—founded Scripps Memorial Hospital and Scripps Metabolic Hospital in 1924, when the heiress was in her 80s. Jamie Burns got her start some 30 years later, in April 1955, when she was born at Mercy Hospital in San Diego. Four decades after that, Scripps bought Burns's birthplace as the non-profit expanded its reach to the present four hospitals and nearly two dozen related facilities.

Burns jokes that the coincidence makes her a Scripps baby, even if she has to toy with the order of things to make it true. "Even before we were Scripps," she says, "I was a Scripps baby."

Burns, one of five siblings, was an unusual child in one respect that would make her especially dependent on medical science throughout her life: she was born without ears. She lacked both the outer cartilaginoid folds of the ears—the pinna—and the canals. Still, she was not technically deaf: her inner ears functioned, and for the first two years of life she could hear, she says, through the vibrations of her skull. This condition—called microtia—occurs once in every 6,000 births, according to Boston Children's Hospital.

Medicine first changed the order of Jamie's life when she was two. It was a happy coincidence. Her father, who worked for the local telephone provider, got an order to install phone lines at an office in downtown San Diego. It turned out the office belonged to a company that made hearing aids. He chatted with the people at the office and told them his daughter suffered from severe hearing problems, and they offered to help in the best way they knew how: by fitting her with hearing aids. The aids, crude by today's standards, amplified the outside world, allowing much more sound to penetrate into her inner ear. The world opened wider.

She wore hearing aids for decades. They helped her through childhood and high school. They helped her into San Diego State University, where she graduated in 1977 with a degree in nutrition and dietetics. And they helped her launch a career working in hospitals around the country. She worked in Los Angeles; she worked in Massachusetts. In 1981, she settled into a job at Bay General Hospital in Chula Vista, halfway between San Diego and the Mexican border.

Then another coincidence with long-lasting consequences intervened in her life: the biggest player in health care in the area took over Bay General in 1986. Burns was now a Scripps Health employee.

The next stage in Jamie's life illustrates how large companies in health and education can leverage their heft and unique position to engender gratitude and loyalty—two emotions that can entice older workers to stay on the job. Companies like Scripps have the money and scope to offer employees extensive health benefits, with access to some of the best doctors in the country. That meant the world to Burns, who in her 30s was ready to move beyond hearing aids toward the complicated surgical construction of real ears.

With support from her bosses, in 1987 she embarked on $50,000 worth of operations, missing weeks of work at a time for each procedure, sometimes three weeks, sometimes six weeks, all on the company clock. Her surgeon was in such high demand that Burns had to get on a stand-by list, meaning sometimes she only had four days, notice before a major operation that could take her off the work schedule for a month. It happened over and over again.

The first stage included five operations. In a biblical flourish, doctors took cartilage from her ribs and fashioned ears they attached to the sides of her head, crafting earlobes from skin grafts. In 1990, doctors drilled an ear canal into the right side of her head, manufacturing eardrums and finally allowing her to properly transmit sound from the outside world to the inner ear. She was now without hearing aids for the first time since she was two.

A canal for the left ear was added in 1994. The sounds of the world came to her with a clarity she'd never before experienced.

But there was one thing Burns says she never heard: a complaint from her bosses at Scripps about all the time off. "I never lost a dime in salary, never anything other than 1,000 percent support," she says. "That's a debt of gratitude I never will be able to pay back."

There are other things Burns feels grateful for.

Scripps bills itself as the kind of place where employees enjoy opportunities in training and education to develop their careers and move into positions with more responsibility and pay. Burns says the company carries through on that promise. She has gone through so many departments and jobs at the company that she's lost count. "Do you want the end of the story, or the 12 or 13 jobs in between?" she asks, laughing.

Burns started with Scripps as a dietitian, and later moved into positions including housekeeping services supervision, project management, and organizational performance. Sometime in the late 1990s, she hit the wall. Jamie had gradually taken on greater responsibility in the company, and that threw her into teams and committees with people at higher and higher levels. People with loftier titles, higher pay, and more extensive backgrounds. And more education. She started noticing at meetings that often she was missing something that everyone else at the table had—a master's degree.

"I realized I didn't have the business background if I was going to continue to grow," she says.

Again, Scripps was there to help. Armed with a company scholarship, Jamie went back to school, taking night classes twice a week at National University to earn an M.B.A. with an emphasis in health care administration. The additional education opened the door to a corporate position in 2000 as a director of leadership management.

It was a rough period at Scripps—the company was suffering operating losses of about $26 million a year, employee turnover of 30 percent, and a high risk of clinic closures because of labor shortages. Then-CEO Stanley Pappelbaum resigned after an emotional standoff with doctors critical of his reform proposals and an exodus of nurses from the company.

Amid the tumult, Burns lasted only eight months in her new job.

"Major organizational chaos, CEO issues and all kinds of stuff" is how Burns describes the tumult at the time. "So here I am in corporate with my MBA, I'm gonna change the world and figured out in three weeks that I might have made a big old career mistake."

So she shifted over to human resources and found it was a much better fit. She picked up a certificate in quality customer service at Chapman University—again, with help from Scripps. She served for nearly five years as director of human resources, where she started a system-wide new employee orientation. Then she settled into her final full-time position as one of the first staffers at the newly formed Scripps Center for Learning & Innovation—an in-house training center—as director of learning and development.

By 2010, her husband Chris was ready to retire after more than three decades as a public school teacher. So he turned to his wife, who was putting in 50-plus hours a week at the time. In a three-decade career, she'd bounced around several hospitals, been through a grueling series of operations, and plowed her way up the ladder at Scripps. Didn't she need a break?

Retire with me, he said.

She wondered if she was ready. A life without work? And what about their finances? Could they even afford it? She was dedicated to her work. At the time, Jamie was deep into running the program for new employees, and, as silly as she says it sounded, she really cared whether Scripps's new hires got off on the right foot.

Plus, Burns says dramatic changes are not her thing. "Surprise," she says, "is not my idea of a good time." Her husband was about to go through a major change with retirement. The last thing their partnership needed, she thought, was to have both of them grappling with life overhauls at the same time. There also were solid financial reasons to stick with her job. She looked around at other boomers and shook her head at their paltry savings. How would they survive in old age? What about health insurance? Her husband was 61, still a few years short of Medicare. Shouldn't she stick with Scripps, where she could carry both of them on her plan?

It just wasn't time.

"No, no," she told her husband. "You figure out how to be retired first."

Sometime in the early 2000s, as Burns was working on her human resources qualifications, a nurse at Scripps had what sounded like a brilliant idea. Many such ideas might never see the light of day. But this time, Scripps officials say, the nurse told her bosses and they listened.

So in 2004, the sprawling non-profit hospital operator, which employs some 13,500 workers, began something called "staged retirement." Jamie Burns didn't know it then, but the program would have a powerful influence on how she would finish out her career at Scripps.

Under the plan, eligible older employees could scale down their work hours, sacrificing some pay but not their all-important full-time health insurance and other benefits. The program is a handy way of keeping talented older workers on the job at least part of the time for a few more years, while the employees get more free time without having to abandon their worklives or break the bank with health insurance bills. The program is limited: supervisor approval is needed, and not everyone can jump on the bandwagon. Staged retirement is offered only to workers 55 or older. And it's only for Scripps long-timers: you need at least 10 years with the company to qualify for partial benefits, 20 years to go into staged retirement with full-time benefits.

So at the end of 2011, once Burns's husband had settled into retirement and started devoting more time to music, she started to wonder if it wasn't time to reconsider her options. Staged retirement was one of them.

It seemed custom-made for her. She had enough time with the company to qualify, and it would be a good way to cut down her hours, but keep her benefits. Her teaching job was such that she could accomplish what she needed in less than five days. And she had options: under the plan, she could work as little as an average of 12 hours a week—or 1.5 days of full-time work—and still qualify. So she thought about it. Dropping down to four days a week wouldn't make much of a difference. Going down to two days would be too little work to make sense. She still liked her job. So Burns settled for three days each week—twice as much as she needed, but just right for her.

So now Burns, who started working part-time at the beginning of 2012, says the program has allowed her to mix the two most important parts her life—work on one side and play and family on the other—more evenly.

She spends Tuesday, Wednesday, and Thursday at Scripps as a teacher and leadership trainer, using the skills she's amassed over a lifetime and engaging with colleagues and students. The experience hasn't been without challenges. She says it was tough to downshift from the 50 to 60 hours a week pace she'd grown used to over the decades.

"It took a few months to kind of get the rhythm down. I made some mistakes that I hadn't made in a while 'cause I lost my five-day-a-week rhythm. And now it's really good," she said, adding that she'd only had to work on her day off only five times in all of 2012.

The other part of her life is play. She says the best part of the week is Thursday evening, when she drives home to a four-day weekend. That's when the music starts. She and her husband—she plays the hammered dulcimer, he plays guitar and keyboards—bill themselves as "Many-Strings," playing Celtic, Americana, and light classical at places like San Diego's Spanish Village Art Center and the Point Loma Farmers Market. When they're not playing music, they take "mini-vacation" trips up the coast, or to visit grandchildren outside Sacramento.

She says the more free time she and Chris have, the more ways they find to use it.

"Oh my gosh, to have time, unbelievable," she says. "And," her voice dropping to a whisper, as if she didn't want anyone else in on her secret, "I knew it would be good. I just didn't know it would be *this* good."

So now Burns's days—the three she spends at work—are occupied by guiding students through Scripps in-house employee training system.

In the classroom, she's a moving target, taking students step by step through Scripps's in-house training program, jumping from computer terminal to terminal to troubleshoot, peppering what could be a dry tutorial with jokes and wry comments about the flaws in the system. At the same time, she treats her students like the adults they are and acknowledges the know-how they bring to the classroom.

"Let me walk you through what I know about LMS, answer a couple of questions," she began one afternoon session. "There's a lot of wisdom in the room, 'cause you all use this, so we'll just answer questions based on the wisdom in the room."

The in-house system, in fact, is emblematic of what employees say they like about Scripps: a constant emphasis on building workers' skills and abilities, allowing them to develop their careers and assume more challenging positions the longer they stay at the company. Burns told her students, most of them newer hires or newly promoted, that the company was on a campaign to get workers into some sort of training program within three months of taking on a fresh position.

"We're trying to streamline the program," she told the students. Sometimes, however, that doesn't happen. "Let's just say it's a work in progress."

A work in progress. Just like Burns's retirement.

When I talked with her in 2012, she had a three-year plan to keep going at Scripps and then give it another look. She has the gift of flexibility: her husband's pension and the couple's savings mean she could quit without crippling their finances, though the extra income helps. Scripps is clearly happy with her work; they have volunteered her for media interviews on their staged retirement program more than once.

She was also having a ball playing music, the chapter in their life that her husband calls "Part Two." And there was still a ton of kayaking and everything else to do.

"If I wanted to work full time, I wouldn't be doing this. The whole point is to work less, 'cause I have this whole other life that I want to spend time doing," she said. "I've been doing this now 11 months, I haven't been able to figure out whether my favorite time now is Thursday as I'm driving home realizing the week is done, Friday morning when I wake up not to an alarm clock, on my way to yoga Friday and Monday mornings, whether it's all the stuff we do, playing music, prepping, playing."

She'd recently bought theater tickets for Sunday nights—a move she never would have made in the days when she had to get up early for work on Monday. These days, Monday means checking in on e-mail for a bit to see what she's missed and getting ready to go back to Scripps on Tuesday.

"Right now this works both for Scripps and for me," she said. "If it ceases to work for Scripps, then it's not gonna work for me, because right now there's a win-win. If it stops working for me, I'll leave. But there's no reason to do that if it's working."

To hear Burns talk, you'd think staged retirement is a gift from the company. But it's far from charity for older workers. Instead, holding on to aging employees makes hard-nosed business sense, particularly in the health industry.

Consider the demographics.

The aging of the population is putting extraordinary burdens on a health care system struggling to balance costs with quality of end-of-life care. Aging also means the industry is catering to a population more likely to appreciate a mature workforce—older doctors, nurses, and hospital staff who are able to empathize more readily with the concerns and attitudes of patients. There's more to it than just being treated by "one of your own." In a world where preconceptions of the aged as feeble and helpless are still prevalent, the presence of older workers in a hospital or clinic can signal to older patients that the company will be sensitive to their needs—without the condescension.

And, as we will see in Japan, specialized skills are important ingredients that can tip the scales for an employer deciding whether to make efforts to hold onto an older workforce. This is of primary importance in health care, where specialized medical knowledge and familiarity with procedures can often be a matter or life or death. Training costs are high. No leading health care operation can long tolerate high turnover rates or bear the burden of continually bringing in new hires while pushing the experienced folks out the door.

So one answer for leading health care providers is to nurture employees, turning—in an odd twist—to the old-style lifetime employment model, where workers stick with the same company for 30 or 40 years, moving through cycles of training and promotion, burnishing skills and increasing their value as employees along the way. And such companies find they need to make another investment: offer the kinds of benefits and other "extras" that build a sense of loyalty between worker and employer, so employees don't take their company-funded skills to a competitor.

A look at the criteria that AARP uses to rank employers will give us a solid idea of how the needs of older workers and the health industry—and other industries as well—can converge with particular policies and vision. AARP looks at recruiting practices, opportunities for training, education and career development, workplace accommodations, alternative work options such as phased retirement, employee health and pension benefits, and extras for retirees. In a point that is often made in these discussions, the policies that benefit older workers are extremely likely to benefit all employees, so it's not necessary that employers have programs targeted exclusively at the 50 and over crowd. The AARP judges include leading researchers in work and retirement, the heads of think-tanks and research institutes, gerontologists, union officials, and experts on aging.

In the organization's 2013 rankings, the top five companies were the National Institutes of Health, Scripps Health, Atlantic Health System, the University of Texas MD Anderson Cancer Center, and Mercy Health System, in that order. The No. 1 choice, NIH, funds more than 300,000 researchers at universities and institutes around the world and it runs 27 centers directly, including the NIH Clinical Center, which the NIH says is the largest hospital in the world dedicated completely to clinical research.

AARP cited NIH for recruiting at 50-plus job fairs and sending its own recent retirees notices of fresh job openings, and offering training benefits such as tuition reimbursement and in-house education. As at Scripps, training is a central feature of being an NIH employee: AARP said that in one 12-month period, all NIH employees had participated in at least one training program. NIH also rotates workers through different departments to help them develop new skills.

Aside from training, NIH offers familiar extras that not only encourage workers to stick around for the long term, but also address their needs as they age: wellness programs with on-site, no-charge exercise classes and health screenings; comprehensive health insurance packages; and flex-time and job-sharing arrangements and phased retirement. It's difficult to measure how much these policies respond to or engender an older workforce, but NIH definitely has plenty of gray heads in its ranks: some 47 percent of its workers are 50-plus, according to AARP, and the average tenure among them is more than 18 years. So these are the long-term employees, the ones who have put a substantial chunk of their lives into the NIH, and have a reasonable expectation that their loyalty should pay off.

Health care is not the only industry where holding onto skilled workers—and outfitting them with new skills as technology advances—is a key to survival and growth. Education is another leading business, and one with a solid future in a knowledge-based economy where employers are waking up to the fact that letting your biggest brains walk out the door into early retirement can be bad for the bottom line. In the health industry, solid health benefits are part of the package. At large universities—such as West Virginia University and Cornell University, both of which have appeared high on recent AARP lists—employers are able to offer a variety of benefits in training and education. It's what they do best. West Virginia, for instance, has a workforce that's 44 percent aged 50 or older, in a state that ranks last in labor force participation rates for older people in the United States. Cornell, meanwhile, has a program called "Encore Cornell Program," which matches Cornell retirees with temporary jobs and volunteer opportunities at the university or in the neighborhood. The program also runs "Encore On-Call," in which retirees register on a call list to offer advice and expertise to the university. "Encore and More" alerts retirees to training and education opportunities on campus. Again, a healthy percentage of the university's employees are 50 or older: 43 percent.

As these policies suggest, attracting and retaining older workers requires putting employees at the center of company policies. In the slash-and-burn labor market of the Great Recession, the guiding wisdom has been that crisis requires rank-and-file employees to come last—last in line for benefits, last in line for pay increases, and, ultimately, last in line for a job. But a look at Scripps shows that in a skills-based industry like health care, survival depends heavily on retaining a talented workforce, even if your workers are in their 50s and 60s.

But even if things make business sense, they don't necessarily get done without some leadership from the top.

Chris Van Gorder knew that according to everything he'd been taught in grad school, the layoffs were necessary.

It was the 1980s, and the health care company he was working for was adjusting to a major shift in Medicare reimbursements. Van Gorder's management team was about twice as big as the bosses thought it needed to be. Blood needed to be let, and it was his job to let it.

It wasn't easy—not for them, and not for him. Not for an ex-cop who nurses the memory of his Teamster father telling him—with tears in his eyes—how the union let him down. How when he'd aged at the end of 40 years working in a milk-bottling plant, he just wasn't needed anymore. "He felt he'd been abandoned by his employer and by his union," Van Gorder recalls.

Van Gorder went ahead with the layoffs, but decided he never wanted to go through that again. The way he grew to see it, those losing their jobs were paying for the mistakes of management, and it wasn't fair. "I never forgot the pain of actually having to really sit down and lay people off," he says. "We're talking about really impacting people's lives, and they didn't create the situation at all."

Van Gorder has been in a position to call the shots since he took over as CEO at Scripps Health in 2000. Only this time he was tasked not with cutting workers but with doing everything he could to keep them from leaving.

Scripps was in a bad place back then. Six months after joining the company as COO, Van Gorder stepped into the top job, replacing a man who'd been drummed out by a revolt among his own medical staff. The non-profit was bleeding money—nearly $26 million a year—and bleeding talent, as turnover rates surged and nurses fled.

So Van Gorder, who moved from the police force to the health business after a head-on, on-the-job car crash landed him in the hospital, launched a campaign to turn that around. And part of that meant putting employees—including older workers—at the center of the company.

That approach, he argues, makes sense in an industry so dependent on the skills and training of its people. "We're a very labor-intensive organization," he told me. "We have lots of technology, but all that technology is delivered by people."

Van Gorder is credited with leading a major reversal—both in finances and in atmosphere—for Scripps. When we spoke the non-profit was mounting an ambitious expansion plan. Turnover was down to a little over 10 percent by 2010, and the nonprofit was in the black, with an operating income of $233 million in 2012. Under his watch, Scripps has established a no-layoff policy, hired a human resources chief—Vic Buzachero—who is also "corporate senior vice-president for innovation," standardized hiring procedures to respond to long-term needs rather than the short-term vagaries of the economy, and strengthened in-house training programs like the one Burns works at. If a position is eliminated, employees can now keep earning pay with benefits at a "career resource center" that helps them look for another job at Scripps or elsewhere. Van Gorder said about 900 people had gone through the program in the previous nine years, and some 90 percent of them had managed to find another job within the company. The staged retirement program started on his watch.

Van Gorder, just a month short of 60 when I spoke with him, considers delayed retirement a benefit to employees that could even prolong their lives. But he was clear that one of the goals of his policies was to instill loyalty in employees, encouraging them to see Scripps as a place where one could develop a career, rather than a stepping-stone to someplace else. Such appeals to loyalty would not be taken seriously without efforts to take care of workers as they move into their 50s and 60s. Nothing can be a greater motivator to look for another job in your 40s than the expectation that your current employer will cut you loose when you're too old to get hired elsewhere. So Scripps has put programs in place to build confidence among its employees and give them the flexibility to adjust their work schedule to changing needs as they get older.

The phased retirement program, however, is still fairly limited. Workers have to get the company's approval to participate, and company officials say quite candidly that the arrangement won't work for the company in every instance, though they are willing to move candidates to parts of the operation where it does work. That's borne out by the numbers: In a company with more than 13,000 employees, about 120—not quite 1 percent—were in the program when I visited, about 40 percent of them nurses. Still, the existence of an active program like that indicates an evolving attitude and an increasing sophistication about how to hold onto talent by making allowances for older workers.

Those older workers are clearly a key component of Scripps's overall workforce. About 36 percent of Scripps employees are 50 or older, and more than 13 percent are 60 or above. The company is also doing an above-average job of holding on to them: the retirement rate for those who hit 65 is 4.9 percent, far below the national average of 17.4 percent, according to Scripps.

The staged retirement plan, limited though it may be, also helps build the loyalty that allows the company to pour resources into training employees without the fear that they'll all jump ship before Scripps can recoup its investment, Van Gorder says.

So, at bottom, it's just business.

"We retain a great person, so we don't have to pay for the replacement and all that kind of stuff," he said. "And I believe that these people will live longer."

Van Gorder's vision is attractive, promising work to anyone who is willing and able to stay on the job. Still, it has its limits. The Scripps program is not a government operation that can be fueled through tough times by politics and deficit-spending; if the American health care industry stumbles or if Scripps's fortunes tank, the program could easily go the way of the fully funded corporate pension.

In the short-term, Van Gorder's vision faces perhaps its starkest challenge in the corridors of the ICU at Scripps Memorial Hospital where Lorraine Pagni-Kiefer dashes from emergency to emergency.

Nurses *are* the health care industry.

There are more than 3 million registered nurses in the United States, the largest group of health care professionals in the country. There are more nurses than surgeons. More than anesthesiologists. More than physical therapists or radiologists or pharmacists or dentists.

They also do some of the most physically demanding work in the industry.

They are on their feet for 12-hour shifts, rushing from cardiac arrest to cardiac arrest, often pinioned between desperately sick patients, distraught families, and overworked doctors. They are the largely unheralded workhorses of the health care industry.

"If you watched Lorraine, you know that you don't sit around too much. You are pretty much all over the place," said Veronica Zaman, Scripps's vice president for human resources and learning, and a nurse herself. "You're circulating, you're constantly moving, so that the fatigue factors also start to play in. You know as you age, your body is less resilient, so we are always very conscious of keeping that safe environment as our workers age."

And while Scripps has taken steps to care for its aging nurses, the profession best illustrates the struggle of health care companies to balance the needs of older employees with the mounting demands of the business.

Nurses are definitely aging. The average age for operating room nurses at Scripps is about 51, Zaman said. Of all Scripps's 4,000-plus nurses, one third are 50 or older, and the average age is 44 and climbing. That's close to the age of nurses nationwide. According to a U.S. Department of Health and Human Services survey, the median age of nurses in America in 2008 was 46 years old, up from 38 years old in 1988. Older nurses make up a much larger percentage: in 1988, only 4.7 percent of nurses were 60 or older; by 2008, that had more than doubled to 10.7 percent. The aging of the nursing profession has far outpaced the aging of the overall labor force.

At the same time that nurses are aging, the demand for their services is soaring—because everyone else is getting older too. Registered nursing is often listed as a top occupation for job growth, and the Bureau of Labor Statistics reports that the number of employed nurses will grow by 26 percent from 2010 to 2020 to 3.45 million. Much of the growth in the legions of nurses expected over the next decade or so will be younger people entering the profession. But seasoned professionals are still seen as essential to the process, and employers like Scripps are under the gun to hold on to them as long as they can—and get them to train the new ones.

That's where someone like Lorraine Pagni-Kiefer comes in.

Like Jamie Burns, Lorraine has a retired husband, but she's young enough—53—to not really be entertaining the idea of retirement yet. In fact, she says she needs to keep working because she's carrying her ex-firefighter husband on her Scripps-sponsored health insurance.

While not yet ready to retire, Lorraine is working in a program that's aimed at making the most of older nurses' expertise: mentorship. Since the mid-2000s, Scripps has drawn on nurses' experience in both training student nurses and new hires, hoping to narrow the difference between the skill levels of the older and younger workers.

Zaman said it could take anywhere between two and five years of work experience for an operating room nurse to get up to snuff, so the older nurses are needed to help train the next generation.

"It's an added advantage that they bring to the table because they have the book knowledge, but then they have that hands-on practical knowledge that they've gained over years of working," said Zaman, who, as the wife of an officer in the Air Force, honed her own nursing skills at a U.S. military hospital in Landstuhl, Germany.

Like others at Scripps, Lorraine had built that knowledge over a career that included alternating bouts of work and formal study.

She grew up in Crockett, California, north of Oakland, coming from an extended family of workers at the C&H sugar refinery that dominates the town's waterfront and its economy. Her parents chose different paths than her aunts and uncles, though: her mother was a nurse and her father was a construction worker who built wineries.

As a child, Lorraine never wanted to work in a hospital when she grew up.

"My mom worked night-shifts, 11 to 7, Christmas and every weekend, and I said I will never be a nurse, never, because I don't want to work weekends and Christmas." She laughed at the way things turned out. "I've probably worked every Christmas for the past 25 years. But that's okay—it's better than being a patient."

By her late teens, she'd changed her mind about her mother's profession. She got her associate's degree in nursing from California State University, Dominguez

Hills in 1983 and went to work at Scripps, moving to the ICU a couple of years later. She returned to school to get her bachelor's in 1992. After another decade of experience, she signed on as a mentor and got so immersed in the job that she went back to school again with help from Scripps tuition reimbursement for a master's degree in nursing education.

When she finished in spring of 2012, colleagues at work asked her what she had planned next. Lorraine's answer: "I said I am going to stay and become the best mentor they had ever seen."

Lorraine says the mentor role offers her a mix of instruction and involvement with treatment she finds engaging.

She clearly thrives on the dynamic life of the hospital.

When her pager rang on the ICU, she shouted into the receiver: "Rapid response is here! I'm Lorraine." She rushed into the room to find an 81-year-old male patient who apparently had been administered too much medication and was having trouble breathing.

She plowed into the room, announcing herself to family members gathered around the bed. I watched from the hallway as she moved among them, taping a drainage tube and overseeing the patient's treatment with other nurses.

According to the standards of a hospital, it was a non-emergency, and Lorraine didn't seem worried. Dashing out of the room for some equipment, she shouted to a co-worker in the hall about a mutual acquaintance she'd run into at the grocery store. "He says hi to everybody."

So this is her day. For 12 hours at a time, she assists and supervises nurses. She buzzes around the ICU with a white smock with a pink, black, and gray flower print. She peeks in on patients and introduces herself, scanning their charts, making sure they're getting the right medication, checking that their alarms are set in case a vital sign goes awry. A big part of her job is also managing her relationship with the younger nurses, being there to help them but not smother them.

It can be a difficult balance in a high-pressured workplace.

"You need to be their friend, because they won't call you if they don't like you," she says during a break. "My goal is to take really excellent care of the patient, not win any popularity contests. But at the same time, you want them to feel comfortable calling you if they're having trouble with a patient."

"I would imagine some of the nurses maybe resent me," she adds, then smiles. "But they don't show it."

But even at just 53, Lorraine already sees the difficulties of pushing forward with such a demanding job into her 60s. The morning we met, she had to handle an 800-pound patient—a serious physical strain on nurses that has become more common amid increasing obesity. Fearing injuries among nurses, Scripps and other health care companies have formed "lift teams" with the expertise—and muscle power—to move larger patients.

A major obstacle to extending the careers of nurses is the 12-hour shift. Originally implemented to offer the benefit of a three-day workweek for nurses, the shifts also reduce the changing of the nursing guard in a hospital from three to two over 24 hours. Shift changes are a major concern at hospitals, since foul-ups on patient care are more likely when the baton is passed from one nurse to the next. Cutting the shift changes has reduced errors.

But the long hours can tip the balance in favor of retirement, particularly for nurses with retired spouses on sufficient pensions. The issue is one of industry-wide concern: the American Nurses Association has a professional panel dedicated to nurse fatigue. At Scripps, the longer shift has proven to be such an impediment to extending careers that the company is considering going back to the eight-hour schedule, despite the medical downsides, said Zaman.

It's certainly a consideration for Lorraine, who wants to hang on as long as she can in the ICU. Looking ahead, she's balancing all the factors that go into such decisions these days. When can she afford to retire? When will her Medicare kick in? How will she pay for health insurance for her husband, who when we talked was just 55 and at least a decade from Medicare?

Lorraine sees those generous Scripps health benefits as a lifesaver—literally. She missed seven months of work the year before we met in a bout with breast cancer. She faced an operation, chemotherapy, radiation, and breast reconstruction. Though she shrugs it off in conversation, it must have been a draining year. But at least the drain wasn't financial: thanks to her benefits package, the cost to her for all that work was nominal.

And so, like many in her position, she is stuck between physical demands at work and the limits of her aging body on one side, and a love of the job and the need to hold onto health insurance on the other side.

"I don't know much longer I'll be able to work 12-hour shifts, but I just got these new shoes," she said, looking down at her feet. "I picture myself hopefully in the next couple of years getting maybe an educator job, but if I have to, I can do this job for nine more years, then I'll be 62 and retire. But the only problem is health benefits. . ."

Lorraine's quandary is about much more than her individual career or even the functioning of the ICU at Scripps—it's a matter for the American economy at large. Scripps and the rest of the health care industry, as well as many other industries in America, are not only struggling to maintain the knowledge and skills embodied in the aging workforce, but also manage the transfer of that knowledge to the next generation.

Close attention to this question is something we see again and again in companies, factories, and professions successfully confronting the demographic challenge across the world's top economies. As Scripps learned in the early 2000s, maintaining such knowledge is not automatic. It is not a matter of fate. The company was well on its way to losing its best people and thereby driving itself into decline. Making the aging worker an organizational priority was a pillar in the effort to turn things around.

Failure can be particularly damaging. As management consultant David W. DeLong points out in his 2004 book, *Lost Knowledge: Confronting the Threat of an Aging Workforce*, humankind has faced losses of critical knowledge over the millennia, from the destruction of the famed Library of Alexandria to the disappearance of the craftsmanship that went into the Stradivarius violins. Now the looming retirements of the World War II baby and the boomer generations, DeLong argues, threatens to erode—or, in some cases, erase—the vast knowledge of the past three decades of tremendous technological change.

These workers carry various kinds of knowledge with them when they walk out the door. First, there are the skills they have as individuals—what they know how to do, and what they understand. Second is what DeLong calls cultural knowledge, workers' ability to operate together as a team. Next is cultural knowledge, the workers' often unstated understanding of how things operate in a particular organization. Finally, we have structured knowledge, the working rules and procedures governing action in a company.

All of this can go out the door with a retiree. For anyone who has worked any length of time in a company, the deficits of the newcomer are readily apparent: rookies need time to learn the ropes. They may lack certain skills, and they need to adapt to the working style, the collaborative process, of their team. They don't yet know "how we do it here," and they have to grow accustomed to the rules and procedures laid out by management.

In an organization with a diverse workforce, where the ages of the staffers are well-distributed, there are plenty of mid- and old-timers to guide the greenhorn into the established way of doing things and to share technical and social knowledge. The company is filled with potential trainers, and the newcomer will have months or even years to attain the skill level of his or her superiors before those superiors leave the company. This provides a smooth transition, so that when the seniors leave, there are well-trained mid-level employees to fill the gap. The loss of crucial knowledge or skills is minimal.

But DeLong shows how the particular circumstances of the boomer generation—a population bulge that came of age in an era of unprecedented technological advances—have created a perilous situation for some of the country's most vital sectors, such as government, manufacturing, energy, aerospace, health care, and education. When the war babies and boomers who flooded into the workforce beginning in the 1970s retire in large numbers, they will take with them vast stores of knowledge. The challenge, DeLong says, is to institute methods of retaining that knowledge—in written or other forms—and transmitting it to younger workers who can carry on after the older generation has left.

At stake is the future viability of the economy, he argues.

"In the long term, you cannot compete effectively in the knowledge economy unless you are serious about knowledge retention," DeLong writes.

As we can see in the case of Scripps and so many other companies, there are powerful forces that make this type of measured, orderly transition increasingly difficult. Heightened globalization and competition, as well as the demands of the stock market, have put pressure on companies to focus increasingly on short-term gains and the bottom line. Layoffs, early retirement, and hiring freezes have hit organizations at both ends of the age spectrum: companies have shed the older, knowledgeable workers, but have not hired enough younger workers to replace them. The less-numerous younger workers themselves can see the writing on the wall: if this is how companies treat older workers, then I'd better get as much as I can while I'm young and get out. This has contributed to the growth of job-jumping as a method of advancement among younger workers. Just as leaders at Scripps feared, this kind of turnover and bleeding of human capital can strangle an organization.

Meanwhile, the laser-beam attention to the bottom line means knowledge retention activities—such as storing instructions, observations, and innovations in written or digital form for later workers to access, or even just "shop talk" among staffers—is discouraged in favor of activities that lead immediately to profits. So workers are kept to the grindstone with little opportunity or incentive to save or share the information in their heads.

DeLong argues that in coming years sectors such as defense, aerospace, secondary education, and the oil and gas industries could be hobbled by retirement departures. "There is little question that many experienced workers will be leaving their jobs in the next decade," he writes. "And that giant sucking sound you will hear is all the knowledge being drained out of organizations by retirements and other forms of turnover."

So companies need to effectively manage retirement, retain mid-career workers, and recruit younger ones. It is only within a reasonably predictable flow of personnel through the life of the company, DeLong says, that an organization can go about capturing and transmitting the knowledge of its older employees.

We've seen how the health care industry is particularly vulnerable to the danger of lost knowledge. The backbone of the sector—nurses—is aging rapidly. But they are not the only ones.

Doctors are also members of an aging profession. A 2007 nationwide survey found that nearly one-quarter of physicians were 60 years or older. The same for dentists: in 2001, more than 80 percent of American dentists were older than 45, and the Institute of Medicine reported in 2008 that the number of people entering dentistry by 2020 would not be enough to replace the retirees.

So hospital systems are under pressure to stave off retirements among its staff for as long as possible. The IOM says that to maintain the current ratio of patients to health care providers, the United States will need an additional 3.5 million providers by 2030—a boost of 35 percent from the current level of nearly 10 million. The needs are spread across the board: nearly 900 more nurses, 284 more doctors, and more than 700 nursing aides will be needed to handle the surging demand for services.

Leading health care providers have been coming to some of the same conclusions as DeLong. Two researchers at the John J. Heldrich Center for Workforce Development at Rutgers University, Laurie Harrington and Maria Heidkamp, found, for example, that Robert Wood Johnson University Hospital in New Brunswick, New Jersey, conducted a workplace assessment in a search for ways of keeping experience nurses from retiring. Some of the steps taken were aimed at easing the effects of long hours of work on aging bodies, such as putting refrigerators on countertops so nurses wouldn't have to bend over to retrieve patients' medications, buying "anti-fatigue" mats so they could rest during downtime, and interviewing nurses considering retiring to identify changes in the work environment that could keep them on the job.

The Institute of Medicine did its own study in 2008, *Retooling for an Aging America: Building the Health Care Workforce*, calling for developing less physically demanding jobs, using technology to help with heavier tasks, and creating more flexible work schedules. The report also suggested retaining older workers as mentors for less experienced colleagues, moving older workers into leadership positions, and offering additional training to retired health care workers to recruit them as geriatric experts or faculty instructors.

The Sloan Center on Aging & Work issued a report in 2010 showing that despite the gains illustrated by outfits such as Scripps, health care operations on average assessed their workforces less than other industries. According to the study, health care companies were lower in percentages of employers who assessed the age of their workforces, the skills they will need in the future, or what abilities their workers have. Of course, these are all key issues. You can't estimate how many workers you're going to lose to retirement if you haven't figured out how many are near retirement age. If you haven't catalogued the array of skills across your workforce, you won't know which skills you are in danger of losing. And if you don't know that, you can't figure out which employees are most important for you to keep on the job, and what your hiring needs are going to be in the future.

"This is interesting because it suggests that many health care organizations, which are among those enterprises most threatened by the aging of the workforce, have limited knowledge of factors that might exacerbate their levels of talent availability risks," the study said.

The most that the Sloan researchers could say was that the health sector was "at least somewhat aware" of the skills shortages headed their way. The abilities that were in short supply were management, sales and marketing, and legal, operations, and computer skills.

One compelling argument the Sloan study makes is based on the gender of the health care workforce: it is overwhelmingly—80 percent—women. Surveys show women feel they have less control over their work schedules than men report, suggesting that flexibility of job schedules may require closer attention in the case of health care than in other industries. The study also recommended giving workers greater decision-making power as a way of increasing their commitment to their jobs and their employers, and thereby diminishing the incentive to retire or move to other jobs or employers. Women, after all, often face a high level of responsibility inside their families. Those over 50 may need to help care for an aging parent. So work-family balance and exhaustion are mounting concerns. The IOM has estimated that nearly 30 percent of nurses work overtime beyond their 12-hour shifts. These are problems that could be at least partially alleviated by greater access to flexible work schedules.

The Sloan study concludes that health sector employers should start by figuring out what information they needed to assess current and future talent needs, assess the workforce to find that information, and plan accordingly. Employers need to develop methods to hold onto high-demand talent, such as more fully engaging the workforce, facilitating transfer of knowledge between generations, and attracting new workers to fill future needs.

Leading options included flexible schedules and flexible career paths, such as "off-ramps" and "on-ramps" that allow workers to come into an organization at different stages of their careers rather than the "hire right out of college, work straight through to retirement" model, and staged retirement. Other possible steps include greater use of technology on the job to lighten physical burdens, such as countering spotty memory with computerized prompts, and so-called smart beds that collect and provide medical information and assist in turning patients. Computer and data systems could also be modified to reduce repetitive stress injury from typing and to simplify methods of data input and retrieval to counter memory lapses among staff and speed workers' ability to get the information they need when they need it.

Many health providers are responding. A 2012 Cornell University study of such responses found a wide variety of steps: flexible work schedules such as weekends-only, work-at-home, and sessional work, or reduced work for short periods without losing benefits; allowing employees to draw on pensions while still working part-time; and allowing retirees to come back within five years without losing benefits.

The stakes, the Sloan study concluded, were not only high for the health sector, but for other parts of the economy as it struggles to accommodate and adjust to the aging workforce. "The health care sector will be one of the leading sources of employment in the forthcoming decade, and many of the talent management practices that employers adopt in this sector will transfer to other sectors," the researchers wrote.

Sometimes the best thing an employer can do is just get out of the way and let their workers get on with it.

Kenn Curzon is a man of his times.

Modern medical technologies—like those showcased at Scripps—have helped to keep his 90-year-old body and mind working far longer than previous generations, at a time when our economic system is increasingly in need of older workers' labor. And his career is the logical outcome of company policy that offers incentives and opportunities for employees to stay on the job for as long as they can.

But Kenn Curzon also possesses a unique mix of physical endurance, mental acuity, and plain old personality—gifts sprung from the mysterious mix of genetics and environment—that have enabled him and a growing number of others like him to keep working deep into old age.

Just like the song sung at his birthday party, Kenn Curzon's road to his career at Scripps has been a long one.

The Blitz was on. The fury of the Nazi war machine came to Britain in September 1940, dropping 337 tons of bombs on London on the first day of an assault that would last until May of the next year. Curzon, then still a couple of months short of 18, had gone into military service, but was dispatched back to his family when his hometown west of the capital came under bombing.

The entire country was mobilized to confront the crisis. Curzon's job was driving a water truck to put out the flames raging from Hitler's incendiary bombs. He recalls rushing into his mother's office where she was shouting into a phone as a volunteer, dispatching fire-fighting units to hard-hit areas. Sirens were wailing.

"They're really bombing heavy!" he cried to his mother.

"I know!" she snapped back. "Why are you bothering me? Get out there and get on with it!"

The Curzon family was very familiar with "getting on with it." Kenn describes his childhood home as a squall of activity, where everyone was busy doing something. Formal employment was a major part of that. His father went into British military intelligence with World War I. His mother started out as a schoolteacher, then went into business for herself training adults for the workforce. Curzon says both of them worked until near the ends of their lives.

"I don't think it's something you inherit," he says of the desire to work. "It's just the thing you do. We were always doing things when I grew up, there was always things going on. So I kind of grew up in an environment where there was nobody just sitting around like, doing nothing."

Curzon's life has gone as far as one can get from "doing nothing." His career reads more like an adventure from Homer's *Odyssey*, with chapters of battle, travel, disguise. And longevity.

By the time he was 18, Curzon had already been getting on with it for some time. Not that he always enjoyed it. When he was 14, his father set him up helping repair cars in garages owned by his uncles because, as his father said, "it's important that you learn this." He hated it, and when he tried to sweeten the deal by asking his father for more money, the elder Curzon refused and told him to look for another job. So he did, he says, at Isleworth Film Studios in London, fetching corned beef sandwiches and hot tea for actors, most notably American Paul Robeson, who was there working on the film *Sanders of the River*, released in 1935.

Then came the war, and the Blitz.

Curzon joined the fight, first as an ammunition expert in the Royal Army Ordnance Corps, then with Britain's Special Air Service, bringing himself into the military intelligence world where his father spent his entire career. The SAS was started as a commando paratrooper unit designed for raids behind enemy lines. He joined in the Allied invasion of Nazi-controlled France at Normandy on D-Day. Curzon avoids talking much on the record about this chapter in his life, claiming the information is "top secret," but whatever he was doing in the war, getting out there and getting on with it had become a habit.

After the war, he studied public service at the University of Bristol, continued his work at SAS for a while, and in 1952 made another big jump in his life—this time across the Atlantic Ocean. Times were tough in postwar Britain, and by then Curzon had a family to feed: he was married with two children. America, everybody told him, was the place to make it. He arrived in Philadelphia and eventually got a job with Chrysler as a service director, staying for 12 years, later striking an alliance with his old battlefield enemies, the Germans, taking a job with carmaker Mercedes in California. Curzon hardly seems to have had an idle hour. He traveled around California for his employer. He worked in the Boy Scouts as a district commissioner and organizer of an annual fundraiser in San Jose. He pursued hobbies in photography and cinematography, shooting film in 8 and 16 mm.

He suffered his share of difficulties and sadness along the way. He and his first wife divorced after 16 years. He married a second time to a Scottish woman who doted on a home garden full of rosebushes, but she struggled with multiple sclerosis and died after a dozen years of marriage. Between his two wives, Curzon had five children.

Time was passing. His career in automotives ended in his early 60s when he retired from Mercedes.

But there were no golf courses or tennis courts or leisurely days beside a sun-dappled pool in a retirement community ahead for Curzon. Just because he retired from one job didn't mean he had to stop working. So he didn't. Instead, Curzon went undercover.

As a bear.

"Two of us used to do it," Curzon says of his six years with the U.S Forest Service in the 1980s portraying Smokey the Bear. "Not everybody could get in the costume—they get claustrophobic."

That wasn't a problem for Curzon.

"I used to feel good in there. You know," he says, smiling, "I was hiding."

The job was more fun than work. Much of it involved publicity shots and social events, like a news correspondents' dinner where Curzon says many of the women were eager to pose for photos with the Bear. "Oh Smokey!" Curzon says, imitating the women in sotto voce "comin' up with all their low-cut gowns." He says he received a letter from the regional chief of the Forest Service joking that "Smokey was dancing and chasing a waitress in the kitchen."

And then in 1990, Curzon made what he expects will be his final career change, going to work for the contractor running parking services for his current home: Scripps Memorial Hospital La Jolla. The quarter-century denouement since then—begun in his late 60s—can actually be seen as the pinnacle of his career. At Scripps he has put together the experience, personal traits, and skills that have defined a relationship to work that has spanned three-quarters of a century.

From a windowless basement office, Kenn Curzon rules over a personal empire of handicapped, visitor, and staff parking stalls, of tickets and time-stamps and automated boom gates. And cars. Vans and SUVs and pick-ups and compacts, Toyotas and Chevys and Fords, hundreds of them coming in and out every day.

But Curzon doesn't preside over the parking lot of an amusement park, a place where people flock for the breathless thrills of a rollercoaster or haunted mansion. The visitors here are worried about the results of a biopsy or distraught over the death of a loved one. They arrive flustered by traffic or on the verge of tears.

"Maybe they're coming here because someone's dying," he said one day in his office, the walls covered with images of London and at least two portraits of the Queen. "It's not like being a cashier out there or an attendant. We make people aware of that, because they look in the car and they see that somebody's sad, and so we just wave them through."

For Curzon, this attention to others—he doesn't use the word, but many would call it empathy—is a quality that comes with age. He says he was first hired because of his age, not despite it. At the time, the hospital was shifting from free to pay parking to discourage students from a nearby university from filling up the lot and taking spots from patients and their families. Officials expected some pushback from irate drivers, Curzon says, and they wanted someone with a cool head to keep things under control through the transition.

Curzon had what he said was an effective recipe for calming down angry drivers and defusing ugly encounters before they spin out of control. "People are going to get upset. You don't get upset with them, you just stand there and just look like you're a giraffe at a zoo or a llama, preferably, just kind of have that look like, 'Oh.' "

There's no doubt that Curzon is well-loved at Scripps, known throughout the company for his storytelling, accent, and old-world habits, such as wearing a full suit and a red, white, and blue tie to work every day. He draws caricatures of colleagues and hands them out.

The affection for him at his surprise party—he calls it a "shock" party—was heartfelt. The preparations were meticulous. His supervisor choked up during his speech about how Curzon had touched the lives of his colleagues. Workmates lined up to hug him and pose for photographs. Upper management loves having him around as well. Van Gorder says he didn't know Curzon's age until the preparations for his birthday party.

"He may walk with a cane, but he's still doing his job. I have no reason to chase him out the door," says Van Gorder. "He's an inspiration for a whole lot of other people who see him, and I know he's an inspiration to the patients. They see him and see that he's still working."

And so Curzon just keeps going. As long as his health holds out and Scripps keeps him on, retirement isn't in the cards. He plays this scenario in his head: he goes to his supervisor and announces he's quitting. What does his supervisor say?

"Oh, no, no, you can't do that. You'll die!"

Curzon laughs.

"What would I do? That's right—I wouldn't do anything," he says. "I'd sit at home. Much better to be doing something and contribute something and be part of a good team, a winning team. And the winning is taking care of people."

He lives alone in a small apartment not far from the hospital. His children are not in the area—a fact that Curzon says he is thankful for, freeing him from any hovering or monitoring of his moves.

His day starts early: he drives into work in his '94 Mercury, arrives between 6 and 6:30 a.m., and works without a computer, depending on direct personal contact to coordinate with his colleagues. "Everything is done the old-fashioned way. Everybody goes, 'Oh my god, he's got a typewriter!' " He writes reports on parking usage, fields calls and complaints, and deals with preparations for special events, such as valet parking for VIPs.

So far, his health is under control. Curzon suffers from lymphedema, which causes his legs to swell, and an aortic aneurysm that requires monitoring. He fainted at work in March 2012, and Scripps doctors had him wear a new device, called a "Zio Patch," which revealed an irregular heartbeat. Doctors implanted a cardiac defibrillator—similar to a pacemaker—in April and Curzon was back to work in five days.

"I don't think I really basically have changed," he says. "I certainly don't go out dancing every night, which I used to do, ballroom dancing, which is good recreation."

"I mean the real thing," he adds, "with a good partner."

And always there is that advice from his mother. There's another piece of advice he remembers, back in the 1950s when he started with Chrysler. The company president, Lester L. Colbert, picked him out as an Englishman for his use of the word "whilst" in a report. At a company meeting with hundreds of people, Colbert called him to the front of the room.

"I knew right away you were British," Curzon quotes Colbert as saying. "I want to tell you, you guys are the best, because you stood on that little island and you fended off everybody."

Later, Cobert took him aside and warned him to beware of too many meetings. "If you guys had been sitting in meetings, Germany would have invaded you."

In other words, Curzon says, don't sit around talking about work.

Just get on with it.

We've seen how progressive company policies can make extended worklives more profitable and enjoyable for older Americans—under the right conditions. Scripps workers are in an enviable, and rare, situation. They toil in an industry that, despite uncertainties and the tough economic climate of recent years, is growing. Many of them have unique skills that are in high demand as society ages. And they have benefited from a business model that capitalizes on their talents and experience.

But that's often not the case in the America of the Great Recession and its bitter aftermath. In fact, as we'll see, the United States has struggled for the past half-century to balance longer lives, personal finance, and the needs of the economy. Now we move to the American post-industrial heartland, Akron, Ohio, where call center trainee Rita Hall is battling a trio of enemies—poverty, unemployment, and precarious health—in her search for a job to keep her afloat until retirement.

This chapter was written based on interviews and information gathered during a visit to Scripps Health, La Jolla, in October 2012, and subsequent e-mails with Lisa Ohmstede, e-mail and phone conversations with Jamie Burns, and a phone interview with the head of human resources, Vic Buzachero, in January 2013.

Rita Hall, 62, eats her daily lunch at the Salvation Army in Akron, Ohio, in January 2013.

3

The Fisherwoman of Akron

AKRON, *Ohio*

In the Bible, Jesus vowed to make his followers into fishers of men.

So on this day, Rita Hall was fishing.

It was January 2013 and she had a live one on the line, a man named Edwin. It was a blessing on a morning—in an age—when no one seems to answer the phone anymore, when most of her calls began and ended talking to voicemail.

"Hello. My name is Rita. I'm calling from Mature Services Employment and Training Solutions. How are you today?" she asked into her mouthpiece, launching into a script she would recite hundreds of times that month.

Edwin grunted a response. Rita pressed ahead.

"The reason for my call," she said, her girlish voice a mixture of sweetness and careful memorization, "is to provide you with information about the free, non-profit training program we have for seniors to help get them back into the workplace."

She waited for his response. Two years before, she had been in the same position as Edwin: out of work, considered too old for a new job but too young for Social Security. Then she found out about the non-profit Mature Services. Since then, she'd put together a resume, brushed up on job-search and interviewing skills, and learned how to manage calls like this one while earning minimum wage. True, she hadn't locked onto a permanent job yet, but she saw signs that was about to change. It was God's will. As she likes to say: "I believe He still wants me to work."

Would Edwin see things this way? His gruff voice scratched through the headphones.

"Oh. . . I'm not interested in training."

"Okay. . .," she said, slowly, the tiniest measure of disappointment peeking into her voice before darting away. "Well, have a great day!"

She hung up with a click of her mouse, checked off a string of boxes on her computer screen, and moved down the list. There were so many more people to call. As her mother—92 at the time—always said: If you got something to do, then do it.

She clicked on the next number, and the phone rang through her earphones. Voicemail answered: At the tone, please leave a message.

"Hello. My name is Rita. I'm calling from Mature Services. . ."

Rita spent more than half of her 62 years working in one of Akron's best-known hospitals as a medical receptionist until she was laid off in 2009. Now she sits in the call center at Mature Services for up to 20 hours a week, calling whomever her bosses at the non-profit tell her to call. She calls jobless older workers like Edwin to invite them to training sessions. She calls companies to entice them to "job fairs" where unemployed workers can meet potential employers. She calls human resource managers to cajole them into training her colleagues.

Over and over. More than 100 times in a four-hour shift. In 2012, she made some 15,000 calls.

That's 1,250 calls a month.

Two-hundred eight-eight calls a week.

Rita's job is part of the only federally run training and employment operation for low-income older workers in the United States, the Senior Community Service Employment Program (SCSEP). SCSEP, overseen by the Department of Labor and operated by non-profits across the country like Mature Services and AARP, is the descendant of a tiny pilot project begun in the heady "Great Society" days of the mid-1960s. It was a time when combating elderly poverty was high on Washington's agenda, and providing light work to older people was seen as a way of strengthening community services while putting some desperately needed cash in seniors' pockets.

Five decades later, as the country struggles to emerge from the joblessness and hardships left behind by the Great Recession and working rates of older Americans increase, SCSEP has expanded far beyond its original scope. Today it commands a budget of $450 million and serves more than 75,000 people aged 55 and over each year. Participants, who must have incomes of 125 percent of the poverty line or less, train for jobs as caretakers or receptionists or factory workers or call-center callers. They learn to use computer programs like Excel and search for jobs on Internet employment sites. They craft resumes. The government reports the program gets nearly half its clients—44.4 percent in 2011—into non-subsidized positions each year.

Rita Hall was hoping to be one of them.

On the day in January 2013 when she spoke with Edwin, Rita was full of that hope. Bursting with it. When I showed up at the call center on that cold northern Ohio morning, it was my second visit with her. She bounced up from her workstation to greet me, held my hand with two warm hands for longer than I expected, and smiled broadly.

Rita had reason to smile. When she'd lost her last hospital job, the economy was hitting rock bottom. She took a year to sort out her life. She'd worked in hospitals since the late 1960s, raised two sons into adulthood with her hard-working husband, Ernie, who owned a body shop. Then in 2005 Ernie died of a heart attack at age 55, leaving Rita on her own. After that, she suffered through health troubles, lost her job, and was skirting the poverty line. What would she do with no job? Unemployment insurance would eventually run out—what then? She'd had to take her pension from the hospital early, locking herself into lower monthly benefits for the rest of her life, and she was still a few years short of Social Security. Her two sons had their own children, their own lives. She didn't want to be a burden.

Then she heard about Mature Services. *There are still about 10 or 15 years left in me to work and do something*, she thought to herself.

So she showed up at the offices on Portage Path in a residential part of Akron, passed the initial screening and orientation, and got to work. Eventually she settled into a routine at the call center: several days a week, she drives her white 2003 Ford Focus just a few minutes from her home, and puts in a half-hour of job-search time at Mature Services. She starts calling at 9 a.m., working with a 15-minute break until 12:30 p.m. She earns minimum wage: $7.85 an hour.

Rita averages at least one job application every two weeks in accordance with SCSEP rules, but in her first two years of searching, she said she had never been offered a job. She'd had only four face-to-face interviews and two more on the phone. And time was running out. It used to be someone like Rita could stay enrolled in SCSEP until retirement. But these days, regulations cap each client at four years of lifetime participation, meaning that sometime in mid-2014, Rita would need to move on—job or no job.

But in January 2013, she thought she might have her chance to leave with a job. A week earlier she'd interviewed at Hudson Dermatology, in Hudson, Ohio, about a 20-minute drive from her house, a bit out of the way for her and an investment in gasoline. But it was a job, a good job, with good hours and solid pay—9 a.m. to 5:30 p.m., a 45-minute break for lunch, $9 an hour to start, going up to $10 after three months. Nothing luxurious but definitely a step up from minimum wage, something that could carry her a few more years into retirement.

Rita liked the $10 an hour part. "I could go for that," she said.

She was expecting a call any day now. There were signs of hope. She didn't want to call them definite signs, not yet. But signs, nonetheless.

First, she was prepared for the interview. As they say at Mature Services, you make your own luck. After finding the job posting on Indeed.com and clinching a sit-down, Rita decided she wanted to present a serious, hard-working, unadorned look. The last time I'd seen her, about eight months before, she had on a red blazer that matched her race-car red fingernails. Now the blazer was gone, replaced with a white blouse and a button-down black sweater. Her nails were trimmed and unpainted.

But she was nervous.

"I thought they were going to look in my car so I cleaned it all out," she said. "I didn't wear any makeup or jewelry."

Then came the interview itself. It lasted only 10 or 15 minutes, but the woman who spoke to Rita made notes all over her resume as they talked. Rita liked that. Then Rita brought up a potential sweetener: a program through Mature Services that would pay her salary for a negotiated period while she got up to speed. Rita felt she scored some points when she showed her preparation by pulling out the paperwork for the program on the spot.

At bottom, Rita just had a gut feeling that she could do this job. After all, she'd worked all those years—nearly 40—in hospitals, taking calls, transcribing doctor's notes, keeping a whole floor running smoothly. A dermatologist's office would be a piece of cake. The only glitch: Rita didn't know about something called EMR—Electronic Medical Records—but the woman said she could be trained, so that didn't seem like a deal-breaker. "I'm used to doing a lot more than that."

There were other reasons to feel good this time. Her age didn't set her apart. The two women working in the office when she visited were in their 50s. And the woman interviewing her was in her 60s. It didn't seem like the kind of place on the lookout for a pretty young thing to answer the phones. The other detail was the head doctor at Hudson—Neera Argawal-Antal—was the daughter of a doctor Rita worked with at Cuyahoga Falls Hospital, Prahladkumar J. Argawal. Or, as Rita called him, PJ.

"It's just such a small world!" she said, thankful and amazed at this gift of coincidence. "That makes for a good relationship."

Rita did the right thing on follow-up, too, dropping a thank-you note in the mail the same day as the interview.

So this is what it all came down to. The resume sessions, the job interview role-playing, the thousands and thousands of phone calls. The little helpers like wage subsidies and quickly posted thank-you notes. The close attention to dress and manner. The fevered, fearful cleaning out of a car just in case a peek inside reveals you to be unworthy of employment. And the prayers, the faith that a God is watching over you and will deliver a job when it's your time.

"I just keep searching," she told me. "I never stop."

On the wall above Rita's workstation hangs a painting: Claude Monet's *The Water Lily Pond* shows a Japanese bridge spanning the water. When would Rita have her shot at crossing over?

Now all she could do was wait.

The United States in the early 1960s faced a tenacious problem: elderly poverty.

As America emerged from the postwar economic expansion, writers and thinkers such as Harvard economist John Kenneth Galbraith, who wrote 1958's *The Affluent Society*, became increasingly alarmed at the yawning gap between the country's wealth as a nation—in terms of gross domestic product, income, and other macro measures of wealth—and the persistent poverty of the underclasses. For Galbraith, society was rich in production and consumption of everything from basic needs to luxury goods, but whole swaths of the population lacked access to education and other crucial public infrastructure. Concern about the stability of the economy rose around the same time with a sharp recession in the late 1950s, spiking joblessness over 7 percent. Another recession followed in the early 1960s, prompting Swedish economist Gunnar Myrdal to open his 1962 book *Challenge to Affluence* with: "For several years the sluggish and jerky development of the American economy has given cause for anxiety."

Attention increasingly turned to the elderly. The U.S. Senate Subcommittee on the Problems of the Aged and Aging in 1960 issued a report titled, "The Aged and Aging in the United States: A National Problem." "It is no longer possible, as it once may have been expedient, to ignore or shrug off these problems and the urgent need to solve them," the report declared. In January of the following year, thousands of delegates converged on Washington for the first White House Conference on Aging, calling for a raft of proposals to lift income levels among the elderly, including expansion of Social Security. It's easy to see the reason for the concern: the statistics from 50 years ago on elder poverty are startling. In 1960, for instance, some 35 percent of seniors 65 or older were considered poor.

Momentum continued to build into the Kennedy era, spurred by works such as the socialist journalist and activist Michael Harrington's *The Other America*, and the Conference on Economic Progress's *Poverty and Deprivation in the United States: The Plight of Two-Fifths of a Nation*. Both published in 1962, these two works helped build momentum for policies to combat inequality across the board, setting the stage for President Lyndon B. Johnson's "Great Society" and the war on poverty.

Harrington and others helped fix the national spotlight on three main areas of deprivation: African-Americans and other minorities, the rural poor in places like Appalachia, and the elderly. From the beginning of the movement, older Americans were a troubling magnet for concern: many considered it shameful that a nation as bountiful as the United States had left a sizeable chunk of its elderly population to fend for itself amid the challenges of loss of work opportunities and income, physical ailments, and general societal abandonment and despair.

Harrington's book crafts a particularly poignant—and enraging—portrait of the indignities of being poor and elderly in early 1960s America. In a chapter sardonically titled "The Golden Years," Harrington plumbs Senate reports on aging for ammunition, taking aim at threadbare, substandard housing; disdainful treatment by stingy, imperious social workers; and the shameful lack of a medical safety net for the sick and old.

Compounding the material deprivation is a spiritual and social isolation:

"This is no country for old men. The physical humiliation and the loneliness are real, but to them is added the indignity of living in a society that is obsessed with youth and tries to ignore age. These people are caught, as one witness before the Senate Committee testified, in a triple 'chain of causality': they are plagued by ill health, they do not have enough money; and they are socially isolated. Some of them are new entrants to the world of the other America, drifting down from a working life of decent wages to an old age of dependency and social workers. A good many are old and poor because they were young and poor, middle-aged and poor. Taken together, they constitute a section of the culture of poverty with over 8,000,000 inhabitants."

Harrington ends the section with a biting indictment of America's cynical treatment of its oldest citizens:

"The brochure writers and the publicist talk of the 'golden years' and of 'senior citizens.' But these are euphemisms to ease the conscience of the callous. America tends to make its people miserable when they become old, and there are not enough phrases in the dictionary to gloss over this ugly reality."

The best known achievements of the Johnson administration's war on poverty were government-funded income supports and other programs, such as the expansion of Social Security and the creation of Medicare in 1965, and the Older Americans Act, which established an Administration on Aging within the Department of Health, Education, and Welfare. But expanding work opportunities for older Americans as a way of boosting income and alleviating poverty was an early focus.

There were a few good reasons for this. Throughout the 1950s, labor force participation rates among older people were dropping sharply as Social Security started drawing more people into retirement and pension and disability payments became more widely available. The working rate for those 65 and older fell by nearly a quarter, from 26.7 percent in 1950 to 20.8 percent in a decade later, though the rate was still 33.1 percent for men. America was on its way to embracing retirement as an ideal, at least for the increasing numbers of those in the middle and upper classes who could afford it. Those who could not were left to fend for themselves—with or without a job.

At the same time, America was clearly aging as medicine and affluence allowed longer lives and reduced infant mortality. In 1900, only 4.1 percent of the population was 65 or older. By 1960, the percentage had more than doubled, to nearly 9 percent. Further increases were forecast, helping to push the issue of aging higher on the list of national priorities. Since then, those forecasts of further increases have come true: today, more than 13 percent of the U.S. population is elderly.

There were other reasons for the attention on aging and work. We also have to take into consideration the vastly different health conditions of the average 60-something in those years. Life expectancy in 1960 was 69.7 years—nearly 10 years less than now. In addition, at that time most work was more physically demanding than today, meaning that workers risked losing their value to employers much sooner in life than they do now. Reports from the era on "older workers" started the clock ticking at age 45 for employees in some occupations. So while 60-somethings in those days were pushed by poverty to get any job they could to subsidize relatively paltry Social Security payouts, they also faced a particularly demanding labor market while dealing with a higher level of physical ailments than our current crop of "65 is the new 45" baby boomers. Circumstances were ripe for government action.

The program that today employs Rita Hall, SCSEP, can trace its DNA back at least to February 21, 1963, when President John F. Kennedy issued a special message to Congress on the elderly, the first time a president had done so. While the message was wide-ranging and included proposals on everything from Social Security and housing to health and taxes, Kennedy made expanding employment one of the priorities of his administration.

"Denial of employment opportunity to older persons is a personal tragedy," he declared. "It is also a national extravagance, wasteful of human resources. No economy can reach its maximum productivity while failing to use the skills, talents, and experience of willing workers."

The president then proposed $10 million a year in matching funds to state and local governments for experimental projects to generate jobs for older Americans. Kennedy's goals were modest, including hiring the elderly to work as school lunch hour relief, child care in centers for working mothers, home care for the handicapped, and assistance in schools, vocational training, and programs to prevent juvenile delinquency. Nodding to the concerns of organized labor, Kennedy said steps would be taken to avoid displacing existing workers, and that wages would be competitive. He also ordered the newly formed President's Council on Aging to study the issue and make recommendations.

The Johnson administration picked up the issue with energy after Kennedy's assassination in November 1963. While the new president considered the findings of the Council, a subcommittee of the Special Senate Committee on Aging in December began a series of hearings on employment of the elderly in three sessions, one each in Washington, DC, Los Angeles, and San Francisco.

The transcripts of these hearings provide a framework for discussing aging and work that we still use today. Senator Jennings Randolph, the West Virginia Democrat who chaired the subcommittee on employment and retirement incomes, shaped the argument for creating jobs for older workers with three main points: one, that the elderly themselves preferred work to government handouts; two, that working for income would alleviate some of the burden on the state, taxpayers, and the younger generations to support the old. His third point—one that we will build on in this book—was that work itself provided the aged with a sense of participation in society that was somehow lacking in retirement.

"Of all the solutions to the financial problems of senior citizens, the one I think which they themselves prefer is to gain full employment, enabling them to continue to be independent, self-sufficient, and productive members of the American society," Randolph told the hearing in Los Angeles in early 1964. Later he added: "Many people of advanced age, while unable to undertake full-time employment, are fully capable of working part-time. They want to do so. Thus they remain in what I call the mainstream of life. They are not shunted aside and they retain a sense of dignity and of usefulness."

Five decades later, Rita Hall and millions of other 50- and 60-somethings would find themselves still struggling to keep their places in the "mainstream of life."

Akron was once all about rubber.

Rubber brought the city its first riches. Dr. Benjamin Franklin Goodrich established the city's first rubber company here in 1870, taking advantage of the area's abundant water, solid transportation links to the outside world, and cheap coal. As the need for transportation grew, so did the demand for rubber. The invention of the pneumatic tire and the ensuing bicycle boom of the 1890s exploded production in Akron, where the U.S. economic crisis had depressed wages, meaning Goodrich could churn out tires at lower prices than competitors.

Other entrepreneurs—imitating Goodrich or simply taking advantage of the same benefits he saw in the city—piled into the business. Firestone. Goodyear. Mayhem played its part: World War I boosted demand for their products, and that was followed by the rise of the American automobile, which rolled across the country on Akron's best. The General Tire and Rubber Company was born, completing the city's transformation into the "Rubber Capital of the World." The Great Depression slowed the action down and threw many out of work, but Pearl Harbor changed all that, pulling America into World War II and setting production at Akron's expanded factories—Goodyear was now making fighter planes and Goodrich churned out aircraft guns—running off the charts. The boom stretched far beyond the war: in the 1950s, the construction of the national highway system, lobbied for by Akron's rubber barons, kept the tiremakers humming.

Rita Sweeney's father was one of them. He worked the nightshift at BF Goodrich for 40 years, and he and his wife ruled over a tightly run home on the east side of the city. They had a family church: Greater Bethel Baptist. Rita's father also taught his family to honor labor—his and theirs. He had a favorite phrase: "Everybody eats at our house and everybody works at our house." If one of the daughters left a spoon unwashed in the sink, then she'd have to wash all the dishes in the house—including the clean ones. It wasn't an idle threat. Rita recalls her sister enduring this punishment. It only took one time for her to learn her lesson.

Rita started working early. During high school she worked after school at O'Neil's department store in downtown Akron from 5 p.m. until 9 p.m. A pretty, slim cheerleader and Homemaker of the Year for her sewing skills, she also modeled clothes for O'Neil's when she was 16. Then, in her last year at Akron Central High School, she fell in love with the man she would be married to for 35 years.

Rita met Ernie Hall on a blind date set up by her younger sister. It was one of those "my date has a buddy who needs a date" arrangements, and Rita obliged, not expecting much. She ended up with a husband.

The war was on in Vietnam, and Ernie was in the Army. He came in uniform. Nearly five decades later, Rita still recalls him with a smile and a single phrase: drop-dead handsome. Ernie proposed a month later, and they were married in a year. And they stayed that way.

"One person. I never married anyone else or was interested in any one else," Rita insists. "It's the same with my job. Don't be jumping here, jumping there."

Not that she didn't move around. She graduated high school in 1968, featured in the yearbook as one of the "Club Queen Candidates." Out of school at 18, she thought she'd better find something to do, and worked as a nursing assistant at Akron General for six months, the first of many hospital jobs. She became ward clerk, then unit clerk, then unit secretary, mostly transcribing doctor's orders. At 20, she and Ernie moved to Los Angeles with their first-born son, just a baby, and she worked at California Lutheran General. They lived in the Crenshaw neighborhood for a year and a half, but Rita says "too many liquor stores and gangs" made it a dangerous place to raise children, and they returned to Akron.

And back to the hospitals. It was a world Rita was familiar with. In 1974, she joined Green Cross Hospital, which became Cuyahoga Falls General Hospital four years later. The work—the place had over 200 beds—kept her racing round the clock: she ordered X-rays, transcribed doctors' orders, managed patients' diets, took incoming calls for ambulances, and did just about every other administrative task that gets done in a hospital. She says she never missed a day on the job, a record that she has kept up at Mature Services, where her supervisor said she'd called in sick only once in two and a half years. She even came in one day in the middle of a snowstorm after missing the call that the office was closed.

At Cuyahoga Falls she stayed. The work was steady and the money helped at home. With her salary and what her husband earned at his body shop business, they raised two boys. But more than that, the hospital was a place where she felt comfortable. She liked working with the people—the patients, doctors, nurses, and the other secretaries.

At home, too, she felt taken care of. Ernie drove her to work and picked her up; he did the grocery shopping. "He had me spoiled," she said. "He was always there to take me where I had to go."

The two boys grew up and moved out, and Rita and Ernie aged into their 50s.

Akron aged too. The tire industry that kept so many thousands of families afloat when Rita and Ernie were young hit on hard times in the 1970s and 1980s. French producer Michelin came out with the radial tire, forcing the Akron rubber-makers to play catch-up. Then crisis hit the Big Three automakers in Detroit. Decline for Akron was swift: in 1987, General Tire sold off its tire plants; Japan's Bridgestone acquired Firestone in 1989. Goodrich merged with Uniroyal, and in 1990 its tire holdings were taken over by Michelin. Goodyear was the only top producer with headquarters in Akron, and its factories were elsewhere. Thousands of jobs were lost. Akron had become a typical Rust Belt has-been.

Rita felt lucky. Her two sons were all grown up. Ernie had his own shop, though she thought he was working far too hard and needed to take better care of himself. And even though the tire business was tanking, the health industry in Akron was growing, as in most places. At work, she felt appreciated and comfortable. She knew her way around. Her colleagues were like her second family; her workplace was her second home. In 2001, she and Ernie bought a modest two-bedroom house, a ranch built in 1940.

Then, in 2005, life suddenly veered for Rita Hall.

In any serious discussion of aging and work these days, several issues are almost guaranteed to be mentioned. One would be that aging workers don't have enough opportunity to work part-time. Another would be that one of the advantages of hiring older workers is that they are flexible on pay and benefits. That is, they are seldom in it to make a lot of money or demand long vacations. Finally, someone would point out that employers have a curious attitude about older workers: the ones already toiling in their companies are among their prized employees, but the ones who show up with job applications in their hands are seen as old, outdated, and set in their ways.

Things weren't much different 50 years ago.

On December 19, 1963, a group of U.S. senators filed into a committee room at the Capitol in Washington, DC, for the first of three hearings that would lead eventually to the program keeping Rita Hall afloat—and set the agenda for five decades of debate about aging and work in the United States.

The Subcommittee on Employment and Retirement Incomes' very first witness, Daniel Moynihan, a future four-term senator from New York who then was a 36-year-old assistant secretary of labor, made an enduring point about part-time work for seniors: there's not enough of it. Just as today, many older would-be workers back then faced the stark choice of either keeping their full-time, 40-hour-a-week jobs or forsaking the work world entirely and becoming 100 percent retired. True, some critics point out that part-time work isn't sufficient for a senior who needs a full-time income. But even today many aging workers are forced to choose between two extremes, when perhaps something in the middle—part-time work, for instance—would be the perfect fit. The argument for part-time work, then and now, is that it can keep people economically active for more years, while carving out more time for elder care or golf or volunteering whatever it is they've been putting off their whole lives.

Another common thread between 50 years ago and today is employers' enduring contradictory attitudes toward the elderly. "In fact, it is one of the anomalies," said Donald Kent, director of the Office of Aging, in the Department of Health, Education and Welfare, "that every time we go to an employer and we say to him, 'Tell us who are your most valuable employees,' he will almost invariably name his older employees, the people who have been with the company for many years. But if for some reason or another, because of automation or because of change in techniques, these people are thrown out of work, the older person finds the greater difficulty in becoming employed."

The list of parallels with the situation today goes on: the concern that laborers and blue-collar workers need to retire earlier than lawyers and other white-collar professionals; hopes that a "silver economy" fueled by older consumers would create comparative advantages for older workers who understand the market; the contradiction between the widespread desire among retirement-age Americans to remain active and the company policies that push them out of the job market.

The hearings also show how local groups were jumping to fill the void left by the absence of federal government help or encouragement, helping older people find work—many times using the same methods used today for Rita Hall at SCSEP. Margaret Schweinhaut, the chairman of the Maryland State Commission on Aging, told the committee of a group of retired business executives in Baltimore who operated an elderly employment service in the basement of a local church. The group had put 89 people to work from April until October in 1963, despite a chronic lack of funding.

In Los Angeles on January 10, 1964, the committee heard from Dr. Margaret E. Bennett, the first chairperson of "Pasadena Jobs After 40," a volunteer group formed in 1959. The group was strikingly well-organized, making connections with employers, labor unions, and civic groups. It held chamber of commerce breakfasts with businesses to advertise the benefits of older workers, and orchestrated day-long forums with lectures on aging employees, job-guidance clinics for individual applicants, and counseling for displaced executives and managers. The group had even conducted a survey of employer attitudes toward older workers.

The committee also heard from Richard Sensor, president of a tiny outfit in Riverside, California, called Hire Older People Enterprises. Sensor concentrated on hiring workers over 60 to manufacture camera accessories and photographic equipment, but found he was increasingly playing the role—free of charge, he said—of a reference for older workers. For instance, he told the committee how he had referred several workers to a woman who called asking for someone to take her husband to the hospital two or three times a week.

Sensor then made a suggestion for a service that sounds remarkably similar to SCSEP, run through the Department of Labor and furnishing part-time work to older Americans. Randolph seemed to recognize the significance of this idea.

"This program of hope for older people... such as you envision can become a reality," Randolph said.

Moves toward that goal had already been gathering pace. More than a year earlier, Congress passed the Manpower Development and Training Act in 1962, aiming to provide a wide range of training opportunities for the unemployed, including older Americans. But clearly more needed to be done specifically for seniors. In September 1964, the Special Committee on Aging recommended the formation of a National Senior Service Corps that would train seniors for jobs such as aides, receptionists, caseworkers in health screening programs, and helpers for elderly discharged from mental hospitals. These types of positions would eventually be referred to as "bridge jobs"—employment that bridges the gap between their former careers and retirement. The President's Council on Aging reported in December 1964 that some 9,000 older workers—then defined as those over 45—had been trained in the preceding fiscal year, and seven pilot programs had been set up around the country aimed at finding new ways of readying workers aged 50 and over for re-entry to the labor force.

In 1965, after Johnson's landslide victory against Barry Goldwater, the committee launched more hearings, this time on "The War on Poverty as it Affects Older Americans" in Washington, Newark, and Boston. Attention focused on the Office of Economic Opportunity, which was created in 1964 to administer programs meant to spearhead Johnson's War on Poverty. What emerges from the hearings is a widespread feeling that, in light of the lack of opportunity in the job market, older workers' needs would be best addressed by a program designed specifically for them.

Johnson's campaign culminated in the 1965 expansion of Social Security and the creation of Medicare and Medicaid. While it also resulted in the Older Americans Act, the precursor to SCSEP was written into the Manpower Development law the same year, calling for meeting the needs of older, chronically unemployed Americans not reached by existing programs.

Thus was born a pilot program called "Operation Mainstream."

Rita Hall is a careful woman.

Hypertensive and diabetic, she takes no salt or sugar with her meals and avoids white bread and potatoes—anything starchy. No alcohol, no chocolate. At work, she sips water and decaf tea. She once had a coffee at Starbucks: "It took me a whole day to drink it, and it kept me up all night." On walks during her 15-minute work break, she wears wraparound sunglasses to protect her cataracts from the sun. Blame her caution on age, or a life spent working in hospitals full of sick people, or just plain personality. One of her mottos, of which she has many, goes like this: "If you're not sure about something, take 10 steps back, think about it, pray about it. And if you're still not sure, don't do it."

It's what life taught her: be careful or disaster will strike.

So Rita flashed with anger when she recalled a phone call eight years before that proved the man she most loved in the world—and most depended on—wasn't careful enough.

It was September 25, 2005. She had one hour left on her shift at the hospital when the phone rang.

It was about Ernie. He hadn't been well. Overwork led to failing health, Rita says, and finally he'd had to sell his body shop and retire. Rita picked up the receiver and heard the news: at the much-too-young age of 55, Ernie had died on the porch of their home.

"He dropped dead on the stoop of a heart attack," she told me, seated in her Ford on lunch break in the Mature Services parking lot.

"They called me up and told me 'We found Ernie dead,' and I had an hour to go at work and I said, 'Why couldn't you call me an hour later?'" She shook her head. "He was tired. I told him he was working too much. But he said, 'Oh no, I'm OK, I'm OK.'"

He wasn't OK. But his widow is determined the same thing isn't going to happen to her. "Well," she said, putting the keys in the ignition, "better him than me. I take my warnings."

Ernie's death was the first in a series of losses Rita would endure as she finished out her 50s and entered her 60s.

Rita had to adjust to this new existence without her husband. He was her rock: he drove her everywhere, ran the household, paid the bills. Now she was on her own. "I had to learn all over again how to survive," she recalled. "I shook it off: You better find out how!"

Somehow, Rita did. And she displayed a remarkable ability to handle whatever life served up. With only a few loaves of bread and some fish, Rita Hall would feed herself for years.

First she faced her own health problems. Aside from diabetes, all the years of working on her feet and running up and down hospital corridors began taking their toll. Now she needed hip replacements—on both sides. As a hospital employee, she was well-positioned to take care of it. In 2007, she took off three months from Cuyahoga for the right hip, then she took another three months off the following year to replace the left. She counted her blessings. The bad luck wasn't as bad as it could have been: thanks to generous benefits as a Summa Health employee, she paid a total of $400 for the $150,000 worth of procedures.

When she went back to work in 2008, more dark news awaited: her employers said she would be limited to 20 hours a week. This she could not accept, not after buying a used Ford that year. She needed full-time money, she said. She held out for what she wanted, and in the end the dispute meant she had no job at all. So she turned to bolstering her skills, studying for a test of medical terminology. Finally, she managed to get the hospital to hire her back full-time in January 2009, and they put her to work in the psychiatric ward on the 2 p.m. to 10:30 p.m. shift.

There was a lot Rita didn't like about this job. For one thing, the hours didn't suit her. She hated driving home in the dark. And the patients were unpredictable. One man there lost control during Rita's shift and tried to escape the ward, leaping over her and running for the exit. He demanded that she open the door, but Rita refused. It took several men to wrestle him to the ground and sedate him.

After that, she moved to the geriatrics unit. That was better. She enjoyed feeding the elderly patients ice cream and chatting with them. But the hours were the same, and she hated coming home to a dark house late at night. She didn't feel safe. Rita was going to be 60, and this just didn't seem like the right thing for an older woman to have to do.

The health industry was changing as well. By 2009, the economic downturn was squeezing everyone, pushing hospital operators into layoffs and consolidations. Summa Health System, which bought Rita's hospital several years before, sold off a 60 percent stake in it to Western Reserve Hospital Partners, and the two companies assumed operations there with plans to open a new 100-bed clinic. Rita Hall's old hospital would be downsized into a senior-care facility. After 35 years on the job, Rita was let go in June that year. Losing the income was one thing, but she also felt like she was losing her family.

"Oh, yeah, I cried," she says. "It was like, 'You're making me leave my home! I love it here.'"

And so, for the first time since Richard Nixon was president, Rita Hall had no hospital job to go to. She sat at home for a year, in that period that many older, suddenly jobless people find themselves in, nibbling at their savings or receiving unemployment insurance, hesitant and uncertain how to begin this new life that seems colder and directionless and—for a widow like Rita—lonely. She'd spent so long in one workplace where she felt fully accepted; now the prospect of finding an employer who would take her seemed remote.

The upheaval brought other changes to Rita's life. In her thinking. In her priorities. In the initial shock of Ernie's death, she'd turned to religion. Sure, she'd always been a churchgoer, but in those painful months of mourning, she grappled for something she could truly put her faith in, something that would never let her down.

Now, after losing her job, she thought back to the party her hospital workmates had thrown on her 35th anniversary, and the big picture they put up of her. How she was at the center of the celebration. Now it seemed to her that she'd been putting work and herself before God. "That's when I really started praying and put my trust in God instead of in man or in myself," she said. Religion is now at the center of Rita's life. She told me she has an altar in her home where she prays several times a day. One day when I visited, she brought Jacques Gillet's *The Consciousness of Jesus* to read during break.

Rita's religion, her adherence to a strict code, her careful attention to her health, also must help soften the hard realities of her life. For Rita is also on the edge of poverty. She's eligible for SCSEP because her income—minus veterans' benefits, certain types of Social Security benefits, and other excluded money—is less than 125 percent of the poverty line, meaning it's below about $14,360 a year, according to 2013 federal guidelines.

But she doesn't talk about poverty or hardship. Instead, she's happy to talk about all the gifts of her life: her faith, her two sons and her three grandchildren, the lessons in discipline passed down from her parents. How she recently egged her sons on to make a New Year's resolution to attend church with her.

There are other gifts she thanks God for—the Salvation Army, for instance, where she has lunch every day for nothing. The free dinner every Wednesday evening at St. Paul's Episcopal Church. And the free breakfast on Sunday at First Grace United Church, the free bread at the Food Pantry. She gets free basic care, insulin, needles, and other medicines at a clinic run by OPEN M—the Opportunity for People Everywhere in Need Ministry. What she can't get free, she gets cheap: her short, wide curls with light brown frosting are done at Akron Beauty School for $6. They do her nails for $4. The engine in the Ford recently started making a loud noise, and a mechanic wanted to charge her $300 to fix it. She didn't have that kind of money, but she found someone who did it for a third of the price. St. Hillary Catholic Church paid her $54 water bill when the utility threatened to turn off her supply.

"God," she said, "has opened many doors for me to live on a little income."

More and more people need those doors opened for them these days. The Great Recession has eaten away at wealth and income, meaning the United States—home to the world's largest economy—is suffering its highest poverty levels since the 1960s. Though poverty rates for children are higher, America's 41 million seniors, most of them living on fixed incomes, are among the most precarious, and they are deeper in poverty the older they get. And women have it worse. A study by the Economic Policy Institute in 2013 showed that most women over the age of 65—52.6 percent—are "economically vulnerable," meaning they have incomes below double the poverty rate. A bump in the road—losing a source of income or a health crisis—could easily push one of these seniors into poverty.

So Rita cuts her expenses wherever she can.

We got into her Focus at the end of her shift to head for lunch. Strictly no frills. The passenger side door doesn't open until she gets in on the driver's side, leans over, and unlocks the door manually. The doors freeze in the cold and Rita had run out of WD-40. She didn't want to spend the money to buy more, but one of her sons got her some restaurant supply non-stick spray from the place he works, and that was just fine. She showed it to me while she let the car warm up.

A cluster of air fresheners dangled from her rearview mirror, scents in the shapes of leaves, one labeled "new car smell," and a handicapped parking tag she got after her hip replacements. We creaked slowly out of the parking lot and headed to the Salvation Army at the Akron Citadel. Rita parked in a handicapped spot and we walked into a basketball court dressed up as a cafeteria.

Rita signed in, but the man taking names—a tall man with glasses—said, "Oh, I know you!" and waved her away. On the menu that day was a meat sauce that Rita passed on, and a mushroom quiche that she took. She skipped the English muffins and gravy, but dug into the apple dumplings, a move she later regretted because they were loaded with sugar, the last thing she needed with her diabetes.

We sat down with an older woman, a friend of Rita's and a fellow Mature Services worker, who was complaining—with an air of paranoia—about the non-profit and the place where she had been placed in a job. Rita plowed through her lunch, telling me I should get some because it's pretty good. The quiche looked like a sponge. She drank water from a plastic Salvation Army cup. Overhead hung a basketball backboard and net. On the wall was the Salvation Army shield and the group's mission statement. A young, stringy couple beside us were making out. Rita didn't seem to notice. When they got up, I could see the woman's cheek-bones protrude—she did not look well. Volunteers started folding up the chairs and cleaning up. We were at the tail end of lunch.

Rita urged her friend to leave her job if she didn't feel right about it. There might be other opportunities. The friend hesitated, but Rita insisted that some-times change could be good.

"You never know where it's going to lead you," Rita counseled. "I'll pray for you."

Rita stood up.

"Truly," she said, "prayer changes things."

Her friend was skeptical. "I don't bother God with my petty stuff."

Rita shook her head as we got up to go. No one's concerns were too small for Rita's God. He'd just provided her with lunch. He'd helped her with so many things. And now she was counting on Him to help her with the job at Hudson Dermatology. Either way, she thought, God would take care of her.

Rita thought He would do the same for her friend.

"You leave it to Him," she said.

Operation Mainstream started out modestly. Aging participants planted flowers in parks. They trimmed hedges along highways. They cut grass in public spaces. The goal was not necessarily to build skills and then funnel workers out to busi-nesses. Instead, the program was aimed at providing useful activity for elders with time and energy on their hands and a need for some extra cash.

The program, which was shifted from Office of Economic Opportunity to the Department of Labor in 1967, had vocal supporters early on. A 1969 con-gressional conference report described Operation Mainstream as "uniquely effective," called for funding an expansion, and added new types of work par-ticipants could take on, including housing, recreation, and day care facilities. The program by that year had nearly $12 million in funding and almost 4,400 enrollees. The following year, the government created 100 new Mainstream projects.

Still, some proponents were frustrated by the small scale of the program. Senator Edward Kennedy, a driving force behind these efforts, noted in 1970 that "a more comprehensive approach is needed to provide increased opportunities for community services by older persons." From then, Congress took some steps to upgrade Operation Mainstream from a pilot into a permanent federal program. In 1973 came the Older American Community Employment Act, which put the program—now the Senior Community Service Employment Program—permanently on the books. In 1978, the project was moved over to the Older Americans Act, fueling its already established steady growth path of funding and enrollment. Appropriations grew from $10 million in 1974 to $200 million in the 1978–79 fiscal year—a 20-fold increase. Enrollment had soared from 3,800 to nearly 50,000.

A report on SCSEP by the National Council on the Aging for a special House committee gave a glowing assessment. The report cited a raft of favorable reports from independent auditing agencies, proponents, and participants—Morgan Management Systems, Inc., the General Accounting Office, Centaur Associates, AARP—over the years attesting to the efficiency and efficacy of the program. "When the concept of an older worker community service employment project first emerged in 1965, there were those who wondered whether it would have sufficient appeal for elderly Americans," Rep. Edward R. Roybal, the chairman of the House Select Committee on Aging, wrote in the preface. "Today—nearly a quarter of a century later—the verdict is clear beyond any reasonable doubt. Older Americans are enthusiastic about participating in community service employment programs as a dignified means to improve their economic well-being in fulfilling and purposeful activity."

SCSEP has, however, also faced serious criticism over the years, particularly as the U.S. debt burden has ballooned and budgets have received greater scrutiny. Critics accuse the program of lacking reliable measures of success or failure, benefiting the non-profits where aging workers like Rita Hall toil rather than the workers themselves. The White House's Office of Management and Budget under President George W. Bush graded the program as "ineffective" in a 2003 assessment, arguing that SCSEP failed to choose grantees such as Mature Services in a competitive way based on past performance, and needed to improve its measurement of success in training and winning jobs for participants. In a March 2011 report on reducing the deficit, the Congressional Budget Office said eliminating SCSEP would save the government some $4 billion between 2012 and 2016. The rationale was that the organizations where participants work could assume the full cost of their wages, instead of the 10 percent they pay now.

Supporters argued that the organizations that employ participants don't have the money, and that people would never get the training they need if they were at the full mercy of the market. In any case, the Labor Department responded to the criticism by instituting a more competitive selection of grantees, resulting in an increase of non-profits administering the program from the long-standing 10 to up to 18. In 2010, the Labor Department also adopted a rule to impose sanctions on grantees who fail to perform up to department standards. The department has bolstered performance assessment, gauging participants' post-program employment levels, wages, satisfaction, and other measures.

Whether or not the program is achieving its goals as well as it should be, SCSEP has certainly been a lifesaver for unemployed older workers like Rita Hall, and its importance as the only federal work program for aging Americans has only increased as the country confronts the Great Recession and its dismal aftermath.

It's May 2012. The recession has been over for nearly three years, but unemployment in the United States is still 8.2 percent. A room at Mature Services fills with the aging unemployed, mostly in their 50s, some of them without college degrees or significant work experience. At least one hasn't worked in 10 years. The economy in Akron has been picking up lately—unemployment is now below the national average—but not for these folks. They are the ones left behind.

Job trainer Laurie Sibila stands before the group and tries to be optimistic.

"Employers come to us looking for workers with experience like yourselves," she tells them, listing job openings ranging from welding to bookkeeping to running a phone at a call center. "They come to us. I'm like their mini HR and I handle it for them, so I think it's pretty amazing they come to us looking for the experienced mature worker."

That's the good news. Then training and placement specialist Chris Walker—himself a graduate of Mature Services and now an employee—takes over.

His news is less upbeat. The SCSEP program administered by Mature Services enjoyed a significant funding boost as part of the financial stimulus package when the bottom fell out of the U.S. economy in 2007 and 2008. But that boost was over by the time I visited in 2012. Federal funding had plunged by more than a third. Positions for SCSEP were down 45 percent—the non-profit closed 7 of 16 offices and laid off 35 people. The program was frozen and Mature Services, at the time, wasn't taking any more participants.

"We hope to be able to enroll sometime soon, but you never know with the federal government," Walker tells the group, moving on to the other non-SCSEP services the non-profit offers, such as a training program called Job Club that prepares students for the arduous, frustrating process of applying and interviewing for openings.

Such was the state of affairs at Mature Services when I showed up to gauge the effect of the recession on the nation's most disadvantaged older workers. Ohio's population of 11.5 million makes it the second-largest state in the Midwest after Illinois and puts it at the center of a manufacturing heartland struggling to transform itself from the Rust Belt wasteland of the 1980s to a post-industrial economy. By some measures, Akron was doing this successfully, maintaining some of its lead in plastics and rubber research and development and diversifying its economy to include a booming health care industry. As Ohio's largest grantee for SCSEP, Mature Services was at the center of the struggle to reach out to the older workers left furthest behind in the deepest economic downturn in 70 years, sharpen their job-search and work skills, and put them on a path to employment and an escape from poverty.

Mature Services has been in the older worker business for a long time. It started out in 1975 as the Senior Workers Action Program, active in Summit County, the county surrounding Akron. The outfit started working with SCSEP in the late 1970s through the national non-profit Senior Services America. SCSEP splits its money, giving 22 percent to states to disburse to local organizations, and the remaining 78 percent directly to national grantees. The Akron operation became a state grantee in 1992, renamed itself Mature Services in 2001, and along the way became one of the 18 or so national grantees, gradually stretching its reach over two large clusters of counties, one in northeastern Ohio encompassing Akron, Cleveland, and Youngstown, and one in the southwest surrounding Cincinnati and Columbus. In 2012 it received $11.2 million in government grants, down sharply from $16.9 million the year before. About 85 percent of that money is for SCSEP.

Aside from employment projects funded with money from SCSEP and another federal job-training scheme under the 1998 Work Investment Act, Mature Services runs programs to help aging substance abusers, provide meals and homecare for disabled seniors, and recruit and place elder community service volunteers. But SCSEP is clearly the core of the operation, meaning the boost in funding in 2010 was a godsend—and the cut in 2012 forced a substantial rollback in services at a time when they were still very much in demand. "The recession was hard," says Paul Mangus, vice president for workforce development. "At the very time we had more people that were hurting, they were starting to pull funds from it."

At the same time, standards were getting tougher. Under beefed-up federal rules, Mangus now has to substantiate what percentage of SCSEP participants get jobs and stick with them for minimum periods of time, and whether their wages increase. In 2011, for the first time he also had to push people out of the program when they reached the new lifetime limit of four years—which has proved a major change for both the participants and the outside organizations Mature Services contracts with.

Part of the challenge, he said, is weaning those employers from an unlimited pool of workers whose wages are paid by SCSEP.

"We're saying wait a minute, it's not all about getting free help here, it's about the individual," says Mangus. "And on the side of the individuals, you need to move on. So that's a big part of managing the programs that we do, making sure that the participants are not exploited, and that they move on so we can make room for new people."

To get to Mature Services, one must drive northwest from central Akron to a road named Portage Path, the present-day incarnation of a trail once used by

Native Americans—the Eries and the Delawares among them—carrying their canoes between the Cuyahoga River in the north and the Tuscarawas River in the south. Back in those days, this vital link would allow one to travel by river from the Great Lakes to the Gulf of Mexico. The eight-mile-long path took on legal and symbolic importance when it formed part of the boundary between the United States and Native American lands in the late 18th century. Today, a statue of a Native American holding a canoe stands at the northern end of the road.

Mature Services' offices form a strip-mall array of outlets—employment, homecare, elder nutrition, adolescent health—all promising, like the road they're located on once did, to transport participants from one point to another, to take them from trouble to stability. Mature Services is not alone. Across the road is the RAMAR drug rehab center and the Horizon House shelter for homeless youth.

Inside Mature Services, housed in a maze of plasterboard corridors, plain white offices, work cubicles, and open meeting spaces, the orientation session mirrors the dual nature of job hunting itself: the hopeful possibilities of fresh beginnings clash continually with the soul-crushing reality of unanswered phone calls, job applications that go nowhere, and interviews that turn sour. The jobs are out there, the unemployed are told, but only if you go out and get them with intelligence and energy. The walls of Mature Services are covered with slogans of tough love. One poster proclaims: "Determination can Overcome any Obstacle: STICK WITH IT!" Another warns would-be slackers: "An Excuse Only Sounds Good to the Person Who Says It." The rhetoric holds out the hope that with some elbow grease, a chipper attitude, and development of the right strategy and the right skills, you will clinch that job, the job that is out there waiting for the savvy, prepared, and determined applicant. And if you don't put in the effort, they seem to say, you won't get a free lunch here.

Mature Services counselors themselves wrestle with treading the path between these two ideas. Sibila, for instance, says much of what Mature Services and other similar outfits do is provide emotional care for those going through the trauma of losing a job later in life.

"They need the direction, they need positive reinforcement," she told me the day before the orientation session. "Being unemployed is very hard emotionally, it takes an emotional toll on people. You're at a time when you need to feel most positive about yourself, but you're probably at the lowest point in your life. You have to act like, 'Yeah, I'm at the top of my game,' and you're the saddest you've ever been because everything you worked for is gone. There's a great need for what we do."

And so Mature Services attempts to guide its clients through the process one step at a time. A major first step is a program they call Job Club, a three-week crash course in looking for employment. Participants learn how to construct resumes, conduct mock interviews, and manage a bewildering mélange of Internet-based job search engines, sites, and scams. Job Club started in 1987. The 30 or so people who run through the program every month critique each other's work, get comments from real-world employers, and network with Mature Services clients in other parts of the state through video conferences.

They also enjoy the services of Chris Walker—one of their own, in a sense. Walker, a 63-year-old no-nonsense former computer programmer with master's degrees in East Asian studies and library science, moved through a series of jobs for three decades purely on the power of personal contacts and happenstance. When he hit a dead-end in 2008 with a commission-only job that wasn't bringing him any commissions, he went back out into the job market—with no success. He landed interviews, but he kept striking out in the end.

"It finally dawned on me that, well, since you never had a job interview before, maybe you don't know what you're doing in a job interview. And I remembered reading an article about this place, and so I called them up and signed up for an orientation, and went through Job Club and found that I did *not* know what I was doing in a job interview. I also didn't know how to look for good opportunities."

Walker says the program turned things around for him. Not that it took him that far afield—he ended up landing a job right here with Mature Services. The experience, though, makes him particularly effective at what he does, giving him street-cred with participants. He runs his charges through a series of mottos, which he says drive home essential truths about the job-search process:

1. Job-seekers must learn to think like employers, not like employees. Keep the focus on what you can offer the company, rather than on what you have to gain from it.
2. Choosing whom to hire is a process of elimination more than a process of selection. Successful candidates need to avoid being eliminated because of silly mistakes, such as typos in a cover letter.
3. Nothing lasts forever. When you get your job, start looking for the next one.

"It's not about what the employer can do for you," Walker told the group one morning. "It's about what you can do for the employer. The employer already knows what he can do for you. What they don't know is you and what you can do for them. So when they ask you in the interview, 'So, Diana, why should we hire you?' and you say, 'Well I got a lot of credit card debt,' that's not how we want to approach it."

The lessons can be a tough sell for a group of people who haven't looked for a job in many years, sometimes decades, and are at the moment crushed under the burden of unemployment, mounting debts, and fear—or the reality—of poverty.

To drive these messages home and give participants a sense they are making progress, Walker videotapes mock interviews with each one at the outset of the course. Later in the course, after the group has discussed the job-application process more deeply, he tapes another round—and brings in an employer to give them a real-world critique.

"We all sit down together and talk about what they did good and what they did bad," he tells me after a Job Club session. "It's amazing. I'm sorry that I can't keep some of them. There was one where the opening question is, 'So, tell me a little bit about yourself,' and this lady launches into like five or seven minutes of surgeries, divorces, grandchildren. Not one single word about work." He laughs. "But we want all their mistakes to be made here, not out there, when they're doing the real thing."

Of course, even a well-constructed resume and sharp interviewing skills can't save you from a lack of useful job skills, so training is a key component of what Mature Services does. While there are in-house operations like the call center where Rita works, much of the training SCSEP participants receive is done at non-profits, government agencies, and businesses around the state who have deals with Mature Services. Under the employer-based training program, Mature Services pays a participant's wages for a negotiated period of time while he or she trains in the real world. Once that time is up, the employer has the option to hire the person or not. This is another balancing act for Mangus's team to perform: how to encourage area employers to participate without allowing the program to become—as some say it already has—just an opportunity to get temp workers for free.

Mature Services is also always on the lookout for potential permanent employers. It's a matter of survival. The non-profit has to report to the Labor Department every year how many of its participants were able to shift into independent jobs—the higher the percentage, the better position Mature Services is when it comes time to renew or expand its federal grant.

It comes down to a lot of massaging.

Much of that massaging is done by Don Zirkle. One of his many duties, aside from running Job Club and helping to screen applicants, is reaching out to businesses in the area to enlist their help. He cajoles them into taking on trainees, hiring his clients and donating cell phones and other equipment Mature Services can sell to raise money.

I went one morning to a conference room at telemarketing giant InfoCision's headquarters in Akron for what Zirkle calls the Business Advisory Board. Every quarter, Zirkle and others from Mature Services meet with one or two dozen representatives from area businesses to feel out the job market and round up supporters. On this particular morning, people from about 18 employers file in—the Chamber of Commerce, a podiatrist's office, LaserQuest, insurance, security, and health care companies, Lowe's.

Zirkle is good at this. He knows the names of everyone in the room, and he and Chris Walker trade riffs.

"I don't really have an agenda other than to get in touch with you guys," Zirkle tells them.

Chris Walker interrupts: "Oh yes you do!"

That gets a few chuckles from the room.

Zirkle continues. "Chris is looking for somebody to do mock interviews. Do we have any volunteers? We have a job club that's going on. . ."

Chris: "Tuesday or Wednesday next week."

"Believe it or not, we have some pretty good success," Zirkle continues. "We've had quite a few placements in the last few months."

And so on. Zirkle rounds up more volunteers to conduct HR presentations for participants and help out with the mock interviews. The Mature Services guys also advertise for the Employer-Based Training program. Businesses, meanwhile, use the occasion to advertise themselves to the others in the room and figure out ways they can benefit from the SCSEP labor pool.

Laura Leonti is one of them. In her late 40s she started a second career when she went into business with her adult son to start a homecare agency for the elderly. Over the next three or four years, the business expanded to include two training centers with about 400 students. When we talked, she was in the midst of setting up a training program with Mature Services to bring participants into a field that needs more workers all the time—especially older ones.

Elderly customers, she said, often will ask for someone more their age to help them get around town, do the shopping, and run their homes. "I think the companionship aspect of it is where the difference is," she said.

Given the dire circumstances, it's difficult for some at Mature Services—both staffers and participants—not to get a little weary with the process. Many here will admit that for some people, just latching onto a 20-hour-a-week gig at minimum wage through SCSEP is the goal, rather than a real-world job that can seem permanently out of reach.

Project Director David DeShon, 62, and training specialist Sue Dukeman, 66, work as a team. As Dukeman likes to say, both of them failed retirement. She worked for years in workforce development for state government, and his last job was for Akron's city census bureau. While both of them believe in the mission, it can be a struggle to get participants to set their sights on something higher than just the crutch of a SCSEP position.

"We are constantly reminding them this is not a job. It's easy to forget," DeShon said. "They like it and they start to think, 'If I hang on here long enough, maybe the agency will pick up a little money from somewhere and they'll be able to hire somebody. They really like me so they'll probably hire me, and I like being here anyway. . .' And they become institutionalized."

Dukeman nodded. "Learned helplessness."

"They stop looking," DeShon continued. "And the training part of it is a good lever to shake them out of those ruts and get them to start thinking in new ways."

The goal, he said, was to get participants back in jobs six months to a year after they show up at Mature Services. That doesn't always work out, particularly if they have some other government benefits to add to what they can make working part-time through SCSEP.

"They learn they can make it between Social Security and this, they're like 'Well, I can do this,'" Dukeman said. "So they reach that comfort zone."

"You wouldn't think anybody would want to do that," DeShon added, "but they do."

There's frustration on the other side of the equation as well.

After orientation one morning, Chris and other supervisors left the room, and the attendees, most of them women, started to banter and gossip. The discussion—punctuated by teasing and bursts of laughter—swirled with a mixture of bitterness over jobs just lost, questions about what could be gained at Mature Services, and shared tips on how to qualify for Ohio's "Buckeye" card, which gets holders—older residents and those with disabilities—discounts on prescriptions and other items.

The talk also illustrated the challenges faced by many at Mature Services.

Vanessa Claxton, 56, wasn't sure she was going to get much out of this if SCSEP's funding was frozen. After stints working at a parking garage and medical offices, she'd taken 10 years off to raise two grandchildren, surviving off Social Security disability payments. Missing a leg since birth, she said only a sedentary job would work for her these days.

She visited Mature Services the year before and went to fairs where older workers can meet potential employers, but she said nothing came of it.

"They say 'orientation,' but I got to get work," she said. "It was more like a waiting game. I got my name on the pad for them to call me for the job fairs, so I was going to job fairs, and it ain't what they say it is, it's just not. You go, put in your resume and you wait, you wait, you wait, and then I'm back here."

She shook her head. "I say eventually, if I keep coming, maybe something will happen."

That's just what Rita Hall was hoping for: something to happen. She'd played her cards the best she could. She'd kept close tabs on her health, she'd put in the hours and the effort at training, she'd saved her money by eating at Salvation Army and getting that free bread and free medical care.

Now it was all up to Hudson Dermatology.

They declined.

That was how Rita put it when Hudson Dermatology turned her down for a job: *They declined.*

It was okay, Rita reasoned. That 20-minute commute each way was a little farther than she really wanted to travel every day. No point in putting so much of your paycheck into the gas tank. It was a matter of fate.

"I don't like to drive," she said. "I guess it really wasn't meant to be."

So Rita, 62 and on her way to 63, was still on the job market—and still at the call center at Mature Services. Still making dozens of phone calls before noon and gossiping with her friends at the Salvation Army over lunch. Still scraping by on Social Security—she'd qualified for reduced retirement benefits starting in January 2013—and minimum wage at SCSEP.

Changes were afoot at Mature Services. Brian Deeds, Rita's supervisor, took a job raising money for the Cleveland Orchestra, and Rita's new boss had upped the job application quota to four a week. That's fine with Rita: "Whatever they tell me to do, I do it." The next big project was preparation for the annual job fair, which brings together about 35 employers and hundreds of older job-seekers at a convention hall in Akron. Rita's job was to call companies around Ohio and try to get them to set up a booth. Helping her out now at the phone bank was Vanessa Claxton, who after some waiting was accepted into SCSEP when slots became available, thanks to increased funding in 2013.

Over the next year and a half, Rita would push ahead at Mature Services, though she said she felt herself slowing down. Her diabetes had flared up, causing her to drop 35 pounds, though she gained it back after adjusting her medication. I was surprised one morning to call her at 10 a.m. and find her asleep. Two jobs would come available, but at 63, Rita was getting more selective: she turned down one offer because it required driving at night, which was getting more difficult because of her cataracts; the other offer was for full-time work, and with her health the way it was, she thought it would be too much. "My mind is good," she said, "but my body says, 'No, you can't do that anymore.'"

In March 2014, she transferred to a front desk receptionist job at Mature Services, fielding phone calls from the public. She said that between her reduced pension, Social Security and part-time work, she was okay for now. "I have the three checks and I'm doing fine," she said. She talked vaguely about a "significant other," a man from North Carolina who called her "morning, noon and night." She would continue at the front desk, she said, until her SCSEP eligibility was exhausted on July 27, 2014. Then, she figured, she'd get something else part-time if she could.

So had the system really worked? After all, between a reduced pension, Social Security, and a part-time job at minimum wage—combined with the various freebies and services she'd scouted around Akron—Rita had managed to jerry-rig an existence that could carry her into a retirement of sorts. But she was on the precipice: a devastating illness, a financial calamity, or the loss of one of her sources of income could push her over the edge. She had family, sisters in Ohio and in the south, but that didn't mean she wasn't vulnerable.

Rita's greatest strength seemed to be an indomitable faith, a sunny outlook that brightened everything that happened in her life.

One winter afternoon I went with Rita to a mini job fair organized by Mature Services. A handful of local employers—Cardinal Maintenance, Lowe's, Interim Health, the Akron Zoo—made presentations to a few dozen older people. The jobs on tap were part-time offerings at low pay: vacuuming and dusting offices at night, home-health aides, selling tickets at the zoo, escorting lost shoppers at Lowe's to the garden hoses or lighting section. Light bridge jobs that many seniors use these days to span the gap between the end of a career and the beginning of retirement.

A sales representative for Avon said selling her products was a perfect job for older workers. "It's something you can work into the rest of your life," she said.

Rita turned to me. She'd detailed for me that afternoon how every three months she gets medical supplies, waiting in line for hours at Open M. Insulin. Syringes. Levamir. How she gets bread at the Food Pantry. How cosmetology students do her hair for cheap.

Her philosophy, she said, would get her through.

"I don't worry about anything. My mother taught me that. 'So Mom, I'm not allowed to worry about anything?'—'No!' That's the secret: Do not worry about nothing. Don't *allow* yourself to worry about it."

Take her hip replacements. The discomfort could easily have forced her into a sedentary life, allowing her muscles to atrophy. But her strictly followed regime of taking daily walks was helping. So much so that her son had come by a few days earlier and put her walker in the basement. She didn't need it anymore.

"Every step of the way," she said, "God's been there."

It would be easy to argue that Rita Hall, for all her intelligence, charm, and determination, just has too many strikes against her. She suffers from chronic health problems. Her husband died young, leaving her without support. She doesn't have a college degree. Without those problems, one might say, she wouldn't have found herself in such a dire situation.

Ron Dziuda didn't have those strikes against him. Like many Americans, Dziuda had planned his life around the old model, the one that had brought prosperity and a measure of happiness in the postwar world. According to the playbook, we were supposed to get an education. Check. Ron Dziuda did that the old-fashioned way, working by day and studying by night. Then he went about constructing a solid middle-class life: he worked hard, got married, bought a house in the suburbs. He and his wife guided the kids through life, shepherded them into college. A few hiccups aside, until the first decade of the 21st century, the American middle-class model was operating more or less according to plan for him.

By 2009, the second half of Ron's life was already in view. Soon it would be payoff time: you wrap up a career, finish with a decent nest egg and Social Security, and settle into a modest but comfortable retirement. That's the least of what we were promised, right? The least we should get from all that hard work and child-raising. Nothing extravagant. Maybe some fishing up in Canada. Maybe some grandchildren to dote on as the kids work on their own model of the American dream.

And then something unforeseen happened to Ron Dziuda.

The model fell apart.

This chapter was reported primarily in visits to Akron in May 2012 and January 2013, and phone conversations with Rita Hall and Paul Mangus. Unless otherwise noted, figures are provided by Mature Services or listed in the National Association of States United for Aging and Disabilities' primer on Senior Community Service Employment Program.

Ron Dziuda, 57, looks at his computerized list of more than 650 job applications during three years of underemployment at his home in Plainfield, Illinois, in October 2012.

4

Nobody Loves You (When You're Down and Out)

PLAINFIELD, *Illinois*

"But remember how you went eighty-seven days without fish and then we
caught big ones every day for three weeks."
"I remember," the old man said. "I know you did not leave me because you
doubted."
"It was papa made me leave. I am a boy and I must obey him."
"I know," the old man said. "It is quite normal."
"He hasn't much faith."
"No," the old man said. "But we have. Haven't we?"
"Yes," the boy said.
—*The Old Man and the Sea*, Ernest Hemingway

Ron Dziuda had something important to say one Tuesday evening at St. Mary Immaculate Church in Plainfield, Illinois.

It was May 2012 and he'd been waiting a long time for this moment. At the depths, he had started to doubt it would ever come. But it was finally here, *his* moment, after three years of living under what his kids came to call "the black cloud." In his mid-50s, he'd lost his job, suffered the humiliation of welfare, and burned down his savings and retirement accounts one by one. He'd borrowed from his own children to pay the mortgage; he'd racked up credit card debt to put food on the table. He'd applied for 800 jobs and been rejected. He'd turned to his wife one night and told her he didn't think he'd ever get back on his feet again.

After all that, Ron Dziuda, 57, finally stood up and spoke.

"I landed a week ago," he said. "It felt great."

His audience—frustrated, jobless men and women like himself in their 40s, 50s, and 60s—stood up with him to applaud. After three years in the wilderness, Ron Dziuda had landed a job at last, a real job with real benefits and a real salary, not the peanuts they paid him at Target to change light bulbs and unclog toilets. He was a sales specialist and it was a sales job. He couldn't be happier.

Now was also a time for thanks. Dziuda—pronounced "Dah-ZOO-dah"—credited his Catholic faith for leading him through that long, dark tunnel.

"About nine months ago, I realized this whole situation was really bigger than I was, so I handed that over to God. And sure enough, I had two job offers," he said as heads around the room nodded. "I had to let go. That's the toughest part. Let it go. Let God. We continue to use our God-given skills to find that job."

"Very few people understand what we're going through," he continued. "But God understands."

"Continue to find that job," he counseled the group he was now finally ready to put behind him. "It's out there."

The 2007–2009 Great Recession, triggered by a housing loan crisis that quickly spread its contagion into distant corners of the global economy, took down financial behemoths such as Lehman Brothers, and bankrupted entire countries. It felled Ireland's Celtic Tiger economy in its tracks, spun Spain and Greece into depressionary spirals, and plunged much of Europe into a punishing debt crisis. In Japan, it deepened the economic malaise that has beset the country since its own stock and real estate bubble burst in the early 1990s. The recession also took down millions of people like Dziuda. At the time he stood up and announced his good luck at St. Mary, five years after the onset of the downturn, joblessness in the United States still seemed locked above the 8 percent mark. Unemployment had emerged as a key issue in the 2012 presidential race, and Republican nominee Mitt Romney's campaign hit hard—and ultimately unsuccessfully—at the Obama administration for failing to craft a robust economic recovery that restored the overall unemployment rate to its pre-recession level of 5 percent.

The meltdown brought pain to many Americans. But the Great Recession was devastating in very specific ways for many older workers. It upended the last decade or two of their careers, draining their nest eggs and sentencing them to years of scraping on the unforgiving rockface of the job market. The recession and late-life job loss has dealt a blow to the confidence of a generation of Americans at a time when many of them hoped to be on the verge of a comfortable retirement. The effects will be with us for decades—whether or not the economy roars back to pre-recession growth rates. Above all, the recession, in concert with longer-term trends such as the disappearance of the traditional retirement-to-grave pension plan and the failure of the 401 (k) model to replace it, has created a core group of older Americans in their 50s and 60s who will need to work many more years to maintain their lifestyles and rebuild a financial cushion to sustain them in retirement. Many will never get there.

The most apparent effect of the recession on older Americans was a sharp spike in joblessness. In May 2012, the unemployment rate for workers aged 55 and older stood at 6.5 percent—less than the overall rate that month of 8.2 percent, but double what it was for older workers five years earlier. And losing a job at 55 isn't the same as losing one at 25. It takes 55-year-olds significantly longer to land a new gig when they do get laid off. The U.S. Government Accountability Office reported to the U.S. Senate in April 2012 that the median length of time out-of-work Americans aged 55 need to find another job had tripled from 10 weeks in 2007 to 35 weeks in 2011. Over the same time period, the median unemployed spell for younger job-seekers rose from 9 weeks to 26 weeks—a significant wait for another job, but still much shorter than that of older workers. And cases of "long-term" unemployed older workers like Dziuda, defined as those out of work for more than six months, or 27 weeks, exploded in the years after the meltdown. The GAO report said that before the recession, less than a quarter of unemployed older workers were out of a job for more than six months. But by 2011, more than half of them—55 percent—were classified as long-term jobless, and one-third were unemployed for more than a year. For older Americans, the search for work can continue for several years: only 31 percent of workers aged 55–64 who lost their jobs between 2007 and 2009 had found full-time employment by the beginning of 2010, the GAO said.

The struggles of older jobless have persisted even as the economy has emerged from the recession. An AARP analysis of April 2014 labor numbers showed unemployed workers aged 55 and older were jobless for an average of 51 weeks, compared to 35 weeks for younger Americans.

The bottom line is that an older worker who lost a job in the recession could look forward to many months—or even years—struggling to get hired again.

That's exactly what happened to Ron Dziuda.

The axe was about to fall. He could feel it.

It was July 2009 and the economy had bottomed out. Unemployment was at 9.5 percent and still headed south, and Dziuda was happy to have a job. He had been working for Misumi USA in Schaumberg, Illinois, about 40 miles north of his home in Plainfield, for more than five years. The company makes industrial components, the guts of larger machines: switches and sensors and ball screws. He'd started in sales, then shifted gears to start up the company's marketing department. Once that was up and running, he moved back over to beef up the "inside sales" operation as manager, tasked with running a five-member team aimed at drumming up new business. The group started with cold calls to potential customers, offering to send free catalogues. Then they'd follow up, and once they had a buyer interested in a product, they'd shift the account over to sales and marketing.

But this morning in July, he had a bad feeling, a feeling that had been building for a while. Starting in the spring that year, his managers told him his performance was falling short. Dziuda thought that couldn't be. To his mind, the problem was unrealistic expectations. In the middle of the worst recession in decades, Misumi's sales targets were just too high, he argued. The system in place for tracking customers needed an overhaul. Dziuda had ideas about how to fix those things, but he says that when he went to management with new proposals to boost the numbers, the boss just shrugged. "Nothing was coming back," Dziuda said. He saw it as an end-of-the-road scenario: while his bosses were demanding a better performance, they weren't letting him do anything to improve.

Then it got worse. His supervisors told him to train someone else in the software system the company used to track customer relations. Until that point, Dziuda had been the main operator of the system, but now they wanted him to transfer that knowledge to someone in IT. Dziuda's prospects darkened. Were they using him to train his replacement? "It was coming," he said. "The writing was on the wall."

Still, Dziuda wasn't panicked at the thought of losing a job. A Detroit native, he'd seen his father spend his entire career at one company, General Motors, and then eagerly take an early retirement package at 55 in the mid-1980s. But Dziuda was a veteran of American industry in the age of Clinton and Bush. Things were different these days. After getting a night-school degree in marketing from University of Detroit in 1985, Dziuda—the oldest of five children—worked at a series of employers across the Midwest, from Detroit to St. Louis and finally to the Chicago area. Ask him for the names of his former employers and they spill rapid-fire off his tongue: Fanuc-Robotics, Panasonic Factory Automation, Cimetrix, ABB, K&S Services. Sometimes he was downsized. Sometimes the economy tanked and his company fell apart. Sometimes the job was a bad fit and he quit or was let go. Dziuda always managed to land on his feet, keeping up a solid middle-class lifestyle. In the late 1990s, he and his family—wife Sue and four children—settled into a comfortable four-bedroom home in a suburban Plainfield subdivision called Wesmere Estates, a tidy collection of neighborhoods of beige aluminum siding and SUVs, where people sweep the sidewalks and plant azaleas in flowerbeds below their bay windows and install sprinkler systems to keep their quarter-acres of sod a solid green. Portraits of the Dziudas' four children hang in the wall along the carpeted stairs in their home. Stenciled in script above the photos is the legend, "All Because Two People Fell in Love."

Still, Dziuda and his family were subject to the ebb and flow of the economy, moving in and out of jobs every few years. Chance and coincidence seemed to play a large role in his life. Laid off in the turmoil of the dot-com bubble and the aftermath of the September 11, 2001, terrorist attacks, Dziuda picked up a part-time job at Target to tide him over between jobs, starting a relationship that would one day keep him from losing his house. Part-time positions at Target in those days came with benefits, which turned out to be a lifesaver when Dziuda was diagnosed with prostate cancer that year. An operation cured his illness, but he says it also cost him a job: he was offered a position in his field right before he went in for surgery, but the offer was rescinded when the employer found out he couldn't start right away. After recovering from the operation, Dziuda was back at Target, this time at 40 hours a week.

Then Misumi came along in 2004 with an offer that fit perfectly. He liked them, they liked him, and Dziuda hoped the years of bouncing from job to job were over.

By July 2009, he'd gotten a good five-year ride from Misumi. But now Dziuda was waiting for something bad to happen. He knew it couldn't come at a worse time. As a salesman, Dziuda had seen firsthand how the economy was eating away at the customer base. He could be the next casualty. Sue started finding personal work files in his study: he'd already begun cleaning out his desk at Misumi.

"He had that feeling," she recalled. "He didn't tell me. I'd find them out on the bench, and oh, you were just waiting for it."

Still, Dziuda hadn't lost all hope. If only he could hold on for a while longer, he thought, his star might rise again. The company was in the middle of a leadership change, and that could bring a new direction. *Maybe things will turn around,* he thought. *Maybe this won't happen.* One morning a human resources manager called and asked if he would be around that day at 5. Of course, Dziuda said, I'm always here till at least 6, right?

But it was a bad sign. That was the only way he could take it: *This is it.*

He walked into the conference room for his meeting, and both the outgoing president and the new president filed in. According to Dziuda, it was over quickly, efficiently, a smooth sequence of events. No drama, no ugly confrontation, no emotions. They told him this was his last day. They asked for his keys and his company credit card. They had him sign an agreement not to take a job with a competitor for a year in exchange for a three-month severance package. And he was out.

Dziuda had seen it coming. But that didn't make much difference.

"It still caught me by surprise," he recalled in his dining room one day, expressing the shock that many job-losers feel, no matter how clear the warning signs. "I didn't know what they were thinking or what the timing was. And all of a sudden I was gone."

He was 54, out of a job at the bottom of the worst recession since the 1930s, with one kid in college, another one about to enter. And it would be a long time before he got back on his feet.

From his vantage point solidly in the middle of the country, Dziuda could see he was part of a growing wave. From the outset of the recession in December 2007 until his last full month at Misumi, the number of unemployed 50-plus workers more than doubled, from 1.4 million to 3.2 million. And it was quickly becoming more difficult for people like Dziuda to get back in the game. The AARP Public Policy Institute, in a 2012 study titled "Boomers and the Great Recession," calculated that the average out-of-work spell for these older job-seekers lengthened from 21.1 weeks in December 2007, to 28.8 weeks in June 2009, right before Dziuda lost his job. And the situation was only going to get worse: by October 2010, the average "between jobs" lull for these workers had ballooned to 43.2 weeks.

So in July 2009, as Dziuda cleaned off his desk in Schaumberg, he faced a long journey to his next job. But first came the anger. Dziuda would dwell on his years at Misumi, remembering the long hours spent building a marketing division from scratch, and, more recently, the scraping on the phone to get new business as the economy melted down. In the end, he thought ruefully, none of that sweat seemed to matter. *I'd given them nothing less than 200 percent, but it wasn't good enough.* Still, he knew that holding onto that sense of betrayal was a dead-end. He'd seen other people go through it, he'd seen them allow the anger and hurt and bitterness to eat away at them, to harden into scowls on their faces, that damaging chip on the shoulder. Some needed months to shake it off. Some never succeeded, letting the sourness take over their lives. And Dziuda knew the last thing an employer wants is to take a chance on an angry, suspicious, embittered older worker.

So he decided to move on, like he'd done so many times before. Had Dziuda succeeded in swallowing the bitter aftertaste of losing his job? It was hard to tell. As we talked at his dining room table in October 2012, more than three years after he'd been let go from Misumi, he still seemed indignant, but was always careful to follow an angry comment with a hopeful one, one that showed he was over it.

Dziuda's first move when he lost his job was not to panic. With his three months' severance in hand, he and his family went ahead with their previous plans to travel to two lakeside cabins in Canada, one owned by his mother, the other by his in-laws, to cool off for a couple of weeks. The time away seemed to clear his mind. Once he was back home in Plainfield, he was ready to get started on his new life. Thanks to previous bouts of unemployment, he knew the drill. He updated his resume. He signed up at job clubs like the one at St. Mary. He called up people he used to work with, applied for every job he could find. He registered on Internet job boards like Monster and Careerbuilder. He sucked it up and went to collect unemployment, despite the humiliation; he had a family to feed. He lined up interviews. Dziuda pumped himself up. *I am going to beat this, I'm not going to be one of the long-term unemployed. I'm going to find something in three months. Because I'm still marketable, and my experience is recent and I can do this.*

His confidence didn't feel misplaced. Interviews were a little harder to come by than they had been in the past, but things were moving. He had reason for his faith: Dziuda has an easy smile, an honest, open-faced manner. He shifts his persona effortlessly between intelligent, experienced salesman and a regular guy from the neighborhood, a true asset when negotiating working relationships on the factory floor and the head office. Over the next few months, he had four or five of what he considered successful interviews. He'd sold himself, communicated his ideas and the value he'd bring to the company. He'd met company officials over several hours in the morning, gone to lunch, parted with warm handshakes and vows to be in touch. It was coming together.

And then nothing happened.

Sometimes he would never hear from the company again. The answers, if there were answers at all, were noncommittal at best, definite rejections at worst. "We're not hiring for that position now," or, "We've decided to wait," or, "We're just not interested." The world, Dziuda was starting to realize in late 2009 and early 2010, was not going to give him a break so easily. Something was different about this recession—the one that economists said was already over. So where was the recovery?

Wow, he thought. *What is going on?*

Dziuda's bout with unemployment took him from the tidy lawns and well-swept front porches of Wesmere into America's rapidly expanding network of job-seeker support groups, government training and education outposts and a confusing welter of online job-search engines. Such places have long been packed with young people struggling to get a foothold in the job market, the cyclically or chronically underemployed, and those displaced by the decades-long decline of manufacturing America. Each of those groups swelled with the Great Recession, driving the proliferation of meeting places. But the downturn also dropped a relatively new group into the mix: older workers who last had to look for a job in the 1980s. They gathered in churches, public schools, city halls, and community centers and occupational training offices in search of companionship, job-searching tips, and that spark of luck that can push a 56-year-old has-been into the gainfully employed column. In Plainfield alone, an orderly city of some 40,000 with a recycling program and designated Halloween trick-and-treat hours, jobless middle-class folks have their pick of employment meetings: at St. Mary and other houses of worship, at the public library, at the local Goodwill, at the workforce development center in nearby Joliet, and online meeting places like Facebook.

The job club at St. Mary met for the first time in January 2008, as the recession was taking its first painful bites out of the economy and people who hadn't had to look for employment for decades were suddenly cast adrift. I showed up there one Tuesday night after seeing a flyer about the meeting at an employment training center in nearby Joliet, an old limestone, railroads, and steel mill center once called the "Pittsburgh of the West." These days, though, the city is well-known as home to the prison—Joliet Correctional Center—that figured in the John Belushi movie *The Blues Brothers.*

St. Mary is similar to other job clubs in the area and across the nation. The jobless get together for presentations and discussion sessions on how to craft a resume, interviewing techniques, and networking in the Internet age. For many older workers, none of this is second nature anymore. "A lot of people who have been working at one place for 15 years and find themselves out of a job, they have no clue what a handbill or an elevator speech is," said David Bachtel, a job search coach at St. Mary. "It's a huge problem, especially for folks who haven't faced that for a long time."

Indeed. The older workers we're talking about were born in the 1940s and 1950s. As adults they saw the arrival of mobile phones, faxes, video games, and the explosion of the Internet. The white-collar folks used computers at work and are familiar with e-mail. They know how to surf the Web and are aware of social media, even if they only dabble with Facebook from time to time, or not at all. But for the guys on the factory floors, all that stuff is only dimly connected to their lives. Even e-mail, which became commonplace in the 1990s, may be something remotely alien.

Yet job searching these days requires applicants to plug into all the latest technologies. At places like St. Mary, they learn how to write resumes that focus on skills and abilities, and—like Dziuda—how to leave out dates and other details that will give precise clues about their ages. They learn how to set up pages on Facebook and LinkedIn and manage job-search engines. They learn skills such as compiling lists of "key words" from job postings and making sure those terms appear in resumes and cover letters. In the old days, they'd apply for a job by going to the company, filling out a two-page form, and handing in their resume and then waiting for a call-back. At least one human would look at your materials. But these days, you fill out applications online, upload your resume and cover letter, and a computer scans the materials for essential phrases. It's only if you can get picked out of the pile in that initial automated screening that you can get a call-back from a person. Job club attendees also develop quick-hit strategies for the next stages to give them an edge with finicky recruiters such as handbills—self-promotional flyers—and elevator speeches, 30-second presentations a job-seeker can deliver quickly if she finds herself between the lobby and the 18th floor with the personnel director.

The night Dziuda made his big announcement, older job-seekers filed into the meeting room at St. Mary and settled in at the large round tables. Attendees updated each other on their job searches, or compared the merits of Monster versus Careerbuilder—and illustrated how the emotional suffering and dislocation of joblessness was deeply intertwined with its economic troubles. The job search itself was profoundly frustrating. Recruiters were in no hurry to hire, and applicants felt companies had the luxury of being extremely picky when it came to hiring. They also struggled with health insurance. One woman fretted that she was out of work at age 63, two years before she'd be eligible for Medicare. Another man railed against the challenges of ferreting out job offers in the immensity of the Internet.

"It was so much easier," he said, "when it was in the newspaper."

Still, Dziuda and the others at St. Mary are the lucky ones in many ways. They have skills and work experience, and are firmly embedded in middle-class

America, even if their grip on that lifestyle has slipped. By banding together with the support of community groups, they can exchange ideas and information, give each other advice and generally pool their experiences for mutual benefit. Many have college degrees. If there is a skill or knowledge set they need, in general they have the resources and information to go out and get it. Dziuda, for all his troubles, still had relevant skills. He had the education, the marketing and sales experience, and the tech savvy.

The only thing he and his buddies at St. Mary didn't have was a job.

Dziuda knew the main reason he and so many others were striking out on work applications. The economy was a mess, and unemployment rates were high across the board. Yet he couldn't help feeling there was another reason why he couldn't get a job: his age.

The last time he'd looked for a job was in 2004, when he was in his late 40s. Now he was in his mid-50s, with more gray on the sides and deeper wrinkles around his eyes. The recruiters interviewing him seemed to get younger every year—and he was getting older. Employers prize their older workers for their work ethic, loyalty, and years of valuable experience. But negative stereotypes persist, particularly for job-seekers: Older workers are slow to learn; older workers miss more work due to illness; older workers won't take orders from younger superiors; older workers can't use technology. Like many other older job-seekers, Dziuda took steps to draw attention to his qualifications rather than his age. When crafting resumes and job applications, Dziuda would carefully omit references and dates—such as birthdate or date of high school graduation—that could reveal he was in his mid-50s. He included his college graduation date, 1985, but since he'd studied part-time while working a day job, that statistic made him appear seven years younger than he was. Soft-peddling his age gave him a window to impress potential employers with his skills and experience before they got a look at his gray hair.

But not everyone was happy to see a 55-year-old job sit down for an interview. He would walk into the room and feel the body language of his interviewers change sharply when they saw his face. He'd dutifully go through his carefully constructed PowerPoint presentation about his career and experience, all his capabilities and the value he'd bring to the job. He'd make his case, but he felt like he was just talking to himself. His interviewers just seemed to be biding their time, waiting for him to finish. Dziuda would walk out, chastened but still hanging on to a thread of hope that his impressions were wrong, that they'd been listening to every word, that maybe this was the time he'd get a call-back.

"But you don't get that call," he said, "and it's over." Dziuda concluded age discrimination was real. He struggled not to be angry about it. *There's nothing you can do about it,* he told himself. Still, it rankled. A 48-year-old applicant might land a job by satisfying 8 out of 10 of the employer's requirements, he reasoned, but a

56-year-old applicant needs to satisfy all the requirements to get the same job. "If you don't have all 10 outcomes," he says, "forget it."

There ought to be a law against it—and there is.

The United States enacted the landmark Age Discrimination in Employment Act in 1967. However, it has not erased perceptions of age discrimination from the job market. Ageism charges filed with the U.S. Equal Employment Opportunity Commission have soared 42 percent since the onset of the recession, from 16,548 cases in 2006 to 23,485 percent in 2011, peaking at 24,582 in 2008. A federal court in March 2012 awarded $1.868 million to a former Hoffman-La Roche Inc. drug company sales executive, Randy Dossat, who claimed age-based harassment by his manager by calling him "old school" and making other discriminatory remarks about his tenure with the company and his suitability to deal with new conditions. Dossat was 55 at the time.

Certainly many older workers perceive persistent discrimination on the job. AARP released a national survey of voters aged 50 or older in May 2012 showing that one-third of respondents said they or someone they knew had faced age discrimination in the workplace, and 81 percent said it was important for Congress to take further action to bolster workplace protections against discrimination. An earlier, wider survey of 50-plus boomers either employed or looking for work, conducted in October 2010 and August 2011, found that between one-third and one-half of respondents who had recently sought work felt age discrimination was a barrier. About one in eight respondents contended it was the most important barrier to finding a job. More than half the unemployed respondents said discrimination had a somewhat or very negative impact on their job search; nearly one in three listed age as a possible or certain reason for losing their previous jobs.

Still, Dziuda, in typical fashion, worked hard to shrug it all off. He would go into interviews, feel the negative atmosphere and figure, *I'm not going to get called back on this one.* And sometimes he would go in, get through what he thought was a great session, come out and never hear from them again. Was it age discrimination? Maybe. Maybe it was something else. Dziuda knew there were so many variables in the process, there was no way he could pick a single factor that tipped the balance.

His answer: suck it up and move on.

By 2010, Dziuda's situation was looking increasingly desperate, despite his years of work experience, tech knowledge, and education. That begged the question: what would happen to the older workers *really* in need of an update? Those with outdated skills or only a high school education or less, those with no chance of cutting it in today's labor market? The United States has a market economy, and market forces determine the shape of the jobs on offer. But what happens when a calamity like the Great Recession wipes out companies and shrinks whole industries, dumping the unskilled or those with the wrong skills into the street? They'd worked hard for years at jobs that no longer exist. Employers don't want them. Where would they get those new skills to compete in the workplace?

Not on the job. In the United States and across the developed world, older workers are often passed over for in-house training, thanks in large part to the perception, increasingly outdated, that it makes no sense to train someone who could be retiring in 5 to 10 years. Surveys show workers aged 55 or older engage in far less training than other age groups, though it's not clear how much of that is because older workers tend to need less training. In any case, the recession forced many companies to curtail or phase out training as a way to cut costs and remain competitive. Companies see training as an investment: they lay out the funds now to train workers, then reap the benefits in increased productivity. The longer a worker sticks with the company after that training, the more benefits the company receives. At least that's how it worked in the past, when workers tended to remain with single companies for longer periods of time. These days, however, with companies appearing and disappearing at a feverish rate and declining expectations that corporations will care for their workers from cradle to grave, younger workers are just as likely as older employees—in fact more likely—to jump ship after only a few years at any one company.

Older workers are often passed over for in-house training, but these days there is much less in-house training to go around. Increasingly, the responsibility for training is falling on the individual worker. And that's a major problem for aging workers who are out of a job and whose top priority is putting food on the table, saving for retirement or paying their children's college tuition. Sadly, critics say the government is not stepping in to the extent needed to provide training for those who would benefit from it.

"Our policies need to make sure that everyone is employable," Sara Rix, a widely respected economist specializing in older workers with AARP's Public Policy Institute, told me in an interview in March 2012. "A lot of people can't afford the training. We don't have the labor market policies to help. We're not giving workers the information to access the right program. It's pretty hard for a middle-aged worker to go back to school."

Sensing an opening, community colleges are attempting to target this new segment of the education market. In 2008, the American Association of Community Colleges launched the Plus 50 Initiative with funding from The Atlantic Philanthropies, founded by Duty Free Shoppers owner Charles Feeney. The initiative disbursed funds among 13 selected colleges for them to create training and education programs for older students or boost existing programs. Joliet Junior College received funding for a three-year pilot program that enabled it to provide free classes on computer programs, career training and other services to aging students looking to retrain for new jobs or brush up on skills to keep them competitive. The funding ended in 2011, but when I visited in May 2012 the college was in the midst of applying for a follow-up "completion" grant to support the training programs and track students as they apply for jobs and work to establish themselves in new positions. The college was offering the same classes, but no longer for free, meaning many students had stopped their coursework or went in search of cheaper alternatives.

Kelly Lapetino, Joliet's workplace skills manager at the college's city campus, said older workers were a burgeoning market for higher education. Over the three years of the pilot program, Lapetino said JCC enrolled about 700 students in the program. Seven percent of the school's 14,000-member student body is aged 50 or older. "That 50–65 age group is that untapped audience that nobody really focuses on," she said. "We wanted to gear toward that age group." But with her department funded entirely by grants, Lapetino said she was having some trouble offering sufficient support for the population in need of help. "It's hard to sustain it if you don't have any financial support from the college," she said of the three-year pilot program. "We got wonderful PR in the process, but budgets are tight everywhere."

Like other operations aimed at worker training and education, the Joliet center where Lapetino works is a welter of offices with affiliated organizations, funding sources, and programs. In the same complex are the Workforce Services Division of Will County, the Workforce Investment Board of Will County, and the Illinois workNet Center. Clients and students come by for everything from classes in remedial math to free used clothing to use for interviews and on the job. Upstairs, Mary Gajcak runs a weekly Career Café that dispenses advice, training, and companionship to the older unemployed. She says most of her attendees have come through the Plus 50 program.

"A lot of these people had one other job in their life and they've been laid off," she said. "It's been slow for them, but I have just a small handful of people who have been here for a long time. Most of the others have found jobs."

One morning, about 10 people filtered into the room, grabbing plastic foam cups of coffee from the coffee maker in the corner and gathering around tables arranged in a circle. They were a diverse bunch. John was a luthier looking for training and work in graphic arts. Fran was a former school bus driver who wanted to train in operating systems. Louise, suffering a bout of laryngitis, had just whispered her way through two phone interviews for jobs in pricing and contract administration. On the agenda that day was social media, a major challenge for folks who found their first jobs in the newspaper want ads. The over-50 age group tends to be more skeptical of social media than younger Americans, even if they are already on the Internet. The Pew Research Center, for instance, released a report in August 2011 showing that 61 percent of online Americans under 30 use social networking sites on a typical day, while only 32 percent of Internet-savvy baby boomers, aged 50–64, do so.

After initial introductions, Mary opened the meeting with a pep-talk: industries are growing, 9 of 10 companies expect growth, 13 industrial sectors were hiring and had positive outlooks, small businesses are adding jobs, and so on. "Across the board, things are looking way better, way better than they were," she said. If anything, human resource departments around the nation were worried about losing the workers they had, she said.

The concerns that day in Joliet focused largely on privacy and questions about whether any of this job search stuff was much use. John Heinz, 57, an out-of-work guitar and cabinet-maker looking for a job in graphic design, was frustrated. He went back to school in his late 40s and early 50s to finish his bachelor's degree in arts and media communications after, in his words, being replaced by cabinet-making machines that can "do three times the work that you can do in a year." Things weren't working out, despite the extra education: he went back to school for a degree in graphic arts, only to get out and find that the only jobs available required five years of experience.

"I'm almost 60," he said. "I'd like to be able to have some retirement when I retire."

In the meantime, he found he was spending so much energy searching for a job that he didn't have the time to devote to building a home guitar-making business. "If I'm actually going to do anything with this stuff from home, then I actually have to spend some time doing it. I can't be spending that full-time job on the computer every day searching sites, and I'm not finding anything that's actually useful," he said.

Heinz is already on Facebook and LinkedIn, but he wasn't initially impressed with the prospect of setting up a Google profile page. "It doesn't seem like there's a whole lot that you can do with it," he told the group.

For Mary Gajcak, that's a problem.

"Any job-seeker that doesn't have that profile on Google is missing out," she told the group. The reason was simple: any potential employer is going to Google an applicant's name. Job-seekers can make sure a professional-looking resume and presentation shows up first, instead of those drunken college photos on Facebook, by setting up a profile page. Gajcak cut no corners: Without a social media presence these days, job-seekers can just give up. The jobless should get on the Web and follow companies, giving them first word of openings. "If you just use newspapers alone for your job postings, you're going to be unemployed for a long time. We need to step outside of our box and get ourselves into the competition."

Networking is also high on her agenda. "If you don't network and you just do your job search at home, it just doesn't work." She urged the group to get out into job-support organizations and reach out to friends, former colleagues, and basically everyone the job-seekers know to get the word out that they're looking for work. If you're really interested in a company that an acquaintance is working for, there's a chance that there's a perk for that employee to put your name in the hat for a job. Companies, she said, would rather trust their employees to bring in good referrals than go through a pile of resumes they got through the Internet.

"That's big," she said. "If there's a company you really like and you know someone that works there, I would be their best friend for a while, for sure."

By the opening of 2010, best friends like that were in short supply.

The economy wasn't going to roar back into shape anytime soon. Instead of getting better with the official end of the recession in June 2009, things seemed to be getting worse. Unemployment was higher than when Dziuda was laid off, edging up to 9.7 percent. The U.S. economy had lost 8.7 million jobs between December 2007 and early 2010. For Dziuda, what had looked like another few months in search of a new position was turning to something much more serious. He was plugging away part-time at Target, making as much as he could at $13 an hour without hitting the limit that he could collect in unemployment benefits, using the free time to pound the pavement.

His family struggled to adjust to this emerging reality. Sue loaded on the jobs. Over the years, she'd started subbing at the local school district and eventually got hired on—with benefits—as a teachers' aide. In the late afternoons she sold fragrances at the mall. After dinner, she gave fitness classes. Back home at 10 p.m., she worked till midnight marking standardized tests online. She was going full-steam seven days a week.

"My fitness training was actually my sanity," Sue told me when I visited their home in Plainfield in April 2014. "I needed to work out at that point—otherwise I would have cried."

Dziuda's doubts began to gnaw at him as the months went by, and the Excel log of job applications he kept on his computer ran to the dozens, and then the hundreds. Before he knew it, he was part of that statistic he'd so feared when he set out on his initial job search: the long-term unemployed.

The longer it went on, the harder it got. Dziuda says Sue kept any doubts she had largely to herself, but he could almost hear the tape of thoughts running through her mind: *What do you think? You think you're going to find something? Really? Do you really think you're going to find something?*

By the second half of 2010, Dziuda was in deep unemployment, marking his first year out of a job. His second oldest son graduated from Michigan State and his daughter started at University of Iowa. Both financed their out-of-state tuitions with loans. Dziuda's job applications piled up at the rate of five a week, in accordance with unemployment insurance rules, but it had become one part routine, one part hopeless endeavor. He wasn't getting many bites, and interviews (when they came) seemed to lead into the same black hole of no job.

Making ends meet was getting harder and harder. And so he began to consume the nest eggs that had been meant to grow, hatch and mature, providing sustenance in retirement, supplementing Social Security benefits that these days were becoming less and less of a sure thing. First he and his wife emptied out the bank accounts. Then the family started chipping away at their modest retirement savings. One by one, these keepsakes of Dziuda's employment history were taken from the safe and sold off.

The $4,000 pension left over from Panasonic.

Gone.

The $4,000 IRA.

Vanished.

The $5,000 in stock from his days at GM and Detroit Edison.

Turned to dust when GM filed for bankruptcy.

Each item represented the tangible fruits of his labor. That money was meant to pay for trips to visit the grandkids. It was meant to pay for quiet vacations at the cabins in Canada. It was meant to pay for a nice meal out with Sue long after the kids had grown up and left the house. Now it was putting food on the table for their children. It was paying the mortgage in what should have been the family's peak earning years. Dziuda was eager and able to work. These were the years he was supposed to be padding his nest. Instead, he was selling it off piece by piece at bargain prices.

Then 2010 turned into 2011. Another year with dwindling faith. The unemployment rate in Illinois at the time was 9 percent. Things weren't going to get better soon. By December 2011, the jobless rate would grow to 9.8 percent. Things would soon get worse for Dziuda as well.

While his wife worked at the school, or in the aerobics studio, or at the mall selling fragrances, Dziuda was at home loading the washer or unloading the dryer, vacuuming the living room carpet. They bickered over the way he folded the laundry. The new job wasn't materializing, and the money just wasn't coming in. But the water bill arrived every month on time. And the electricity bill. And the gas bill. And the mortgage.

With their savings depleted, the couple took a deep breath and did what many desperate families of the Great Recession did: they went into debt. Dziuda had to turn to his own son, the eldest, a Purdue grad with an engineering job, for a $5,000 loan—taken in dribs and drabs over the months—to make the house payment and avoid foreclosure. Then came a second mortgage on the house. They dipped into their daughter's student loan fund and ended up owing her $3,000.

All the while, prospective employers seemed impossible to please. They were looking for the perfect candidate. The companies were just too scared to hire, holding out for a sure thing, leaving hopefuls—by August 2011, 3.3 million 50-plus workers were jobless and looking for employment—to wallow for months while they deliberated. Or, Dziuda found, employers would hold his experience against him. You're over-qualified, they told him, and even if we hire you, you'll be out the door once something better comes along. So he had to advertise himself, but not too much. "But wait a minute, don't you want somebody that can hit the ground running and perform from day one?" Dziuda would ask. "I've been out of work for 24 months and I'm working at Target—I'm not a quitter."

His resolve would face a further test in September 2011, when his unemployment insurance tapped out. Now the Dziudas were truly on their own.

Dziuda had already extended his benefits once, and now there was no option. He would have to take whatever full-time work he could find to stay afloat. With nothing better on the horizon, Target, where he'd worked off and on since 2002, was the logical choice. The open position was called Store Facilities Technician, but some of the duties—which included tending to clogged toilets and blown-out light bulbs—weren't so technical. Dziuda, a man with a degree in marketing and two decades of experience in sales, a man who'd worked at Target for some eight years, seemed like a cinch for the job. He was desperate and willing to work hard for the sake of boosting his hourly pay by three bucks, from $13 to $16.

So he applied, and got a first interview. No problem. With eight years' experience with the company, he didn't expect much competition. Then came another interview, which was no surprise in these times. Then came a third round, and Dziuda figured that would be enough. But his bosses at Target weren't done screening their prospects. There were a lot of choices, and these days, you couldn't be too picky. So on it went: a fourth meeting, a fifth meeting. A sixth, and then a seventh. He thought this over: *It just can't be right. What are they looking for? I'm not a hot-head, I'm not an 'angry white man.' It's incredible.* And then there were the people passing judgment on him, people he called kids, 25 or 26 years old, barely out of college, with men and women in their 30s running the whole store. Dziuda looked around at them working. *I could do that.*

Finally, they offered him the job. After nine interviews, he won an annual salary of about $30,000—a fraction of what he'd made in his former life. *That's all you pay?* Dziuda thought to himself. That was above the poverty line for a family of four in 2011, but not by much. Then he got a look at the benefits package and realized he couldn't even afford it. Here he was lucky: he and the kids were covered under his wife's job with the school district. But he looked around with new eyes at his work colleagues, the ones carrying whole families on the same salary without his options. *My god,* he thought, *how do you do it?*

Dziuda was thankful: Target had saved him from poverty. But rock bottom was not that far away. Dziuda had applied for 653 jobs in two years, fully documented on the family computer, with at least another 100 on top of that—with not a single viable offer. They had stopped buying anything beyond bedrock essentials, scraped by just to get clothes for the kids at Christmas. Retirement gone. The credit cards were close to maxed out; Sue was using them for food and gas.

Their children struggled to understand.

"My kids were embarrassed that their dad worked at Target and their daddy substitute taught and they were like, 'Don't come to my school, I don't want anybody to know,' " said Sue. "It was very embarrassing."

Sue wrestled with her emotions quietly. In front of Ron, she showed a brave face, believing she needed extra strength to save him from his own doubts, the excitement and crushing disappointment that followed each fruitless job interview. Privately, her world darkened. Government aid only seemed available for others deeper in poverty, or, in her view, those less willing to work round the clock to overcome adversity. The Church only seemed more interested in keeping up her weekly contributions than in helping out her family. She was fiercely determined to hold onto her house, not to fall into foreclosure like so many others. Yet family accused her of driving Ron too hard in his quest to rise above his job at Target. She looked out their window of their home on Poplar Glen Ct. and eyed a neighbor going off to work, spoke silently in her thoughts. *Why does he have a job? He's such a loser. Why does he have a job and you don't? It's not fair.*

"I cried a lot, but not in front of Ron," she said. "He was already down. I wasn't going to make him feel worse. I jumped in and worked it off—I worked off my emotions. My fitness class all heard it, you know, it's like 'We're going to beat it.'"

Was Target the best he could hope for? Was this the end of the road? One of his sons had joined him working there part-time over the summer, and Ron pointed out the other older guys toiling away—just like he did—without benefits.

"Come here to work and look around," Dziuda told his son. "*That's* why you go to college."

It was an ironic lesson. After all, Dziuda himself had worked himself through night school for that college degree, then paid his dues at several companies, amassing decades of experience in sales and marketing. And he ended up in the same place, at Target. Now that he was full-time, he would have to squeeze in his job search on evenings or days off. He started to think the unthinkable: was searching even worth it?

He turned to Sue. When they were putting together their 2011 taxes, they compared income—and Sue came out on top by about $10,000. Their combined income was $70,000—down some 40 percent from what they made when he was with Misumi. He shook his head, partly in sadness and partly in gratitude. But Sue was filled with resentment. Why had she given so much over the years, raising a family instead of building a career, only to end up being the breadwinner?

"It was hard for me to swallow that," she said. "That was kind of a reality check, because I'd never made more (than Ron). It didn't make me feel good—it kinda made me feel bad. It shouldn't have been that way."

True, his wife's earnings were more than his, but he could provide much more—if only he had a shot at a job in his specialty. Would things ever change? He was starting to lose faith. They talked about just stopping payments and giving up the house, the tidy four-bedroom home on a quarter acre in the Wesmere Glens subdivision. The one with the portraits of their four children along the stairway below the stenciled legend, "All Because Two People Fell in Love." He thought it might be time to scale back their expectations. There's only so much you can hope for on $16 an hour at Target.

"You know what?" he told her. "This might be it. I hate to say it, and I'll never stop looking for something better. But this might be it."

Sue shook her head.

"No, you've gone this far, you can't stop," she told him. "There's something out there for you and you have to believe and you just have to keep going for it."

Dziuda can't be blamed for suspecting that an hourly job at Target was the end of the line for him. The American economy had long been suffering from the hollowing out of the industrial workforce, the rot now burrowing a tunnel underneath his middle-class existence and that of many 50-something workers in the upper Midwest. Workers who cut their teeth in a postwar industrial America that led the world in production of automobiles, aircraft, electronics, and just about everything else must now face the sad fact that their skills are in far less demand in an economy increasingly looking to technology and services for growth. The Information Technology & Innovation Foundation, a non-partisan think-tank based in Washington, DC, issued a report in March 2012 estimating that U.S. manufacturing had shed a third of its jobs, about 5.7 million positions, since 2000. And when older industries decline, they take older workers with them. According to the GAO, 66 percent of jobless older workers in manufacturing were out of work a half year or more in 2011, and one in five were jobless for more than two years. Highlighting the long-term trends in the U.S. economy, education and health services workers are faring better. Less than half—46 percent—of jobless older workers in those fields were out of luck for 27 or more weeks.

The bottom line? For many aging workers in aging industries, the day when they "land" may never come. "We've seen job loss," says AARP economist Sara Rix, "and those jobs are not coming back."

Instead, many of these workers will end up with lower-paying, lower-skilled replacement work. The National Employment Law Project, a think-tank that advocates on behalf of lower-wage workers and is led by a former public policy chief at the AFL-CIO, reported in August 2012 that "mid-wage" occupations— such as electricians, truck drivers, and carpenters—made up 60 percent of the jobs lost in the recession, but only 22 percent of the positions created in the recovery. Meanwhile, the report said, "lower-wage" occupations, including retail salespeople, waiters and waitresses, and "food preparation workers," constituted 21 percent of the jobs lost and a robust 58 percent of jobs gained in the recovery.

What this all means, according to the report, is blue-collar workers who made $14 to $21 an hour yesterday are losing their jobs and coming back as burger-flippers making roughly half that. Or they feel lucky to score a part-time $13-an-hour job at Target like the one that kept Ron Dziuda afloat for two years.

Older workers who lose their jobs on average take new positions at lower pay no matter what they do. An Urban Institute study in 2012 showed that workers aged 50–61 who lost their jobs in the recession and then found other work between 2008 and 2011 saw their median hourly wage fall from $16.40 to $12.90—a drop of 21 percent.

Dziuda was still on the higher end of that scale, but he'd fallen a long way, and there was no sign he'd even get back what he'd lost.

By early 2012 Dziuda was trying—trying really hard—to feel lucky. Stripped of the trappings of the solid middle-class existence, the steady, well-paying job, the benefits and security, the independence and pride in pulling your own weight, he was turning to the basics for sustenance. His 30-year marriage. The health of his four children, the youngest of which was now heading off to college (and taking out substantial loans) in the fall.

And his faith. Dziuda had been a steadily practicing Catholic, carrying on the religion his family had brought with them from Poland in the early 20th century. He'd memorized a prayer for the unemployed which he recited to himself. And now, in his resignation, he and Sue were ready to—as he said that day at St. Mary—put their fate in God's hands.

You know what? Let's stop making the house payment. God will take care of us. He always has. And we'll just move on from here.

Well, where are we going to go?

I don't know, let's get an apartment, and now there's only the two of us here, so we can downsize. . .

Can God get you a job? Dziuda says He can. That's how he explains the mystery that once he acknowledged his exhaustion and leaned on his faith for help, a door opened.

Dziuda came across a job ad on the Internet for selling sandblasters. Pangborn Group. Around since 1904. The job caught his eye because of his background in sales and knowledge of industrial equipment. Yes, but he didn't know anything about sandblasters. *Maybe I'll sit on that one a bit*, he thought, so he filed it away and it slipped his mind. Until a guy he knew at St. Mary pointed out the position. *Did you see this ad?* the guy said. *I thought of you when I saw it.* Pangborn again. Now Dziuda had to have a second look. Was this the sign he was waiting for? Fate? Divine intervention? He applied.

And that was the beginning of everything. Before he knew it, he was at a hotel in Chicago for an interview with two managers. Two guys his age, no impression that his gray hair or wrinkles around the eyes bothered them. After that came the plane ride to headquarters in Atlanta for more talks.

And then he tried to put it out of his mind. Dziuda had been down this road many times over the previous three years: hopeful job application, smooth interviews, smiles and handshakes. And then silence. Besides, things were starting to loosen up. Another company contacted him, invited him down to North Carolina for an interview. Two months went by without a word from Pangborn.

One day the phone rang.

One of the recruiters Dziuda had met in Atlanta was going up to Chicago for work and he asked to meet. Sure, Dziuda said, how about Longhorn Steakhouse, off I-55, about a half-hour north of Dziuda's home? He put on a tie and jacket, drove up, and walked into the restaurant.

The recruiter took one look at Dziuda's tie and shook his head. There was no reason for a tie. He could have come dressed casually. After all, the tough part was over: the Pangborn recruiter was there to make Dziuda an offer.

A job offer.

Dziuda listened to the details, but his head was already drifting into the clouds. He asked for time to run it by his wife, and the two left the restaurant. What had just happened? He got in his car and pulled carefully out of the parking lot, trying to contain his excitement.

He drove home with the same thoughts over and over running through his head: *My God, I got a job. I actually have a job. Oh my God, I never thought this would happen.*

I have a job.

He called Sue at work. She was excited, but was this what he wanted to do? Other companies seemed interested, so when she got home, they sat down and wrote out the pros and cons on a sheet of paper. Bottom line was: Pangborn was the best fit. It was all starting to sink in. Was this really the end to three years of struggle?

"I don't think we could believe it," Sue said. "It was too good to believe."

And that was it. Three years of searching were at an end. The eating up the savings, the racking up of credit card debt, the sad, desperate move to borrow money from their own children. The dinners of instant ramen and hot dogs. But Dziuda says there were no tears of gratitude. Instead, they just sighed heavily with exhausted relief. They could start making the house payment again.

It was a few days later when I watched him stand up at St. Mary and make his announcement.

The time for celebration was short. Now he had a long struggle ahead to dig himself and his family out of a financial hole. Dziuda and his wife have started making payments on their mortgage from their income again, and their youngest child, a son, left the house for the University of Wisconsin, Madison, in August 2012. The retirement funds are all gone, the savings are tapped out, and the credit cards are mired in debt. His house is barely worth what he owes on it.

When his eldest son got married in June that year, Dziuda had to beg off some of the obligations the groom's family typically pays for, such as the wedding rehearsal dinner. *I got a job May 1st. I'm sorry, but that's not going to happen.* He's started paying the interest on his son's college loans to try to limit the growth of his debt, but anything more than that was still beyond the family's reach. His children resigned themselves to facing college debt loads when they go out into the work world.

In the meantime, Dziuda pushed ahead with the Pangborn job. He estimated he was on the road about 80 percent of the time, handling sales in Michigan, Illinois, and Indiana, driving his brand new 2012 Dodge Journey—and putting 18,000 miles on it in the first five months on the job.

The position brought new challenges with it. Dziuda had never sold shot-blast equipment, so now he had to learn a whole new industry. Instead of going to work in a shirt and tie and doing business on the phone, he pulls on old jeans and steel-toed shoes and drives from foundry to foundry across the upper Midwest, demonstrating equipment and troubleshooting for customers.

His enthusiasm is still high.

"It's all been good, it's all good," he said five months into the new job. "I'm like a sponge, throw me in anywhere and I'll learn, just pick it up and I can run with it."

Still, the scars—financial and emotional—from his three-year battle with the job market are still there. They may never fade entirely. He's kept his part-time job at Target, working five hours on Saturday and Sunday mornings, partly out of gratitude, partly out of the lingering fear that this secure, stable calm he's found could shatter at any time. Will the job at Pangborn still be here next year? Can he learn shot-blast equipment fast enough and well enough to be successful? Will he be able to retire from this job, or will he again be on the job-search rollercoaster at an even older age? Pangborn was growing, so what would his next move be? Is there a promotion down the road?

Dziuda's answer to all those questions is the same: I don't know.

"I guess my biggest thing is: how long is this going to last?"

The world, in some ways, has dimmed. The past several years have been ones of disappointment and humiliation. He'd lost his job, gone on unemployment, struggled with job discrimination, and faced three years of rejection. He and Sue work seven days a week now out of the fear that his main job could be taken away at any moment. The future is uncertain. He sees his kids graduating with loads of debt, moving into a shaky job market. It doesn't seem fair. He said a young man with a marketing degree worked side-by-side with him at Target for a decade before finally scoring a full-time position with benefits. Now he drives a truck for Frito-Lay.

The legacy of their struggle shows itself in the little things. Their kids call it "the black cloud"—that shadow of bad luck that seems to be right over their shoulders. "We have a black cloud that looms," said Sue. "When Andrew had a job offer rescinded—there's the black cloud. Britt feels the black cloud now on her shoulders with trying to get in the medical profession. There's the black cloud again." The cloud hovered over them at Ron and Sue's 30th wedding anniversary celebration in the fall of 2013, when they hesitated to buy themselves a nice dinner out, thinking about how much it would cost.

"There's a guilt that comes with everything we do now, and my kids are like, `You gotta stop that,"' said Sue. "Because sometimes I think it's too good, it's gonna end. Is it gonna be taken away from us again? I don't like that feeling, but that's what this experience has done. It's like I don't ever feel secure."

At the same time, though, Dziuda is deeply thankful he and his family were spared from even greater misfortune. In the end, he kept his house. At the point of his deepest despair, he nailed a steady job that pulled him back from falling permanently away from the middle class. Now, with some luck, he has a chance to scrape his way back to solvency. His 30-year marriage survived the storm intact, arguments about how to fold the laundry aside; his four kids are healthy.

And he'd kept his faith.

"Seeing other people going through it, and seeing how fortunate I am, the upbringing, my experience. I think I'm so much better off. God, thank you. I'm much more thankful for what I have now."

"Even if I had to work at Target for the rest of my life, it is what it is."

Dziuda is clear about one thing: he'll probably never retire.

His experience mirrors that of other baby boomers who have weathered the recession, especially those who struggled with unemployment. The AARP survey showed that 43 percent of respondents said they planned to work at least part-time in retirement, and 36 percent—more than one-third—said they would postpone the date of their retirement. Of those like Dziuda who lost their jobs and regained employment, 42 percent said they would put off the date of their final exit from the workforce to make up lost ground. These numbers make sense when one considers the way the Great Recession has eroded the optimism of boomers overall.

While a typical reaction to lowered confidence is to increase savings, Dziuda says that won't be an option for his family until they tame the debts run up during his years at Target. Pangborn, for instance, has a 401 (k), but Dziuda didn't have the surplus income to start making deposits until 2014—nearly two years after he'd started his new job.

At this point, he's hoping to stay healthy enough to work for at least for 15 years to rebuild—putting him in his 70s before he can downshift. But for now, he's putting all expectations of retirement out of his mind. There's too much catching up to do. And then even if he manages to clear the credit card debt and start chipping away at his mortgage, he still needs to rebuild a nest egg that would sustain him and his wife into old age—much of it without the help of a resurgent post-recession stock market.

"In one way, shape or form, or another," he said, "I will probably work for the rest of my life."

For all his struggles, Ron Dziuda is luckier than many. He has a college degree, decades of experience, a working spouse, and family to support him. And, though it took a long time, in the end the system came through for him—unemployment insurance and work at Target sustained him through the low points, and he eventually scored a solid job despite his age and time in the wilderness. Now, with some luck and continued good health, he has the chance to regain at least part of what he lost.

But he'd be the first to tell you it wasn't easy. Could there have been systems in place, some policy or mechanism to ease and speed his passage from one job to another, sparing him three years of heartbreak and despair? Is there a better way? Each society confronting the demographic and economic challenges of the early 21st century will need to find its own path. And yet, we all—from Kamikatsu to Akron to Stockholm—are facing similar strains. How are others dealing with these sea-changes?

Now we head overseas, to the "Rest of the Rich"—those highly developed countries of Europe and East Asia where aging is even more advanced than in the United States. Our first stop is Sweden, where Kjell-Åke Ericsson fell out of his job—and landed in the hands of one of the country's largest job training programs.

This chapter was reported primarily in three visits to Joliet and Plainfield in May and October 2012, and April 2014.

Morgan Svensson, 72, shows photos of his work as a carpenter at the Pensionärspoolen temporary work agency for older people in Gothenburg, Sweden, in May 2013.

5

The Swedish Way

Kjell-Åke Ericsson has spent a lifetime in jewelry. Thirty years ago, at the age of 21, he inherited the family wholesale business in Stockholm, importing fashion accessories—earrings, necklaces, armbands, studs—from Asia for sale and distribution in Europe. At the company's height, he oversaw 30 employees and sales offices elsewhere in Sweden, in Gothenburg in the west and Malmö in the south.

Over the years, he built an expertise in sales and forged contacts and relationships in Asia, particularly China. But the 1990s were not kind to the Swedish economy. Businesses went under, unemployment spiked, and chain stores started wiping out the single-owner accessory outlets that formed Ericsson's customer base. With clients dwindling, he folded the business in June 2001 and defected to his rivals: he signed on as a strategic buyer with Glitter International, a Stockholm-based fashion chain.

There he stayed for 12 years, managing relations with suppliers and traveling to product fairs in China, South Korea, the Philippines, India, and Taiwan, sourcing new products and taking care of vendor contracts. It wasn't a bad deal: during the years Ericsson was there, Glitter expanded its reach from under 50 stores to some 250 outlets in Sweden, Norway, Denmark, Finland, and Poland.

But in the spring of 2013, Glitter reorganized its buying department, and Ericsson was suddenly out of a job.

"Of course, I was surprised," he said. "This reorganization, I didn't know anything about that. This came from nowhere."

It could have been a disaster for Ericsson, who is married with a pair of teenaged daughters. He had two major strikes against him as he ventured out into the job market for the first time in more than a decade. First, he had never gone to college. As many in the United States in the Great Recession have found, that fact alone would exclude him from many jobs, and those without a university degree have a higher unemployment rate than college grads. Strike two is another big one: he's 51. As we've seen already, workers in their 50s who are laid off have a much harder time finding new work than younger colleagues.

But Ericsson hasn't found himself out on the street—far from it. The first thing he did when he got his pink slip was go to his union—Unionen, one of two major retail workers' unions in Sweden—for a consultation and support. There he found out that anyone over 45 with more than five years with the same company was entitled to six months severance at full pay. And then his company added another six months of pay for his agreement, brokered with the help of the union, not to legally fight his dismissal. With another month thrown in for vacation pay, Ericsson has a total of 13 months at full-pay.

That's a pretty good deal, but severance is only as good as it lasts; eventually it runs out, and what a laid-off 51-year-old needs most is a steady job. But in Sweden, there's help for that too: after he stopped work at Glitter, Ericsson was at TRR Trygghetsrådet, one of the country's largest so-called job security councils, organizations jointly set up by employers and unions who receive, retrain, and otherwise prepare laid-off workers to compete in the job market.

In his first month at TRR, Ericsson went to a seminar on putting his resume in order and gearing up mentally for his job search and swapped notes with other jobless workers at the council in a meeting aimed at sharing contacts. He met with a personal counselor to map out a search plan, and started making contacts with more specialized employment agencies. A couple of days after I met him in May 2013, he was scheduled to go to a separate agency for job interview coaching—paid for by TRR.

So now, Ericsson has a new routine: instead of sitting around at home or sleeping in, he gets up early, comes to TRR's Stockholm offices, plunks down at a computer terminal and works on his resume, makes appointments, or attends job search seminars.

"So far it has given me a place to start from," he told me in a TRR conference room one afternoon. "It's given me an office. It's given me some seminars, some information, what to think about, given me a coach. But they don't give me the key—you have to find it yourself. It just gives you support, and I'm quite impressed so far. I won't say they will be my savior, but it gives me a base to go from. That's very good, I think."

If he sticks with it, Ericsson's chances of landing a job are excellent. TRR officials say they have a 90 percent success rate for clients who keep searching, with the spell between jobs averaging about six or seven months.

Job councils like TRR are the grease of the Swedish labor system, and one of the many reasons why this country of barely 10 million people has emerged as a model for many in Europe who are struggling to boost work levels among older people. On a continent that has long been associated with an early retirement culture, Sweden and its northern neighbors—Norway, Finland, and Denmark—stand out as countries that have managed to safeguard the bulk of the welfare state while smoothing out some of the inconsistencies in the labor market.

True, unemployment amid the European crisis is still high in Sweden—it hovered near 9 percent when I spoke with Ericsson in May 2013—but the country has been largely successful at keeping people engaged in the work market until retirement at age 65. Labor force participation for people aged 55–64 has risen from 73 percent in 2008 to nearly 78 percent in 2013. And that's not just because there are a lot of jobless older Swedes looking for work: employment of those aged 55 to 64 has increased from under 62 percent in 1995 to over 73 percent today. So Swedes in their 60s are participating extensively in the job market. Unemployment for that age group in 2013 was around 5.5 percent—higher than it was in 2008, but lower than in the United States.

The labor force participation figures have drawn attention from around the continent, and the world. Bureaucrats as far away as Japan include Sweden in their presentations on building older workforces. The officials I spoke to at TRR said bureaucrats from the Italian government had just visited, and more from France were expected later in the week.

"Sweden is a very good example of what can be done," said Anne-Marie Guillemard, an aging worker specialist at University of Paris Descartes Sorbonne in Paris. "They have been developing a proactive labor market policy, not toward older workers, but . . . for all ages. But it helps to make older workers more efficient at the workplace so they are not fired."

Sweden has managed this, curiously, without any major programs specifically for older workers. Instead, the Swedes have set up agencies designed to catch workers of all ages before they fall into long-term unemployment, retool them for new job market realities, and get them back out working. As society has aged, they have tweaked the various agencies to offer older workers special benefits, such as longer spells of unemployment insurance and other higher levels of support.

TRR and other job security councils are considered key. The councils were first set up in the 1970s as economic growth slowed across Europe and the first oil shock jarred finances across the Western world. The wealthy nations of the continent now had to deal with a new problem they hadn't encountered in the heady postwar years of expansion: rising unemployment. While many nations like France, which we'll look at later in the book, responded by investing heavily in early retirement schemes, Sweden took a different path. In the decades since, employers in different sectors of the economy—finance, construction, health care, public agencies, even churches and theaters—have gotten together with their respective unions and brokered deals to create the councils. The agencies are funded by contributions from companies and covered workers, who pay 0.3 percent of their salaries in exchange for having a place like TRR to go when they get laid off. Today there are about a dozen major job councils in the country covering some 2 million workers, and TRR is one of the largest.

There are several factors that make the system possible. One is the pervasiveness of union membership in Sweden: nearly 70 percent. True, this is down from the 80 percent of a decade ago, but it is still remarkably high. Union membership in the United States, in comparison, is less than 12 percent. This means that workers in Sweden in nearly every industry are covered by unions, and those unions can negotiate with greater legitimacy and weight. Swedish labor laws passed in the 1970s also play a role in managing the labor market. One such law requires employers to have "just cause" in dismissing workers, thereby attempting to regulate swings in employment. Another law requires employers bound by collective agreements to consult with unions on any changes effecting labor relations— meaning restructuring plans have to be worked out with the unions.

The councils are a logical extension of these circumstances. The arrangement gives businesses the flexibility to unload workers in tough times with less threat of union backlash or bad press for dumping its employees in the streets. Laid-off workers, meanwhile, secure a financial cushion and support and direction in finding the next job. System-wide, the councils promote labor mobility, moving workers from companies in dire straits toward companies in growing industries.

The framework appeals to the Swedish quest for stability and cohesiveness as it competes economically in a European Union dominated by Germany, France, and Britain. "We are a small country," said Ann-Sofi Sjöberg, the TRR spokeswoman who showed me around the offices, where everything seemed to have a fresh coat of paint. "We have to be quick, we have to solve our internal problems by ourselves . . . with a smooth way of handling the workforce to keep our little country fit for the competition."

TRR was at the forefront of the job council movement. It was the first established in 1974, in an agreement between a leading business federation, the Confederation of Swedish Enterprise, and a white-collar union, the Federation of Salaried Employees in Industry and Services. TRR is sprawling—it covers some 700,000 workers in 32,000 companies—including top names in Swedish industry such as telecom and mobile phone giant Ericsson and leading automaker Volvo. Annual spending is around 1 billion Swedish krona, about $150 million, and has helped some 175,000 workers over the past decade. It also has earned excellent marks for transitioning workers from one job to another: it claims that 90 percent of its clients who actively seek work find it, with 90 percent of those finding a position equal to or better than the job they had before. TRR has outposts all over Sweden: it employs 230 people in nearly 40 offices around the country. When I visited, they had 18,000 job-seekers on the books.

The councils operate as independent non-profits, meaning they are nimbler than government agencies and more responsive to individual job-seeker's needs, officials say. They can also expand in short order in response to rising need. When I dropped by, TRR had just taken over an additional floor in an office building in downtown Stockholm to accommodate several hundred workers recently let go by Ericsson. The council did the same when carmaker Saab struggled with insolvency. Sjöberg said that of the 1,500 former Saab employees who walked through the doors when the company filed for bankruptcy in December 2011, at least 1,250 of them had found jobs within a year and a half.

As the first job council, TRR has set the standard for how to handle redundant workers and prepare them for re-employment. On one hand, the method is heavy on personal attention, ego-massaging, and post-layoff psychic healing, along with a dollop of financial support to cushion the blow. On the other hand, the councils like TRR are firm in their insistence that their services are aimed at getting a job, not a form of permanent welfare. Services are open only to those workers laid off for economic reasons; those fired for poor work performance need to go to the state for help. Participation in the job councils is voluntary, and most people can only participate in a council for a maximum of two years, though extensions are possible.

Sometimes, TRR will invite workers about to lose their jobs to come in for a consultation even before they've been let go.

"We focus from day one," said Sjöberg. "When you've been made redundant from a company, we say come to us as soon as possible, we don't want you to wait, because we know that even though you might have had six months pay or one year, if you start being at home, 'I'm just going to paint the house,' then you start to lose energy."

While the job councils are open to all covered workers, in practice their services are geared toward job-seekers in mid-career or later. At TRR, a worker needs to have worked more than 16 hours a week at the same company for at least a year to be eligible for help. For additional "redundancy pay," which fills some of the gap between state-funded unemployment insurance and a worker's former salary, clients need to be 40 or older with five years at the same company. Two-thirds of the workers who get new jobs in any given year at TRR are between 40 and 59.

Councils like TRR boast of their personal touch. At the center of that claim are people like Louise Lagerling, a TRR job counselor whose job it is to guide clients like Ericsson through the process.

Lagerling, who is trained in cognitive behavioral therapy, came to TRR eight years earlier, after a few years as a recruiter for IT companies. She has a roster of some 60 clients who meet with her one-on-one—some more regularly than others, depending on their own wishes—as she takes them through a series of steps she says will deliver them from joblessness to employment. "The focus is always the client and the meeting with the client and process," she said. "We follow them from start, till the goal, which is of course a new job."

The first step in the process is an assessment of skills and goals. What can they do? What are their abilities? What kind of job do they want? When do they want to go back to work? Right away, or in three months? Once that has been ironed out, Lagerling—backed with her knowledge of the job market—coaches them on whether they need to develop new skills to find employment, and, if so, how to go about doing that.

And what if, say, the out-of-work newspaper writer wants to take a course on multimedia reporting skills at a local university? With Lagerling's approval, TRR will pay for it. Each counselor has 1 million kronor—about $150,000—to lavish on her clients as she sees fit. TRR has contracts with numerous outside educational and training companies to handle their clients, or job-seekers can come forward with their own ideas. "Everything—IT, sales courses, certificates, project management, economy, etc. Everything," Lagerling said. "We have a lot of companies that we work with in that sense as specialties, but the client can also come and say, 'I would like to do this, is it possible?' So we can buy from others rather than our own suppliers."

Still, the counselor has the final say on what TRR will finance for a particular client, giving the organization a powerful influence over participants' future job choices. "If it's a well-known course or education, then you can tell this is going to lead to work, because as a counselor you have to know the job market," said Lagerling. But counselors can turn down requests they doubt will strengthen the client's job prospects.

"We have a lot of people who have been sitting by a desk all of their lives in front of a computer, and they come to us and say, 'OK, I've been doing this for 30 years and now I want to be a massage therapist or a florist.' OK, that's not going to lead you anywhere close to a job."

The other big piece of what TRR and other job councils do—and one of their trickiest tasks—is teaching people how to look for a job: they work on resume building, interviewing, and working personal networks to find out about available positions. Clients are taught how to set up social media accounts, update their resumes, and stand out in job interviews.

Like many older job-seekers who have been relatively secure for 10, 20, or 30 years in the same company, Ericsson said his first real bout with joblessness had been disorienting.

"The main thing now is to concentrate on getting my CV organized, to get all my data, to get . . . LinkedIn," he told me. "Do you have a LinkedIn? Do you understand how it all works, and how you update the whole thing? This TRR, they organize LinkedIn seminars, so you can get to know it and understand it, because we all are plus-45, and we all worked so hard and we never thought about LinkedIn. I mean, what was that? Do you really need it? Can't you just phone me?"

One of the toughest tasks is prodding older workers raised in more modest times to adjust to a competitive job market that demands a high level of self-promotion. "You have to present yourself in a more 'selling' way," said Ericsson. "You have to be like a salesperson and sell yourself and say, 'Look how good I am! I've improved this and I've done that, the company increased, or I made this!' " he said.

Lagerling said this is particularly difficult for older job-seekers in Sweden, where quiet teamwork has traditionally been valued over boasting and American-style individualism. "Swedes in particular are quite shy and they don't like to talk about themselves. It's very hard for a Swede to say, 'I was the top team member in my group.' So we have to learn how to rethink, how to reformulate. The younger ones who are in their 20s or 30s, they don't have the same problem as the older ones. They are so influenced from the Internet and TV and media and American TV shows, etc. We have the culture here. But the older ones, they're not really adopting that."

It was difficult to gauge how much further Ericsson had to go in his effort to land a new job. He credited his four weeks at TRR with forcing him to reconsider his CV, establish a presence online, and reach out to more specialized employment agencies. He'd met with an agency that specialized in the fashion industry the week before and had posted his resume on their website; a meeting with another agency had been set up for the following week.

He also seemed to be reconfiguring his ideas about what type of job he could perform. When he arrived at TRR in April, he more or less assumed he'd be going into the same business he'd always worked in. But by May, his ideas were evolving. One issue he was facing was that his age and his gender put him out of step in an industry he said is dominated by women in their late 20s. So he was starting to look into sales jobs related to so-called fast-moving consumer goods such as disposable cameras, soft drinks, and toiletries.

"I could do that as well if it's from Asia, because I know how Asia works," he said. "I can source things . . . . If you look at the consumer goods, there's only buying and selling. I understand that part, so I might be able to find companies who are selling fast-moving consumer goods of all kinds of things. It doesn't have to be fashion."

In an environment that many American job-seekers would consider nearly luxurious—when we talked, Ericsson still had 12 more months at full salary—he was clearly unmoored by his status as a job-seeker. Neither his wife, a British citizen who works as a head-mistress at a school, nor his two teenage daughters seemed to be particularly upset about his joblessness.

"They're worried but not too much. I'm more worried," he said. "Time is ticking."

The job councils are a unique feature of the Swedish labor market that bears close attention and perhaps some emulation, particularly in their obvious success in finding new jobs for clients. Still, they enjoy special advantages that make such success more likely. First, they are entirely voluntary, meaning job-seekers already bring high levels of motivation to the table. In the case of TRR, we are also talking about some of the most educated, well-trained workers in the Swedish economy, Ericsson's lack of a college degree notwithstanding. These workers bring with them years of experience with top-line companies and a wealth of contacts. According to statistics compiled by Ola Bergström, an economist at Sweden's Gothenburg University, between 80 and 90 percent of clients find jobs within seven or eight months.

What happens to the 20 percent who don't make it? They end up in the hands of the state.

The Swedish Public Employment Service, the headquarters of which are housed in a functional glass, steel, and cement structure on the northern end of Stockholm's center, near a highway and a dusty construction site, is the country's go-to place for the jobless. It's at one of the service's 330 offices around Sweden where Swedes down on their luck can register to collect unemployment insurance, sign up for vocational training, brush up on their resume-writing skills, and find leads that will get them back on the job.

The service—known by its 18-letter Swedish name, Arbetsförmedlingen—offers a smorgasbord of programs. Its 13,000 employees—including some 1,800 psychologists and other specialists—provide dole payments, wage subsidies for workers with disabilities of up to 100 percent of their salaries, temporary jobs for the jobless, and training programs. The service has a budget of 70 billion krona, or more than $10 billion, about $1,000 for every inhabitant in the country. The service reaches out to thousands of employers to secure jobs for its clients, handling some 600,000 job vacancies a year. All told, the service had more than 400,000 clients registered in March 2013, two months before I visited. In 2010–2011, they found jobs for more than half a million people.

And the agency is becoming more important all the time. One reason is a change in emphasis in public policy. Sweden has fine-tuned its prodigious welfare state over the past two decades, pointing more people—those on disability insurance, for instance, or newly arrived immigrants—in the agency's direction in hopes of shifting them from dependence on government largesse to participation in the labor market. The other less purposeful reason is that unemployment is increasing in Sweden. Economic growth stalled at the end of 2012, and joblessness stood at 8.8 percent in March 2013, up from 7.8 percent in 2012. For the agency, greater unemployment means a higher budget.

"More unemployment, more funding," said Tord Strannefors, head forecaster in the Service's analysis division. "The sum has increased, and I think it will also do so next year and the next year."

But like the job councils, there's one program the Arbetsförmedlingen doesn't have: one specifically for older workers.

Strannefors might argue there's no need for one. Sweden is doing a fine job keeping older Swedes in the workforce. As we've seen, labor force participation rates for Swedes aged 55–64—right before the long-standing retirement age of 65—is remarkably high, particularly when compared to more southerly neighbors like France and the Mediterranean countries. Sweden is second in Europe only behind Iceland.

Strannefors's first move when I went to visit his office was to lay several graphs before me. One shows the labor participation rate for older Swedes on an upward, if uneven, trend since the late 1980s, with dips for the Swedish economic crisis in the early to mid-1990s, another smaller drop in 1998, and then some stagnation from 2005 until 2008 before taking off, reaching 78 percent in 2013. So Swedes in their 60s are participating relatively successfully in the job market.

So, aside from job council, what are the Swedes doing right? One might expect that the Swedish welfare state would bring greater benefits in health and education, and that would make older people easier to employ. After all, there is a vast difference between a 63-year-old in robust health with an advanced academic degree and one in poor health with little education. And yet, educational attainment in Sweden, though admirable, is roughly the same as the United States, at least in terms of a high school degree or its equivalent. Average life expectancy in Sweden is 82—higher than 79 in the United States, but not remarkably so. Sweden has great levels of equality, at least as measured by the Gini coefficient. And they've paid for it. Even today, after the so-called welfare state has gone through serious adjustments to manage costs and bolster incentives for economic growth and achievement, Swedes can still fork over nearly 60 percent of their income in taxes. A system like that wouldn't go over well everywhere. And Swedish society is hardly fissure-free. Riots in immigrant neighborhoods in Stockholm just the week after I left illustrated the divisions and perceptions of inequality lying underneath the placid, egalitarian exterior.

It might be in part a matter of attitude.

Though the welfare state as practiced in some parts of the world is associated with freedom from work—labor contracts that increase vacation times, allow earlier retirement, and so on—the Swedish model mixes generous state support with what is known as the "work first principle." The principle comes down to this idea: the state would rather subsidize wages and keep people at work than let them go jobless and pay them to do nothing. On one level, it smacks of a socialistic "everyone has a job and nobody works" system. But there certainly is something to be said for maintaining work skills and the daily rhythm of keeping a job, even if that job would be unsustainable if exposed to the rigors of the market. Activity, social engagement, and dignity carry their own benefits, this thinking goes, even if the state plays an open role in subsidizing them as a gateway to self-sustaining employment. Economists might say that the cost is a misallocation of labor that could be used more productively elsewhere, but that's a cost governments incur all the time, whether they're helping 60-year-olds find jobs or handing out defense contracts or agricultural subsidies.

In a system as famously state-led as Sweden's, places like Arbetsförmedlingen have been a cornerstone of the country's progress in dealing with the impact of aging on the labor market and the workplace. The service's own promotional literature claims it acts as "the matching engine of the Swedish labor market." The agency provides guidance and advice to job-seekers, employment-training programs, and support to immigrants, of which Sweden accepts some 100,000 a year. The focus is on those who need the extra help: recent arrivals, the disabled, and the long-term unemployed. The help isn't cheap. The service spends 12 billion krona ($1.8 billion) a year in wage and other subsidies for people with disabilities, meaning that the government can help an individual get a job by paying up to 100 percent of that person's wages, depending on the impact the individual's disability has on productivity. About half that sum is spent each year on so-called new start jobs, aimed primarily at those who have been out of work for a time ranging from six months to a year.

Though no particular program at Arbetsförmedlingen is aimed at older workers, the service does make special allowances for them. For instance, while workers aged 26–55 need to be out of work for a year to qualify for a "new start" job, older workers can join the program after only six months unemployed. This benefit is also offered to younger workers aged 21–25. Older workers can stay in the program for twice as long as people in other age categories. Benefits like those have drawn older workers toward particular parts of the service. Workers aged 50 or older, for instance, make up more than 40 percent of the 100,000 people participating in the Job and Development Program, aimed at those who have been out of the workforce for a certain period of time.

"There is a consensus in Sweden that if you want to work, then you should have that opportunity," Strannefors said. "More people want to work longer, but you also have a lot of people who don't want that."

How much longer do they want to work?

When the Swedes introduced the world's first universal state pension system in 1913, they set the retirement age at a lofty 67. It stayed that way until the 1970s, when it was lowered to 65 as Sweden's relatively modest nod to the idea prevalent at the time that older workers should retire a little earlier and make room for younger people.

And there the retirement age has been ever since, widely accepted as the natural time to quit working and enjoy the fruits of one's labor. The number is enshrined in the eligibility age of a state pension. These days, Swedes have the legal "right" to employment until 67, meaning a company can't force its workers to quit earlier. But few employees exercise the right to work that late—80 percent of them retire at 65. While the percentage of workers among Swedes aged 55 to 64 is near the highest in the world, it drops off dramatically after 65. Clearly, to many Swedes, the "work first" principle no longer applies after that magic number.

And that's just what's wrong with Sweden today, according to Ingemar Eriksson.

Eriksson, who has worked in the ministries of Finance, and Health and Social Affairs, and as the economic attaché at the Swedish Embassy in Washington, DC, led a special "Commission on Retirement Age" that issued a 500-page report in April 2013. The report called for, among other things, a raising of the eligibility ages for public and private pensions.

For Eriksson, the "retire at 65" idea is setting an aging Sweden up for economic and political trouble down the road. First, 65 is just too young to opt out of the labor market, he argues. Today's 60-somethings are healthier, more educated, and just plain smarter and more capable than those of a generation ago. Shoving them out to pasture is a waste of resources. On top of that, many older Swedes— as people in many other parts of the developed world these days—say that they would like to keep working beyond the traditional retirement age if conditions were right.

The expectation of retirement at 65 also creates a self-fulfilling prophesy, he argues. Workers who are 55 or 60 see little point in developing their careers or seeking new training. After all, they'll be out of the workforce soon. And employers certainly have little interest in paying to educate a worker who is on the verge of leaving the company, taking her new capacities with her.

More importantly, the aging society just won't be able to keep benefits high enough to maintain support for the pension system, Eriksson says. Right now, the pension is able to replace an average of 60 percent of a person's working-time income. Already, he says, there are signs that this percentage—the replacement rate—is declining because there are fewer workers to pay for the pensions of more old people. On top of that, the Swedish pension system is built to respond to economic conditions. Bad times automatically translate into lower benefits. That not only presages a declining standard of living for tomorrow's pensioners, but it also could undermine the widespread support the pension system enjoys among the population.

"We need to change this behavior rather fast in order to prevent this drop in general trust," he told me. "When people live to 75 or 80, if they retire before 65, which many people do here, they will have a lousy life, really."

And so, Eriksson argues, what they need is a little nudge—in the form of a later retirement age.

"Right now, we nudge people to retire at 65 or earlier, and that makes them unnecessarily unhappy and unnecessarily poor when they are old. So we have to remodel our rules and our information and our education programs in order to nudge people to continue to work."

That nudge is the report Eriksson's commission issued just a few weeks before we met.

The main recommendations seem hardly revolutionary: The minimum eligibility age for certain pension accounts would be raised from 61 to 63 by 2019, and the eligibility age for the state "guaranteed" pension would be raised from 65 to 66 by the same year. Company and private pensions, now available to workers at 55, would be forbidden for anyone under 62 by 2017, and the "employment protection law" would be changed to raise the guarantee the right to work from age 67 to 68 in 2016.

Perhaps the most remarkable proposal is to peg the "recommended retirement age"—which determines eligibility for the state guaranteed pension—to the average life expectance at age 65 in Sweden. This builds a direct link between long lives and the rights to a pension, enshrining the idea that if you live longer, you ought to work longer. It also builds flexibility into the system, so the state would automatically respond to increases in life expectancy, without having to go through the arduous political process every few years of increasing the retirement age.

To smooth out the transition, the report also calls for a wide-ranging program, funded by the savings realized by having higher retirement ages, to improve the work environment in Sweden by alleviating physical demands, health hazards, and stress on the job and spreading best practices on how to adjust workplaces to larger numbers of older employees. The report recommends strengthened measures against age discrimination, new rules making training available to workers at higher ages, and creating more opportunities for part-time work and flexible hours.

The individual recommendations aren't radical, but the wording of the report is considerably strident. The commission dismissed as "myths" the notions that early retirement leads to longer lives, or that old workers need to be cleaned out of the labor force to make room for young people. "Early retirement," the report declares, "can be regarded as a historical remnant that entails a waste of human capital."

Eriksson says the recommendations are needed to change attitudes about the connection between age and work. By forcing people to accept longer worklives, he hopes to encourage Swedes in mid-career or later to seek—and, eventually, to demand—opportunities for training and education into their 50s and early 60s to maintain their relevance in the workplace. Slowly, he said, attitudes about older workers will evolve.

"The attitudes and the negative expectations of old people will disappear quite fast and we will have a new world in which old people are not very special," he said. "They will be ordinary people until a quite high age."

The commission's recommendations are certain to find a receptive audience within parts of the current center-right government. Prime Minister Fredrik Reinfeldt caused a stir in 2012 when he suggested in an interview with the *Dagens Nyheter* daily newspaper that Swedes ought to be working until 75. "To hire someone who is 55 who says 'yes, I plan to work until I'm 75'—that's 20 years, that's a very long and interesting employment relationship compared to a person who at that age plans to start winding down in five or six years," Reinfeldt said. "If people believe that we can live longer and shorten our working life, the pension will for sure be reduced. The next question is then, are people prepared for that? In most cases I don't think so." Reinfeldt argued that 50-somethings, instead of focusing on retirement in a few years if their jobs get too tough, should shift gears and move into work that they can do, perhaps with the help of government study grants.

That said, there are powerful interests expected to oppose any tinkering with the retirement age. Labor of course has based its legitimacy on reducing time at work; it would be a major cultural change for unions to get behind any measure that encourages people to work more. Employers and business federations, too, are loathe to accept any measure that limits their flexibility in hiring and firing. They are expected to fight the proposed increase in the employment guarantee age until 69, and the increase in the eligibility age for private pensions will impinge on their ability to unload aging workers or control labor costs by offering early retirement. While there are many older Swedes who want to work longer, the country is also strongly attached to the welfare state, and the pension system is a strong symbol of social justice and equity.

Many in Sweden see themselves as relatively well-off when compared to other European countries with higher levels of aging and lower levels of older people at work. "It may not be so easy—employees and employers are satisfied," said Roland Kadefors, an expert in aging and work at Gothenburg University's department of work science. "The employers don't see this problem as acute yet."

Eriksson says he doesn't expect the process to be quick.

"It's extremely difficult to have any idea how it will work out. I'm still quite optimistic."

As we've discussed elsewhere, raising retirement ages puts the spotlight on efforts to make sure the measure doesn't just lead to greater unemployment among older people.

The government in Sweden has been relatively effective in shutting early exits from the labor market over the past two decades. The Commission's proposal would insure new doors don't open by making eligibility for sickness benefits and other programs rise in tandem with the retirement age, thereby stopping Swedes from using them as sources of income to tide them over until their pensions kick in.

"Early exit is not an option any more for some people," said Eskil Wadensjö, an economist and pension system expert at the Swedish Institute for Social Research at Stockholm University. "Now you really have to have an illness or a disability of some kind to get a disability pension."

As in many countries facing a similar dilemma, the raising of retirement ages risks exacerbating the growing inequalities between rich and poor in Sweden—a troubling prospect in a nation that is proud of its egalitarian tradition. Over the past decade, the elderly, foreign-born, and those with lower income have benefited far less from economic growth than the young, native-born, and well-off, according to Statistics Sweden, the government's central database. The OECD shows Sweden's Gini coefficient, the statistical marker used to measure income inequality, as rising from 0.21 in 1990 to 0.26 in 2008. That's still not bad comparatively: Sweden still ranks as the country with the seventh most equitable distribution of income in the OECD, while the United States, with a Gini coefficient of 0.38, is 31st out of 34 member countries.

Wadensjö said the rising retirement age could adversely affect those who are already at some disadvantage in the current pension system: those employed in physically demanding jobs, which typically are lower paid and bring lower pension benefits; and foreign-born residents, who are now approaching 15 percent of the population. Another group that loses out in the pension sweepstakes in Sweden is the self-employed, said Wadensjö. Only half of them are covered by occupational pensions related to their jobs, meaning they have to depend on the rather meager guaranteed state pension.

But it's the foreign-born, many of them refugees with limited education and work skills, who will face the toughest times in old age.

"Quite a few are coming as refugees and they will have problems, they already have problems," he said in his office in Stockholm. "When they get the pension they will get a low pension, so I guess we will have more and more discussions about the pensions of the foreign-born in the years to come."

One way to smooth the transition, as we'll see in Japan and other parts of Europe, is to push companies to innovate in ways that create space for older workers on the job. So far, the Swedish approach of managing the labor market for all ages rather than specifically for older workers has functioned well enough across the society. The country has put many of its 60-somethings to work, even without much stand-out innovation among companies. And the government has not yet pushed companies in any attention-grabbing ways to come up with new ideas about how to use older workers.

"It's not very much discussed," said Wadensjö. "It's more discussed in general to make it easier for older workers to be in the workplaces. I don't think we have any special cases."

The answer for some is something called "age management." The guru of the age management movement in Europe and a highly regarded expert in Sweden, Finnish researcher Johani Ilmarinen, argued in a 2013 essay that instead of changing older people so they fit into what companies need, society should concentrate on changing companies so the work they offer is a better fit for older people. "The potential to develop work to become more age-friendly or age-adapted is much greater than the potential to change the aging process," he wrote.

According to Ilmarinen, a longtime professor and researcher at the Finnish Institute of Occupational Health and now a consultant for companies grappling with aging, the responsibilities for lengthening work lives rest with the individual worker, employers, and the government and society. The workers themselves need to maintain their physical and intellectual health and develop work skills throughout their lives. Employers need to design workplaces that are healthy and adapted to the changing capabilities and needs of older employees. Society should implement policies that encourage and reward working longer and remove obstacles, while combating age discrimination and outmoded myths about the abilities of older workers.

"The final goal is to create an aging society where the costs of health care, work disability and unemployment are lower, early exit rates from working life have been reduced and the national economy and welfare system remain at a sustainable level," he wrote in the essay, which was part of the Eriksson commission's deliberations.

Ilmarinen has elaborated a "work ability model" that centers on three questions: Can the individual work longer? Does that individual want to work longer? Is there the opportunity for that individual to work longer? He visualizes this as a house: floor one is health and functional capacities, the second floor contains the worker's skills, and on the third floor we find the worker's motivation, values, and attitudes about work. The fourth floor houses the work environment. The most important nexus is between the third and fourth floors: does the work environment promote motivation and good feelings about work, or does it discourage the older worker, forcing him into retirement? Downsizing and negative attitudes about older workers can sap that motivation, while flexible workplaces where older employees are understood and taken care of can boost that motivation.

"The more positively weighted the third floor is, the more likely it is that one will have a good working life and a longer career," he wrote.

In this mode of thinking, it is crucial for employers to become educated about older workers and put that knowledge into practice in their workplaces. To make that happen, Ilmarinen recommended that Sweden establish a national program for older workers and invest in age management for such things as training for managers, supervisors, and foremen, among other steps.

The European Union is paying some attention to these ideas. In 2010, the European Commission funded a "Best Agers" project in the Baltic Sea region—Sweden, Denmark, Germany, Latvia, Lithuania, Estonia, Poland, and, curiously, Great Britain—to assess age management in the area, spread best practices, and make recommendations. The recommendations for Sweden, made at the end of the project in 2012, included steps such as establishing a network for companies to share their experiences in age management, cracking down on age discrimination, and creating incentives for companies and labor unions to implement age management at the workplace. The project also produced a series of reports, a documentary telling the stories of workers who continued on the job into their 60s and 70s in the region, and a 17-point program for increasing working lives.

Kadefors has been working on the Best Agers project at Gothenburg University. He argued the recommendations now on the table in Sweden ought to pay more attention to age management at the company level. Eriksson's recommendation of putting more money into a government agency on the work environment might help, but it won't be enough, Kadefors said.

"They noted there's a need to reform working conditions, but they don't really have any, I would say, good proposals in this area," he said.

Developments in Germany are particularly compelling for Kadefors and others looking into workplace adjustments. For instance, BMW is getting a lot of attention. In 2007, the company invested 40,000 euros in an experiment to test the working force of the future—an older one. They figured out that their workforce would be an average of 47 years old by 2017, so they staffed one of their production lines in a plant in Dingolfing, southern Germany, to reflect that future demographic.

Then the project—called "Today for Tomorrow"—began in earnest. They made 70 changes in the way the production line operated, including job rotations to stave off boredom and repetitive stress injury; age and health-friendly shift plans; adaptable, ergonomically designed chairs to reduce physical strain; and new magnifying glasses to cut wear and tear on the eyes and make errors less likely. Physiotherapists train workers how to stretch on the factory floor to avoid injury, and workers were given special shoes. The results: productivity on the line increased 7 percent—just as productive as the lines with younger workers.

BMW is now running similar simulations in all its plants, as well as an engine production facility in Steyr, Austria, and twice they've rolled out an advertising campaign in major newspapers and other media touting their age management steps. "They have used this problem and they turned it into a competitive edge," said Kadefors. "I think we can learn a lot from German companies."

Researchers like Kadefors, however, concede that there is still too little evidence of how age management works in companies. One problem is the lack of examples to study. As a result, the same companies seem to come up all the time, such as BMW in Germany or Vita Needle in the United States or Areva in France. In the case of Sweden, Vattenfall AB Nordic, a leading European energy producer and nuclear power plant operator headquartered in Stockholm, is the company used as a prime example. Like many companies in the energy and technology sector, Vattenfall has an aging core of highly trained engineers and technicians, and faced the prospect of mass retirements as these workers hit their late 50s and early 60s. So in 2001 the company set the retirement age at 65, and it developed the "Vattenfall Ageing Workforce Management Programme" in 2003. The program included one-day seminars for older workers aimed at motivating them to prolong their careers, special schedules that allowed older workers to cut their hours by 20 percent, leadership training for managers on aging issues, and a system to transfer skills and knowledge from the older generation to younger workers.

A study by researchers Reidar J. Mykletun and Trude Furunes found mixed results. Some workers resisted the seminars, which were eventually suspended. The flexible schedules, however, were popular among older workers, who felt they helped both maintain their alertness at work and smooth the transition from work to retirement. Managers felt the schedules encouraged workers to be more motivated and engaged in their tasks. The leadership training seminars were well received; the skills transfer project was popular but short-lived. A "senior resource pool" aimed at directing older workers toward roles more suited to their abilities succeeded in finding new jobs within Vattenfall for 180 employees, but the program was eventually suspended due to low demand.

Still, Mykletun and Furunes found significant prolonging of work lives during this period. From 2000 to 2008, workers added an average of five-and-a-half years to their careers, increasing the retirement age from 58.2 to 62.8. In a survey, older workers also reported high levels of managerial interest in their personal development. The program also saved the company money by reducing costs of early retirement, with no observed drop in productivity.

Kadefors said some of those methods had been adopted by other nuclear power plant operators in Sweden as a way of transferring skills from the older workers to the younger ones through a mentorship program.

"This is something they did out of necessity," he said. "Whatever the government says, the companies wouldn't listen until they think it's good business for them."

Other companies just don't appreciate the long-term value of such programs, Kadefors said. While researching automaker Volvo, he found that managers wanted most to hold onto the institutional knowledge of older engineers who had a comprehensive view of how their cars were developed and produced. Yet when Kadefors asked them how they intended to transfer that knowledge to younger workers, they just shrugged. "They said, 'Well, there's so little time to do that.' I think it's a common situation in all organizations," he said. "There's always something that you need to prioritize this week."

Still, Kadefors feels there still are too few examples for researchers to study. He is reaching out to public hospitals in Gothenburg and working with fellow researchers in Latvia, Lithuania, and Poland to try to implement age management methods into the workplace and then monitor the results. "There are so few really good examples and what we want to do here is launch a study where we actually measure the effect of the intervention and to create the examples which you can actually learn from," he said. "Otherwise it's sort of anecdotal learning."

Indeed, government officials argue they can't take much of the age management theory seriously—or spend much money on it—until there is solid enough evidence that it works. I raised this question with Eriksson, and he said that until there are convincing results that show age management actually can keep people at work longer, he would stick to his argument that raising the bar by increasing retirement ages would be incentive enough to force companies to figure this out on their own.

In the meantime, small businesses in Sweden have been searching for ways to turn a profit from the growing need of older people to work—and the growing demand for their services.

Sabina Dubrowska had a long, hard day ahead. It was mid-morning in an apartment house in Gothenburg, Sweden, in early May, and while the rest of the country was enjoying the beginning a four-day national holiday weekend for Day of the Ascension, the 69-year-old Polish immigrant had to scrub down the grimy apartment of a rather unkempt older man to make way for a new occupant. So she pushed some of the furniture and cardboard boxes of clothes and knick-knacks out of the way and headed straight for the toughest job: the grease-caked kitchen.

Cleaning someone else's grime-crusted kitchen might seem like unnecessarily rough work for a woman nearly 70, and Dubrowska might agree. She worked for years as a nurse in Gdina, Poland, but she retired at 55 and moved to Sweden—like so many people from eastern Europe over the past two decades—in search of steady work and a decent wage. Sweden makes it easy with an open-door policy to immigrants and an array of government services aimed at smoothing newcomers' paths into the workplace. For several years she worked as an aide in a nursing home.

But the years eventually caught up with Dubrowska, legally if not physically. Even in Sweden, getting a job can be tough for anyone beyond retirement age of 65. So when Dubrowska turned 66 in 2010, she retired again and was back on the market for something to do.

It didn't take her long to find an answer. She finished at the nursing home in March—and in April she called Pensionärspoolen, one of a growing number of start-ups in Sweden aimed at cashing in on the growing population of older people who are still eager to work and happy to supplement their pensions with a few extra krona. She works between 60 and 70 hours a month as a housecleaner at 115 krona, or about $17, an hour. The work gives her something to do and puts extra cash in her pocket. Thanks to laws encouraging older people to work in Sweden, she pays fewer income taxes than younger earners.

Plus, the activity keeps her sharp, she said.

"What else can I do?" she asked as she maneuvered around the studio apartment, from the disassembled bed, past a tiny TV and a painting of Jesus leaning against the wall behind a black garbage bag of clothes. "I like to move."

Indeed, Pensionärspoolen—based in Gothenburg, Sweden's second-largest city and a main port on the west coast—is an intriguing business idea. The company and others like it, including the largest of its type, Veteranpoolen, target a curious space in the labor market. Entrepreneur Patrik Magneby, a former sailor with the Swedish navy (who suffers, ironically, from severe sea-sickness) and leadership coach at the naval academy, started the company in 2008 after seeing his own mother go through feelings of depression after retiring from a career in retail and store management. "The main thing was I could see she wasn't needed anymore," he told me in a single-desk office he shares with his marketing director Kenneth Kjörnsberg in the "World Trade Center" complex in southeast Gothenburg. "Her mind-set was smaller and smaller—the world shrank for her."

So he set up shop in Härryda, outside Gothenburg, and focused on older workers offering services such as home improvement, cleaning, and gardening. The choice of work was strategic as well. The home improvement industry had operated as a sort of cash business to evade Sweden's heavy taxes, but a change in the tax code allowing homeowners a deduction for 50 percent of such purchases had created a boom in demand for painters, carpenters, and handymen. Magneby saw an opportunity to move in on a fresh market.

Magneby improvised from the very beginning. He scored his first contract in January 2009 to build a bathroom—without knowing anything about the work or having a single employee. With some searching he found an older carpenter to help him and he was on his way. By May that year his workers had performed 500 hours of work, illustrating to him that there was both a demand for services by older workers and an aging population willing to roll up their sleeves. Today, the company has branched out modestly as a franchise business pulling in 20 million krona (about $3 million) in annual revenue, a relatively small piece of what Kjörnsberg estimates is a 600-million-krona industry in Sweden. Pensionärspoolen has branches scattered around Gothenburg and elsewhere, and is starting to draw some national attention. Minister for Children and Elderly Maria Larsson attended the opening of the company's franchise in Stockholm in August 2012.

Today, Magneby has about 800 seniors on his employee list, but only about half of them work regularly. Despite the increased interest in working among 60- and 70-somethings, Magneby said hiring older workers can be tricky. They are already pulling in a pension, so some of them aren't very interested in working much. Sometimes, he says, they can overestimate their abilities, based on pride in what they achieved in the old days. And health problems can strike suddenly, sapping an employee's work skills or even the ability to stay on the job. But overall, Magneby says older workers in Sweden have the advantages that employers all around the world praise them for: experience, maturity, reliability.

"The customers are looking for experienced people," he said, stroking a longish goatee.

And so, at least for now, it's falling to companies like Pensionärspoolen to provide a spot for workers who are too old to fit the "retire at 65" Swedish employment paradigm. These are the true outliers, the iconoclasts who for whatever reason—finances, determination, or just plain restlessness—have chosen to stay on the workplace well beyond the normal boundary.

Morgan Svensson, a 72-year-old former real estate manager who now does carpentry work through Pensionärspoolen, says he fills his days with activities—building backyard decks, chatting on his webpage, which he says gets about 1,000 visitors a week, and listening to music.

Gathered with other Pensionärspoolen workers at company offices in Gothenburg, Svensson was eager to show me photos of some of his work. The whole time we talked he kept a Bluetooth headset hooked on his ear—just in case he got a call.

The grandfather of six figured he worked about 40 hours a week, sometimes 50.

"If you have something to do, you feel good. If you don't have anything to do, then you just don't feel so good," he said. "I feel like I'm 50 years old. If I'm like this when I'm 80, then I'll still be doing this."

As we've seen here, Sweden is being fairly aggressive about using public policy to encourage longer worklives. But companies have been slow to create senior-friendly workplaces, in large part because they haven't had to yet.

Companies in Japan, the world's most rapidly aging leading economy, don't have such luxuries, least of all in the graying countryside beyond Tokyo and Osaka. Now we move to Kudamatsu, where the head of the Yamashita Kogyosho factory looks on his aging workforce not as a liability, but as the company's secret weapon in a battle for survival.

This chapter is based on interviews in Stockholm and Gothenburg in May 2013. Statistics come from organizations cited unless indicated otherwise.

Jiro Kunimura, 67, uses a hammer to shape a bullet train nose cone at Yamashita Kogyosho in July 2012.

6

The Hammer Men

KUDAMATSU, *Japan*

Ching! Ching! Ching! The hammer head slammed down on metal, bounced up, and slammed down again. Ching! The metallic ring echoed across the factory floor like a bell, a rhythmic, industrial worksong. The engine behind this work was no machine, but a trim man, about 5'5", wide at the shoulders and narrow at the hips. With one white-gloved hand, he gripped the wooden shaft of a hammer. With the other, he held a sheet of aluminum that would one day travel 200 miles an hour on the prow of one of the world's fastest trains.

Ching!

The hammer man, Hiroyuki Fujii, 65, works at Yamashita Kogyosho, a company in southwestern Japan that for nearly five decades has practiced a unique labor: making the nose cones of the country's "shinkansen" bullet trains—with hammers. Nowhere else in the world is this work done in the same way for the same purpose. Other companies in Japan use machine presses to shape their nose cones. Around the world, high-speed train nose cones can be made of fiberglass or other composites. Only here, in this tiny corner of Japan facing the Inland Sea, a waterway famed and feared for its pirates in feudal times, do workmen construct high-tech trains with a hammering technique so nuanced they also use it to fashion metal violins and cellos.

I'd come to Yamashita Kogyosho, in the industrial town of Kudamatsu, to interview the company's aging workers. The core hammer men at Yamashita were in their 60s, either nearing the company's retirement age or already past it. Yet Tatsuto Yamashita, who took over as company president for his ailing father in 2007, had realized that these men, despite their age and their roots in the past, carried the very skill—their hammer work—that would transport the company into the future. So he'd enlisted Fujii and other older men to stay on past retirement and join in the work of attracting and mentoring younger would-be artisans. For me, that was the story: how Yamashita, instead of dumping his older workers like so many other companies, was attempting to capitalize on their unique skills to rejuvenate his business.

But first things first. Fujii handed me the hammer.

I sat down at the stool, facing a squat block of iron the size of an old chest, the top covered with a glimmering, pounded skin of steel. Fujii had demonstrated for me how he could hammer a flat, frisbee-sized sheet of aluminum into a perfectly symmetrical bowl in about a minute. I studied his handiwork, the hammer marks in neat distribution across the plate, the bowl's smooth arc. But I had no idea why hitting it would cause it to bend in a particular way.

I didn't realize it at the time, but part of the secret was already in my hands. The hammer itself was a work of art. The Yamashita crew buys ordinary hammers off the shelves and manually extends the shafts to give them more swing power. Gleaning what they've learned from decades of this kind of work, they shave the metal heads to various shapes to achieve different effects on impact. The institutional knowledge of sheet metal hammering techniques at Yamashita is unique in Japan, and perhaps the world.

Now it was my turn to wield the hammer. Fujii gave me a fresh disc of aluminum. I gripped the shaft, lifted the hammer, and immediately realized the other part of his secret, the part I was missing: skill. My wrist struggled to keep the hammer head steady. For me, the longer shaft made it more unwieldy. I banged the aluminum a few times, but instead of the clean "Ching!" I'd heard before, my blows clattered dully on the plate. Instead of the round silver smudges, I'd created lopsided indentations. Despite my best efforts, the hammer head wasn't hitting the aluminum full on, but with the head's edges, creating little sliver-moon scars on the plate. I tried changing the angle of the aluminum, but I still only got that flat, clattering sound, and the blow-marks were misshapen. It just didn't seem right—Fujii had made it look so easy. I kept hitting. My forearm was beginning to ache. I put down the hammer and held up my handiwork—lumpy, lopsided. The work of a preschooler.

"So, how long would it take for someone to learn how to do this?" I asked Fujii, pointing to the symmetrical bowl he'd hammered, wondering how many hours I'd have to spend bent over the anvil to get it right.

"This?" he asked, holding up his work and pursing his lips as if it were the most primitive task possible. "Oh, about a year."

Japan has long been among the world's premier job-creators for the elderly. Older Japanese work at higher rates—about 20 percent of the 65+ population is on the job—than in any advanced industrialized nation on earth. They hammer bullet train nose cones; they toil in the country's thousands of small workshops; they bend over rice fields wedged like terraces on green hillsides.

Some of the credit for Japan's ability to keep its elders at work has to go to cultural factors somewhat specific to Japan. The lifetime employment system, under which workers at larger corporations are all but guaranteed a job for life in exchange for loyalty and dedication, has encouraged many to identify so closely with their companies and trades that life without work is hardly imaginable. The pro-work ethos appears to be outliving the lifetime employment system, which has frayed over the last two decades. Besides that, while many people in America figure they'll work as long as their health holds out, many Japanese see things in reverse: they'll stay healthy as long as they can keep working. Time and again, as I traveled Japan talking to aging farmers, engineers, laborers, and executives, they told me that staying in the game kept them physically fit, engaged with their friends and colleagues, and mentally sharp. Without work, they said, they'd lapse into inactivity and, some feared, senility.

But those factors only account for part of what Japan has achieved in elderly employment. The country is also on a broad campaign to adjust its labor and pension system to keep as many elderly in the workforce as possible. The reason is easy to understand when one considers the country's demographic profile. Japan is among the most rapidly aging nations on earth. In 1989, the 65-plus portion of the population was a little over 11 percent. That's nothing extraordinary; today, for instance, the U.S. rate is 13 percent. But since the late 1980s, that percentage in Japan has doubled to about 25 percent today—a surge that is more rapid than in any other leading industrialized country. By mid-century, some 40 percent of Japanese will be 65 or older, a demographic fact that will shake the country's health, pension, and employment systems to the core. Seen on a graph, Japan's aging has followed the trajectory of a jet taking off.

On the ground, however, Japan's aging revolution looks more like a crash landing: villages populated by octogenarians, school closings that force rural teens to travel hours to regional cities for secondary education, hamlets that have merged with neighbors or simply vanished as their populations aged or died off. The face of Japan, more so than any other nation on the planet, is gray and wizened.

None of this has come as a surprise to Japan's government planners. Population, in fact, has been a long-term Japanese obsession. In the early and mid-20th century, militarists used the fear of overpopulation as an argument for conquest and colonization of the Asian mainland, leading Tokyo on the road to Pearl Harbor and World War II. Population was used as a rallying cry during the fighting, as propagandists cheered on the "100-million strong Japanese," though at the time there were only about 80 million of them. After the war, conquest was replaced by combating poverty and avoiding starvation as leading priorities. Bureaucrats panicked when birthrates soared in the late 1940s, raising fears that too many kids would drain resources from the hoped-for economic revival. The government helped to cut short the baby boom by taking steps such as liberalizing abortion laws, and in the early 1950s birthrates began a long decline.

By the 1960s, Japanese demographers had already realized what they'd done. The rapid end of the baby boom meant Japan would age with lightning speed over the coming decades. That would lead to a sad litany of effects: mounting health and pension costs, a possible contraction of the workforce, and a brake on economic growth. Still, for most Japanese it was hard to take the dire predictions very seriously in the 1960s, when the country was racing from strength to strength, from hosting the Olympics in 1964 to doubling GDP over less than eight years. But starting in the 1970s, bureaucrats began pushing to raise the retirement age from 55 to 60—a feat that was only accomplished in 1986, after overcoming the opposition of leading business associations. Since then, the fretting over the rising percentage of elderly, combined with contributing factors such as chronically low fertility rates, the longest lifespans on earth, and the penchant for young people to delay or even forego marriage, has reached fever pitch. In 2005, the country's total population fell for the first time since World War II. The Health and Welfare Ministry has even attempted to forecast with scientific precision the ultimate demise of the Japanese race. By one estimate by the government in the late 1990s, the last Japanese will be born sometime in the middle of the third millennium.

What a difference a couple of decades can make. Japanese ambitions in the 1980s—and the world's expectations of Japan—knew no bounds. Leading writers had Japan pegged as the successor to the United States as the leading economic power in the world. But by the early 2000s, after more than 10 years into an economic slowdown with no sign of a return to high growth, Japan had downshifted its ambitions considerably. Today, it seems the country's grandest hope—the more assertive stance of Prime Minister Shinzo Abe aside—is to become a sort of Switzerland of Asia, a stable, prosperous minor power. Considering the alternative, this is nothing to be sneered at. But one major obstacle is the fastest-growing segment of its population: old people. Dealing with the so-called demographic time bomb has become a leading national priority.

Tokyo has pursued three main policies to control or adapt to the aging phenomenon. The government has tried, to some extent, to increase fertility rates by literally paying parents for having children and chipping away at roadblocks to motherhood, such as a lack of day care. But the steps have done little to reverse the decline in baby-making in Japan. Even if successful, the results would not be felt in the labor market for decades. So women in Japan forced to choose between a job or raising a family are postponing marriage and childbirth until their 30s or later, keeping fertility at historically low rates.

An alternative pursued by many aging nations in Europe and North America is immigration. In 2008, a group of lawmakers from Japan's conservative Liberal Democratic Party lawmakers proposed boosting the number of foreigners in the country by 10 million over the next half-century. The idea went nowhere. While compelling, such proposals have little traction on Main Street in Japan. The country is still living in the shadow of international isolation during the feudal Edo Period, between the 17th and 19th centuries, when foreigners were barred from Japanese shores and citizens venturing abroad could be executed if they returned home. Even in 21st-century hyperconnected Japan, suspicions of foreigners run deep, and immigration is more commonly associated in public discourse with riots and lawlessness than with a revitalizing influx of hard-working laborers and professionals. Less than 2 percent of the population is non-Japanese. A few years ago, while researching multiculturalism in Japan, I called up the Justice Ministry to confirm numbers of immigrants. The bureaucrat's response was adamant: Japan does not have an immigration policy, so questions about 'immigrants' make no sense.

So who will run the machines, answer the phones, and serve the customers in an aging Japan? For some bureaucrats, there's an easy answer: the elderly. That's not as desperate as it sounds. As in the United States, Japan has a very talented, well-educated, and well-trained baby boom generation on the verge of retirement. The brevity of the baby boom means the cohort in Japan is much smaller—not quite 8 million. But as the boomers go, so goes the nation. These are folks that created the country of bullet trains and robotics and Hello Kitty. They came of age in the revitalized Japan of the 1950s and 1960s, rose to their prime with the booming economy of the 1980s, and matured at the end of one millennium and the beginning of the next. As in America, the boomers' talents and excesses defined an era. And, as in America, forecasts of their en masse retirement as they hit their 60s have so far failed to materialize.

Government policy is taking a leading role in keeping the boomers in the workplace. In 2006, the government approved legislation requiring companies larger than a certain size to do one of three things: raise their minimum retirement age from 60 to 65, abolish retirement age altogether, or come up with a system to rehire retirees and keep them working until 65. At the same time, officials started the clock running on a very gradual increase in the retirement age from 60 to 65. Most of the transition was complete in 2013, but it won't entirely finish until 2025.

That's too little, too late for some people. Atsushi Seike, president of the prestigious Keio University and vocal advocate for elderly employment, has made a career of campaigning for a new retirement age of 70 as a step towards an "ageless society." "Baby boomers are a very important asset," Seike told me within the ivy covered main building on the Keio campus. "Not only because of their huge numbers, but also they have accumulated skills and knowledge during their whole career."

At the same time, the government has turned itself into a one-stop shopping center for companies looking for ways to comply with the requirement to keep 60-somethings on the job. The Japan Organization for Employment of the Elderly and Persons with Disabilities, an arm of the Labor, Health and Welfare Ministry housed in a steel and glass structure in the Tokyo bayside neighborhood of Hamamatsu-cho, bills itself as a warehouse of ideas. The office collects data on company demographics, hands out awards and money to employers who come up with innovative ways to integrate older folks into their workforces, and sends advisors out to help struggling companies.

Tetsuro Kawauchi, who with his slicked back black hair and salt-of-the-earth manner seems more like a 1950s union organizer than a bureaucrat, presides over the work at JEED. "Japan has been worrying about population decline and aging since the 1970s, so we've been thinking about this for more than 30 years," he said at the outset of an interview in which he attempted to move line by line through a government pamphlet in typical bureaucratic style. But his effusive manner got the best of him: he'd get through one line of the pamphlet and then go off on a tangent about, say, his weekend job as a farmer in Nasu, outside Tokyo.

Kawauchi's main function was as an advisor and general cheerleader for companies attempting to comply with the 2006 law. The results had been mixed at the time I spoke with Kawauchi in 2010. While about 95 percent of the companies affected had some kind of program for employing workers until they're 65, only about half could offer jobs for all the post-60 staffers who want them. The numbers dropped off sharply when looking at the over-65 crowd: only 20 percent of companies had any plans to keep workers until they're 70. Labor Ministry bureaucrats said they were determined to boost those numbers, but they didn't have any fresh initiatives to achieve that goal. Kawauchi's outfit works as the ministry's outreach program to companies. It sends government-paid advisors—it has a roster of nearly 500 of them—to companies to find out what problems they're having in complying with the law and come up with strategies to boost their elderly employment numbers. The workload seemed a bit overwhelming: those 500 advisors had a to-do list of some 30,000 companies.

Some of their clients were struggling, Kawauchi told me. One problem is what to do with workers of different capabilities. Some people age more gracefully than others, and the differences between individuals increase the older they get. How do you maintain some semblance of equality and harmony in the company, while at the same time assign appropriate work for both your high-performing elderly employees and the guys who have slowed more with age? Another major problem was how to handle the salaries of the workers you most want to keep. Statistics show that salaries in Japan fall an average of 30 or 40 percent for workers after they pass their 60th birthday, even though many of them still have to do the same job for the same hours, at least until they start drawing a pension and can cut their shifts. "So workers aren't very motivated," Kawauchi said.

The most interesting aspect for him was the motivation of those who have the luxury of a decent pension and could easily just slip into retirement, and yet they still want to work. For him, the answer comes from childhood experiences of deprivation after the war. "Why do they want to work?" Kawauchi asked. "Because they think they're poor! Our mentality from a long time ago is the farmer mentality, thinking that we're on the verge of poverty." In addition to that, there are also people who are artisans, who are in love with their craft and don't care how much they get paid to practice it. "They only get 90,000 yen a month (about US$900 at 2014 exchange rates), but they appreciate the boss. The company is like a family. They feel like they are at home. The company president treats them like family, so if there is this kind of relationship, then their motivation doesn't decline. Instead, they work very hard." He told the story of a guy who worked at a manufacturing plant until he was 96; he retired two years after his own son retired. Kawauchi shook his head. "That's the Japanese for you."

JEED has paired with companies and medical consultants to come up with ways to make the workplace more user-friendly for the elderly. Most of the methods are hardly advanced: they break up 10-kilogram boxes into two five-kilo boxes for easier lifting, install staircases with smaller steps, configure workstations so employees can sit more than stand, and institute frequent breaks in the workday. "If you sit one hour and then take a 15-minute break, that's ideal," Kawauchi said.

Perhaps more than the physical challenges, one of the biggest roadblocks is preparing workers mentally and emotionally for downshifting from high responsibility, prestige and salary to the fewer demands, lower pay, and diminished cachet of post-retirement work. "I give lectures about how to change your mentality, to prepare for that letdown," he said. "After retirement, your responsibility falls—it's more task-based. So we talk about it. The idea is to get them to think: 'The high-pressure work all those years was tough, but now I can relax a little.'"

Despite those drawbacks, it was clear to Kawauchi and many others in the government that there just weren't enough jobs available for the elderly who wanted them. At the same time, companies that really needed their older workers—because younger workers were in short supply or the veterans had skills that couldn't be matched by newcomers—would always find a way to do it. "Companies that face a labor shortage are coming up with their own answers about how to employ older workers," he said. "And then they can share their practices with other companies."

Still, Japan faces an uphill battle. Kawauchi estimates the country will need to keep all its 60-somethings employed and 40 percent of people in their 70s on the job in order to avoid a labor shortage. But the reality is that today's 50-somethings are facing an increasingly tough job market, one that depends on personal connections. Outposts of the government-run Hello Work employment agency are ubiquitous, but only 47 percent of job-seekers over 50 who find new positions get them there, according to JEED. The majority get jobs though people that they know. But even those connections are getting more difficult to capitalize on amid the global economic downturn.

"The economy gets bad, the company looks to cut the oldest people, and then it's hard for them to find a job after that," Kawauchi said. Many of the laid-off end up at the Silver Human Resource Centers, a massive public network of odd-job employment agencies for older folks. The centers are huge—some 700,000 people work at them nationwide. Still, the jobs available, such as cleaning up public parks

or taking tickets at baseball games, are not always challenging, though the centers
are attempting to transform themselves into more dynamic employment centers.
But in the meantime, the network isn't much use for a 60-year-old manager or
engineer looking for work.

So what would be an ideal place for the aging worker revolution to take place?
At a small company in an elderly corner of the countryside, where bonds between
the workers and management are strong.

In other words, at a place like the home of the hammer men, Yamashita
Kogyosho.

Tatsuto Yamashita picked me up at my hotel soon after I'd arrived in Hikari, a
factory town just east of the Yamashita Kogyosho workshops. I'd taken a train
there from Kure, in neighboring Hiroshima Prefecture, and looked through the
window toward the Inland Sea. The coast is often obscured by sprawling plants
producing chemicals or refining oil or forging train cars and engines. The open
spaces between the larger factories are strewn with the usual commercial overflow: smaller companies, workshops, warehouses, and parking lots, or semi-barren
plots of abandoned industrialized land, the trees long gone and weeds or smaller
shrubs taking over. Often, such plots are circled by rusted chain-link fences.

When I contacted Tatsuto for a visit, he was an eager host, recommending a
hotel and offering to set up a dinner with his aging crew. Accommodations in the
area were rare, and Tatsuto urged me to stay at a hotel beside "one of the most
beautiful beaches in Japan." Hotel Matsubaraya, however, had missed its heyday
by about 30 years. Beside the elevator on my floor was a 1980s-era instant noodle
vending machine with a faded photograph of smiling blond children. The beach,
while expansive and filled with white sand, a rarity in Japan, was also pockmarked
with litter. Smokestacks billowed in the distance. The industrial landscape dominates the entire town of Hikari, where narrow alleys lined with aging wooden
homes coexist beside garishly colored chain drugstores and supermarkets.
Chimneys and industrial blocks rose up in the background, giving the city—
home to a suicide submarine training base during World War II—a gritty edge.

Tatsuto, 46, had sounded briskly organized on the phone, but in person his
boyishness was immediately apparent. He parted his bushy brown hair in the
middle in Beatles' Sgt. Pepper's style, and his plaintive eyes blinked behind non-
descript glasses. Tatsuto's voice squeaked when his enthusiasm for just about
everything—the beach, his company, his family—got the best of him, and he
spoke in staccato bursts, frequently exclaiming, "Now, wait a minute!" when he
wanted to make a point.

Though Tatsuto was born and raised in Hikari and neighboring Kudamatsu, his
route to the helm of Yamashita Kogyosho had been circuitous. As a child, he'd been
surrounded by trains. His father, Kiyoto, the original hammer man, had founded a
company dedicated to them. Industrial giant Hitachi, Ltd. was churning out some

of the fastest, most respected locomotives in the world just down the road. When Tatsuto was a baby, his parents lived under one roof with his father's coworkers, Fujii and Jiro Kunimura. As he grew up in the 1960s and 1970s, his hometown of Kudamatsu was transformed into part of a band of intense industrialization that extended from Tokyo, 565 miles away, all the way to Fukuoka in the southwest. This was the smoky, polluted, dynamic engine—the homeland of Toyota and Sony and Mitsubishi—that powered the Japanese economy from the hardscrabble post-war years into the ranks of the richest nations on earth.

But young Tatsuto wanted nothing to do with train work. He saw his future stretching far beyond the confines of his tiny steel and cement corner of Japan. After graduating from high school, he quickly left Kudamatsu behind. He went to university in Tokyo to study finance—not as a way to guide his father's company into the coming years and decades, but as his ticket out. After college, he joined the Japan Credit Bureau and left the country, landing eventually in Sydney, Australia. He married a Japanese woman who'd grown up there and settled down. They had a boy. He spoke English at work with an Aussie accent, living in a country that has never done more than talk about high-speed rail. Trains were firmly in his past.

Then trouble struck. His father, by then in his 70s, suffered a stroke. The man who had made his place in the world by swinging a hammer was now reduced to a frail shadow of himself. Tatsuto was shocked when he came home to visit. "I don't think I'm going to live," his father said. The company, he said, should probably just be sold off to the highest bidder. The main workers were all in their 60s, and they were probably better off hanging up the hammer and taking it easy in retirement, Kiyoto reasoned. There were prospective buyers out there, though everyone knew they were just after Yamashita's access to contracts with Hitachi. Once the company was sold, the elder Yamashita figured, the buyer would just shut down the factory and sell off its components or put them to other uses. He argued there was no other way. "*Sho ga nai,*" he said: there's nothing you can do about it.

Tatsuto knew that was not what his father wanted in his heart. Kiyoto had poured the best decades of his life into the company, into nurturing and developing his unique skills and those of his companions. He'd built everything with his own hands. Of course the old man would want to see the company continue. But Tatsuto knew his father would never ask such a sacrifice from his only son. Tatsuto would have to take that step on his own.

"I realized I hadn't really talked to him since I'd graduated high school. I went off to Tokyo to college. I never really did anything together with him," Tatsuto said, shaking his head. Now, the son had found something—something really big—that he could do with the father. And, after years of travel, he rediscovered his family roots. "I thought if I ignored my struggling father, I would be punished in some way. Also, I thought my son should have some memory of his grandfather."

So he decided to take a radical, risky step: give up his financial career in Sydney, move his young family back to Kudamatsu, and take over his father's graying company. He hoped the presence of their grandchild would help rejuvenate his parents. And he hoped he could find a way to revive Yamashita Kogyosho.

But he knew the odds were against him.

"What do you think?" Tatsuto asked his wife.

"Well," she said, "if you become a beggar, then I'll become a beggar with you."

Between the cities of Hikari and Kudamatsu, the squat corrugated steel building of Yamashita Kogyosho—one of two workshops the company owns—is easy to miss. Its gray-blue walls and tidy, garage-like open workspace rest on a ridge overlooking a road that runs between the chemical behemoth Idemitsu at one end and Hitachi's train manufacturing facility at the other. Tatsuto pulled into the parking lot in front of the modest workshop, got out of the car, and immediately pointed across the entry road to a fence and a mile-long driveway that wound its way to a distant cluster of buildings.

"We're the closest company to Hitachi," he said.

The Tokyo-based conglomerate, founded in 1910 during Japan's fevered drive toward industrialization, is a high-tech giant. A Hitachi factory's proximity is no mere statement of geography. The company is one of Japan's largest manufacturers of "shinkansen" bullet trains and the top customer for Yamashita's metal train parts. That relationship means that 30 percent of the bullet-train nose cones streaming across bridges and ricefields all over the country are fashioned right here at Yamashita. His shop's proximity to Hitachi was at once a point of pride and survival. No Hitachi, no Yamashita. The road linking them was a lifeline that Yamashita would never jeopardize.

At the entrance to the company is a chrome stand displaying black and white photos. The prints are a shrine to Yamashita's early greatest hits: a bullet train prototype worked on by the elder Yamashita in June 1962; a photo of Japan's first passenger monorail, the Inoyama Park Line, from March of the same year. One photo showed the wooden frames Kiyoto and his workmen built to help them shape sheet metal into the famed original bullet nose cone. Beside them is a photo of a farewell ceremony for the 1000 model—a train that had been in operation for 44 years, from 1964 until 2008. "My father made the face of that train with his hands," Tatsuto said, opening his palms to make the point.

His words drew a clear image of the body's relationship to the work. This is something I found wherever I interviewed aging workers in Japan, this intimate relationship with materials and products. Tsuneko Hariki of Kamikatsu had dirt crusted under her fingernails as she sorted sprigs of Japanese maple; 85-year-old Hirohisa Matsumoto bent closely over his workbench on the tiny island of Okikamuro as he tempered the fishhooks he forged by hand. Manufacturing, when broken down to its Latin roots, means "making by hand." In Kudamatsu,

I'd found a product not normally associated with artisans and handiwork—a high-speed train—that had roots as elemental as subsistence farming or medieval blacksmithing. The Japanese use the word "monodzukuri," or the art of making things, and the culture is very attuned to the idea of an object embodying the labor of its creator. Buddhist temples in Japan will even have "funeral" services for things such as pinball machines that are being retired to honor the workmanship that went into their making, the pleasure they've given customers, and the profit they've generated for owners. So "making things" is an honored calling. Kiyoto was proof enough: he'd been awarded the prestigious Monodzukuri Nippon Grand Award in 2007—a fact that came up several times during my visits with the Yamashitas.

Perhaps the prize meant so much to them because of Kiyoto's humble beginnings. Like much else in Japan, Yamashita Kogyosho's roots are planted firmly in the devastation of World War II. Even before the atomic bombings of Hiroshima and Nagasaki, Allied incendiaries had burned dozens of Japanese cities to the ground. The experience of growing up in wartime Japan had affected him deeply, as I learned when I joined Tatsuto for a dinner to introduce me to Kiyoto, 75, and two workers who had been with him from the beginning, Fujii and Kunimura. The restaurant was in the old style, with rough-hewn dark wood gables and tightly woven straw "tatami" mat floors. On the menu for the evening was pike conger eel, and the whitish creatures—predators with jagged teeth that sink into its prey and don't let go—slithered and slinked through the water in a tank in the hallway that led to our private dining room.

Kiyoto Yamashita's father died when the boy was four, in 1939, and Kiyoto knew a life of work from an early age. As a nine-year-old when the Japanese war machine was crumbling under Allied assault, he would climb into the mountains of Yamaguchi Prefecture to scavenge pine tree roots to crush for oil as part of a national campaign to supplement dwindling fuel supplies. The entire nation was girding for an eventual invasion. Authorities told them that as Japanese they would have to fight to the last man, woman, and child. Students at his school were ordered to forget about their studies and instead planted potatoes in the playground to survive. All the trees were cut down for firewood.

"We had no information from the outside. It was just like North Korea is today," Kiyoto said. "We were shaving bamboo staves. That was what we were going to use to fight against the B-52? But this was supposed to be the country of the gods. So even if you thought it was stupid to fight with sticks, you couldn't say anything."

Then came the U.S. atomic bomb attacks on nearby Hiroshima and Nagasaki. Suddenly the war was over, and Japan's long struggle out of devastation began.

In those hardscrabble years after the war, Yamashita went back to studying, but he never finished high school. By the time he was 17, in 1952, at the end of the U.S. postwar occupation, he was working here and there at part-time jobs. He landed some work at a car repair shop. It may be hard to imagine this now, at a time when Toyota, Honda, Nissan, and Mazda are household names the world over, but back then, cars were few and far between in Japan, possessions of the American occupiers or the Japanese elite. But Yamashita said he had the feeling at the time that one day, ordinary Japanese would have their own cars, and he wanted to be in on the action.

Yamashita was ahead of his time. It would be years before anyone would make much money fixing cars. With too few autos on the road, he and his co-workers started looking for other opportunities. Then Hitachi came calling.

The company had won a contract to help India construct a national railroad, and needed craftsmen to do the metal work. Yamashita's car repair shop was chosen for the job and called in a group of workers from Hiroshima who were famous in the region for their ability to shape metal into any form using the simplest of tools: the hammer. The encounter would change Yamashita's life.

The Hiroshima hammer men had honed their skills in the atomic rubble of their city. Cars on the road back then faced a harsh environment. Japan after the war was a nightmare for bodies and suspension systems. Dirt and mud roads were common, and what paved roads existed were strewn with potholes and craters. Many of the cars were old, battered, and in need of inventive repair. Pieces ordered from the United States were expensive and would take too long to arrive. So these men had adapted the skills of the forge to the modern era, learning to make nearly anything with a hammer. Young Yamashita took naturally to the concentration, patience, and hand-eye coordination needed to fashion steel into smooth shapes and arching curves, and after a few years he was considered among the best. The reputation would serve him well.

Eventually, the company Yamashita worked for ran into financial troubles and stopped paying salaries. The hammer men quit and went back home to Hiroshima. But Yamashita nurtured the techniques he'd learned, as both an art and a way to stay employed. Hitachi, which was expanding in the area, took notice and started calling Yamashita in for special hammering jobs. "I started making things. They didn't always work out, but it was OK," he said. "I built connections, I developed the most in that period. I built confidence back then."

Yamashita moved to Okayama Steel Works, and there he formed bonds with the men who would stay with him for the next five decades.

As a child in rural Yamaguchi Prefecture in the 1950s, Jiro Kunimura dreamed of working on cars. "When I was a kid, I saw car-dealers and I thought I wanted to do that. We were poor, so my parents wanted me to get out of the house as quickly as possible," he told me in an upstairs office with photos of bullet trains, design plans, and awards hanging from the walls. He'd been born in Kyoto. His parents worked in restaurants but soon came down to Yamaguchi with their brood of six children. Jiro moved out and came to Kudamatsu in 1961 when he was 17, finding work in the garage where Yamashita worked. But then Yamashita left, and Kunimura went off to school with his friend Fujii to study sheet metal. But the threesome wasn't split up for long. Kunimura and Fujii were two of the seven students at the technical school who got jobs at Okayama, which he joined in April 1962, reuniting with Yamashita.

That's when their real apprenticeship in hammering began in earnest. Yamashita trained them in the technique, and the three of them worked on a project for Hitachi making steel tanks for oil trucks. Yamashita laughed when he told me this, looking over at his two companions during dinner. "How many hundreds of them did we have to make?" he asked. But then Okayama also started suffering troubles.

"Pretty much everyone else quit. Back then working with a hammer—I didn't think I'd last until the summer at that work," Kunimura said. Getting a job with Hitachi, a top-of-the-line employer in the area, was a possibility, but Kunimura wasn't eager. "I didn't want to join a big company. That's how you lose your freedom."

So instead, they all scattered. Yamashita left to do projects with Hitachi. Fujii and Kunimura hung on as long as they could, but eventually they quit as well. "We were the last two left," Fujii said. It was the early 1960s. Kunimura went back to his family in Yamaguchi city to attend technical school. Fujii took off for the bright lights of Tokyo. But they wouldn't be separated for long.

In 1962, Yamashita found himself involved in a high-priority government project: the fastest train in the world. By then, Japan had dug itself out of the gaping crater—a physical as well as psychological one—left by the wreckage of World War II. The economy was roaring back, and Prime Minister Hayato Ikeda had set a stunning goal of doubling national production, a benchmark that would be met and surpassed by decade's end. Tokyo was to bask in the global spotlight as the host of the 1964 Olympics. Now the country's engineers were working on a train that would symbolize the emergence of a peaceful, modern, and prosperous Japan—and Yamashita was on the front end of it, hammer in hand.

Armed with designs for one of the prototypes of the "shinkansen," or "new trunk line," he went to work on the nose cone for Hitachi. He built a wooden frame in accordance with the design's specifications and hammered sheets of aluminum into the original "bullet." The prototype was a success: in March 1963, the Class 1000 shinkansen reached 159 miles per hour (256 km per hour)—a world record at the time. The train then moved to full production, meaning much more hammering work ahead. Yamashita was ready to put together a formal team. But he had a problem: his favorite workers were spread out over Japan.

The first key was roping in Kunimura. That was easily done. Yamashita contacted him and Kunimura quit school and came back to Kudamatsu. Kunimura says he didn't have any illusions about hammer work. "I never would have guessed I'd stay at it so long," he says. "I planned to just try it for a year."

Fujii was harder to track down. He'd gone up to Tokyo and lost contact with his old co-workers. So Yamashita went up to the capital on his own and found Fujii living the life of a wild young bachelor. Fujii's exploits and reputation as a bon vivant have become company legend. "It was a real mess," Kunimura says, shaking his head and smiling. Yet Yamashita prevailed and somehow enticed Fujii to give up the big city and come back to Kudamatsu.

The team was formally put together in September 1963, and they went to work on the first bullet trains. Yamashita Kogyosho was soon incorporated. The first shinkansen went into service with Yamashita's handiwork on the front of it in 1964, and weeks later Tokyo hosted the Olympics. The New Japan had arrived on the international stage less than two decades after the end of World War II.

A photo from those early days hangs on the wall at the company offices. Six workers stand in front of a car and a bicycle. Train tracks snake by in the background. Yamashita is thin, clearly older and wiser than the rest, in a cap and sports coat. Kunimura is beside him, with a boyishly full head of hair, bangs to his eyebrows. The men are comfortable with each other. To the right, one worker drapes his arm around another's shoulder. At the center is Fujii, in a bomber jacket, his thick black hair combed back Elvis Presley–style and hands rakishly on his hips.

Japanese companies often advertise themselves as surrogate families for their workers, a warm, fuzzy place where employees work hard but enjoy the security that they will be taken care of their whole lives. Yamashita Kogyosho really was like a family. In the early and mid-1960s, money was tight. Yamashita, his wife, Fujii, and Kunimura actually lived under the same roof for several years. Tatsuto was born in 1964, and he jokes around about how the two workers were like his uncles, changing his diapers and playing with him when he was a baby. Fujii and Kunimura eventually moved out, but even then the two of them lived together in an apartment for a while. It was only when they got married that they went their own ways.

After the initial high of the first bullet trains, times were tough. Contracts from Hitachi were few and far between, yet would arrive suddenly with impossibly tight deadlines. Yamashita's men would work around the clock until the project was done, and then just as suddenly they would have nothing to do—and no income. In the sometimes lengthy lulls between train contracts, the hammer men turned to any work that could make a yen. Kunimura, for instance, remembers making display cases for fish shops, molds for concrete, any sheet metal work he could find. So the train contracts, when they came, were precious, and Yamashita's crew felt they had to overcome any obstacle to get the work done or risk losing Hitachi's faith and then not getting the next contract.

The men stuck with the hammer through it all. In retrospect, they can see today how those hardships, the need to use their skills to make just about anything out of aluminum, forced them to develop their art. And even when the train contracts came, new technology would throw up roadblocks that had to be surmounted if the company were to survive.

Yamashita's next big break came in the 1970s, when Japan began experimenting with magnetic levitation trains, which glide above the track, kept afloat by powerful magnetic fields. Kunimura was the central workman for the contract, and he struggled for weeks with the nose cone of the ML500, which was to run on an experimental track in southern Japan. He had to work with .8mm-thick sheets of "2024," a particularly light but strong aluminum alloy. But he ran into a serious difficulty: the metal wouldn't curve under his hammering the way other types of aluminum did. Normally, Kunimura would hammer from the center of a piece. The force of the hammer would thin the metal under the blow, pushing it outward and causing a curvature in the sheet. Then he would spread out his blows to the rest of the sheet. But 2024 wouldn't curve when Kunimura hit it with his usual force, and putting more muscle into it just damaged it. He became obsessed; if they couldn't mold the metal with hammers, they would lose the contract. He experimented endlessly and desperately, with the weight of the company firmly on his shoulders. He was willing to try anything. Finally, he made a breakthrough, discovering entirely by accident that, for whatever reason, hitting the sheet off-center and closer to the edges would create the curvature he wanted. Kunimura, through trial and error, had developed his own method for hammering 2024 in time to work day and night to fill the contract.

The train was a success. The ML500 set a world record of 517 kph (321 mph) in 1979, winning accolades for its engineers and keeping Yamashita in business. In the years since then, the hammer men worked on some of the most technologically advanced trains on earth: the Class 500 that debuted in the 1990s as the Nozomi service, with operating speeds of 300 kph; the 700T, which was the first shinkansen exported, began service in Taiwan in 2007. When I first visited Yamashita in 2010, they were working on the E5, slated for debut in March the following year, with eventual top operating speeds of 320 kph, the fastest in Japan.

It isn't easy work, even in good times. The deadline pressure from a demanding, big-name company like Hitachi is intense. The bullet train is considered the pride of Japan, and high levels of workmanship and performance were national priorities—heady stuff for a bunch of blue-collar guys from Yamaguchi. It took its toll as they aged. Both Fujii and Kunimura confessed to wanting to leave at some points.

Fujii seems to have come the closest to bailing out. After three decades with Yamashita, he got restless, and he began taking days off to look for other work. The others must have known about his wandering, because he spoke of it openly after a couple of beers and some sake at dinner, and nobody flinched. "Until about 10 years ago, I might have left the company. At that time, I just wanted to quit and get an easier job," Fujii said. "I'd been doing the same thing since I was 17 years old, and I was in a slump. I hated the job. I'd take a day off and go to an employment agency, but they didn't have anything for me."

Fujii shrugged.

"So I would take a couple of days off, refresh myself, and come back," he said.

Fujii and Kunimura now say a mixture of loyalty, friendship with each other and the Yamashitas, and pride in their own workmanship gave them the strength to keep going. These are the elements seen time and time again in companies with a successfully aging workforce. Employees who have bonds with each other and management, a commitment to the company, and a sense of satisfaction from the work—some meaning beyond the purely economic function of their labor—are more highly motivated to stay on the job. These are some of the central reasons why in Japan, smaller companies like Yamashita Kogyosho can often be better equipped to adjust to the country's graying workforce, earning them greater attention as the country grapples with the realities of a super-aged society.

In Yamashita Kogyosho's case, these elements had been in place for decades.

"We made a good team with the boss," Kunimura said. "He's a good person, and he took care of us. Fujii, too. If we had a problem, we could talk about it. If I were alone, I might have quit."

Not everyone in Japan is as lucky.

Within the gleaming steel and glass tower of the Tokyo Job Center, executive coach Kumiko Watanabe held forth with the perky enthusiasm of a tour guide. She spoke clearly and brightly as she moved before the white board, punctuating her advice with wide smiles. Her aging students needed the boost: many of them were jobless employees of big-name corporations now forced to lower their sights to smaller companies.

But if they were expecting a warm and fuzzy group hug from Watanabe, they were mistaken. She had a stern message for these select members of the "Expert Human Resource Development" program: Forget pride.

Her rules were clear: No looking down on smaller companies. No boasting about the glory days with Sanyo or Toshiba. No complaining about the modest pay offers.

You are starting over, she counseled them, and you need the humility of the beginner.

"Set your former self aside," she said.

This ego-deflating lesson was at the core of a unique program—by the center's own reckoning, the only one in Japan at the time—to retrain former big company white-collar employees for jobs in small and medium-sized firms. Started in 2007, the program is limited to about 100 students a year. The government-run center says that some 60 percent of participants get jobs after finishing the 12-day course, though officials said they did not have data on what kinds of jobs they got or whether they were satisfied with them.

But the program fits well with the idea voiced time and time again by government officials and academics that today's 50- and 60-somethings have valuable skills and knowledge that need to be retained in the workforce, and that the easiest place to use those talents is in Japan's plentiful supply of smaller companies. Places like Yamashita Kogyosho, located in smaller cities with little name recognition or prestige, lack the sparkle to attract today's college graduates. They are located in areas packed with aging populations. So the printers and car parts manufacturers and small-time machine-makers look to older, more serious, less-demanding employees to keep them afloat.

At the same time, the program illustrates a fact that older workers across the developed world are struggling with: it's much easier to move among jobs within the same company than it is to be laid-off or retired and have to search for work elsewhere. The research is clear on this: Employers and managers value their older workers highly, but tend to ascribe negative "aging worker" stereotypes when facing older job applicants. So the same worker is likely to face less discrimination within a home company than as a job applicant on the outside. This is even truer in Japan, where job-hopping is rare and in general frowned upon. Job seekers, particularly those in their 50s and 60s, can be looked on with suspicion as "damaged goods."

Yet in a society where one's worth is calculated perhaps in larger measure than in the West by what groups the individual belongs to, workers often still cling to the prestige of their former employers.

That's a major turn-off for potential bosses and colleagues at smaller, less glamorous companies. So Watanabe was on a mission to rip that attitude out by the root.

She led the class of 19 students—18 men and 1 woman—through a series of role-playing exercises in which they mostly practiced self-introduction, teamwork, and problem solving, followed by self-reflection and criticism. Some of her instructions would be familiar to anyone who has read a self-help manual or career counseling book.

"Remember, just talking on and on is not a self-introduction," she said. "You want to leave people wanting to hear more about you. So self-check!"

Despite all the talk about super-sized pride, Watanabe really couldn't have asked for a more earnest group of students. Her charges obediently gathered in groups for role-plays and enthusiastically assumed their tasks, whether it was team leader or timekeeper. They bowed reverently to the instructor at the beginning and end of each session, and embraced the dramatic aspect of the class.

In one session, for instance, they split into groups to practice job interviews. Applicants would walk to the door and knock on it, simulating the actual experience. Then some of them, swept away with the moment, suffered from real jitters, even though the setting was entirely artificial. One extremely eager student bowed after his interview and walked to the door and opened it slightly as if he were really leaving to better approximate the day in which he would take the stage and then exit it.

It was easy, though, to understand why they took it all so seriously: They faced some precise expectations. The interview instructor even dictated to his students that the proper way to grip the door handle on the way out of the interview room was with two hands. A student raised his hand.

"What if you're carrying a briefcase?"

The teacher thought a moment.

"In that case," he said, "it's OK to use just one hand."

But Watanabe and the other trainers were pushovers compared to the new "big men" in the students' lives: presidents of small companies. Kouichi Ohishi, president of Daiwa Hightechs, which developed a machine that wraps books in plastic to stop bookshop browsers from reading them, was brought before the group to serve up a stiff dose of humility.

People from big companies, he said, are opinionated, overly critical, and think they have nothing more to learn. They ignore the needs of clients. In any case, Ohishi said, he wasn't hiring.

"We're not looking for older workers right now," he said.

The second company president, Masashi Kumei, of Nikko Electric Co., was even gruffer.

"I've hired four or five people from big companies," he said, frowning at the somber group. "None of them worked out."

The browbeating didn't discourage "experts" course student Takashi Suzuki. The 62-year-old had a passion that kept up his spirits: semiconductors.

In 23 years at Tokyo-based telecoms firm Iwasaki Tsushin, Suzuki honed his knowledge in quality control of the silicon chips at the core of modern electronics. The sky was the limit in 1970 in booming Japan, and Suzuki figured he'd ride the job-for-life model with the same company all the way to retirement.

"Companies were doing well in the high growth economy," he said. "So I figured I would follow the seniority-based salary system."

But then Iwasaki did something unexpected. After the bursting of the economic bubble in the early 1990s, the company discontinued its semiconductor business. By then, Suzuki had amassed skill and knowledge about computer chips, and he wasn't about to give all that up just stay with his company. So he did something highly unusual: he quit and went looking for a company where he could use his expertise. He jumped to LSI Logic, where he worked for six years, and then to AMD, where he was employed for nine years.

And then he retired. But the idea of puttering around the garden and shooting nine holes in the afternoon didn't hold his attention for long.

"How old were you when you retired?" I asked.

"Sixty-two," he said.

"And how old are you now?"

"Sixty-two."

Suzuki's retirement had lasted about five months. What drew him out? His own belief that what he's learned in his life can be useful to society. For four decades, he'd crunched budgets, managed personnel, and tested semiconductors. Surely, he thought, that ought to count for something.

He just didn't know what.

"What is the best way for me to go? I don't know," he said, shrugging. "But through this program, I might get a better idea."

In January 2007, as Tatsuto Yamashita settled into his new position as chief of his father's company, he crunched some numbers on a calculator. The results shocked him: the average worker at his company was only a few years away from retirement.

"There were no 20- or 30-year-olds working here. They were all in their 50s," he said. That created a real problem for the company. Many of the workers on staff had put in 30 or 40 years at this work. Their knowledge and skills were unique in Japan and probably in the world. And there was no one to follow them: It would take at least a decade of training to get a new employee up to anywhere near the skill level of the aging hammer men. Without quick action to bring new people into the fold, the older workers would retire and leave behind a crew without the skills to carry the company forward. Tatsuto had to act right away.

"Making something beautiful, producing a train—it's like learning to play an instrument," he said. "I thought this was terrible. What were we going to do when people retired? You can't just hire somebody and expect them to become a craftsman right away."

Yamashita naturally turned to the vocational schools in the area. Here, he thought, he could find some budding hammer men for his future workforce. But that only led him to his next surprise: almost nobody there had ever heard of the hammer work going on at Yamashita's workshop. He was flabbergasted. The methods that had built Japan's crowning achievement in transportation, a train whose face was recognized around the world, were basically a company secret. People living in the shadow of his workshops, his neighbors, had no idea what these workmen were doing.

"They didn't even tell students about this skill in technical high schools in Kudamatsu!" he said. "Only 10 percent of those kids even knew that trains were made in Kudamatsu. I was shocked."

Tatsuto realized he needed to accomplish one task before he could even dream of embarking on a rejuvenation of his outfit: he had to make sure his most talented older workers—Kunimura and Fujii among them—would stay with the company for as many years as they could.

So he faced the same dilemma faced by thousands of companies in Japan, particularly those founded on crucial specialized skills. Craftsmen at work in places like Yamashita Kogyosho seem to have been passed over by time, honing their skills hidden in tiny machine shops around the country, toiling in anonymity for little pay and little recognition beyond the factory walls. The rest of society moves on its way, young people running—like the younger Yamashita once did—to the big cities for jobs in finance or business or high-tech in companies that are household names. Yet much of the "stuff" that fills our lives, our trains and vehicles, our computers and the machines that make them depend heavily on the arcane abilities of men like Fujii and Kunimura. Now the prospect of their leaving the scene has triggered a sense of urgency: there is no one to take their places. It turns out that they were indispensable after all. So while some large companies have struggled to find suitable work for their older workers beyond retirement age, Yamashita Kogyosho found that it could not survive without them.

Tatsuto moved quickly. His oldest workmen were in their early 60s, already at or even past standard retirement ages in Japan. So Tatsuto revamped the company guidelines, setting the retirement age at 65, five years later than the norm. Alongside that, he created a system under which workers who want to stick around but not work full-time can officially "retire," start receiving pension benefits, and come back to work as part-timers. Such systems have gained popularity in Japan. They meet government requirements by keeping able-bodied workers in the shop, but since the workers already have access to at least some of their pension benefits, employers can pay out less money in wages.

But Tatsuto was not motivated by government orders or the wish to trim costs. It was all about necessity. Without these older men, his company would fall apart. Yamashita had joined companies all over Japan in a vast experiment in how to keep aging workers around. Time and time again, they found that flexible hours and giving elders positions of respect and responsibility within the company could go a long way to encourage seniors to postpone full retirement.

"They're all very energetic," Tatsuto said of his own workers. "In a big company, they want you to quit once you're 65 if you don't have a special skill. But in a small company like this one, the number of employees is small. You want a really good craftsman to work until his last breath. You're grateful for that."

Tatsuto could count on another advantage in his effort to keep his retirement-age workers around: deep personal bonds with his workers.

Kunimura said that sense of obligation on his part grew in part out of the elder Yamashita's own management style. When times were tough, everyone pulled in their belts and worked harder. When times were good, the boss shared the spoils with his workers. This was the attitude that had got them through the tough times in the 1960s and 1970s, and it would get them through these new hard times as well.

"Work is for living, of course, but it's also for the company," Kunimura explained. "Of course, there are troubles. We've had a long relationship, so money isn't the issue. If the company has trouble, you feel like you have to do something."

Tatsuto was already giving some thought to what that something might be.

The construction of trains hardly sounds like beautiful or attractive work. It is industry and all that brings to mind: chemicals and machines and grit and smoke, steel pounding against steel. Hammering in a drafty cement and corrugated steel workshop seems very far from any kind of art. So Yamashita faced a challenge: make this work come to life in a way that would attract a younger generation without the hunger or burning ambition of the Japanese who lived through World War II.

"I thought, 'Wait a minute! I want people to know about this!'" Yamashita said. "I needed something that would make people say, 'Oh, there is such as thing as this.'"

So Yamashita turned to art—in the form of a violin. It wasn't an entirely original idea. Violins had been made of metal before. The beginning of aluminum-making in the 19th century had led to musical experimenting, and metallic violins were produced in the United States in the 1890s. They never really took off in popularity and are still considered mostly curiosity pieces in the music world. Hammers and violins had crossed paths in other ways. The most expensive violin in the world is known as the "Hammer Stradivarius." And musicologists can resort to banging hammers next to a violin to test the instrument's capacity for resonance.

But Yamashita had something new in mind: his violins would be *shaped* by hammers.

The instruments suited Yamashita's purposes. He wasn't after a perfect sound. He needed a beautifully crafted object that would capture a future worker's imagination. And he could do more than just show it off like an objet d'art—he could get someone to play it. The aging hammer men were crucial to the project. Yamashita's father, now recovered, fashioned the first aluminum cello. Fujii also got to work on a violin. As always, there were complications. For instance, it turns out aluminum is much heavier than wood, and the metal instruments—particularly the violin—were too heavy to play comfortably. So the Yamashita team looked for a lighter metal and came up with magnesium in 1-mm-thick sheets. The gleaming instruments are lined up in a demonstration room on the second floor of Yamashita's factory.

For presentations at schools in the region, Tatsuto brings along violinist Makiko Miyoshi. She lifted one of the instruments out of its case on one of the days I was at Yamashita's and started playing. Even to untrained ears, the magnesium violin has a slightly flat tone. Miyoshi agreed the sound doesn't come close to a wooden instrument, but she said that doesn't matter. "I'm not looking for the same sound to come out of a metal violin. But I hope it will get better and better. Of course, it took centuries to perfect the wooden violin, so maybe we'll see the same thing with metal violins."

Tatsuto didn't seem satisfied yet. Some people have approached Yamashita about buying the instruments, but he refuses, insisting they're just for demonstration.

"I hope we can make a lighter, louder sound," he said. "As long as we have this company, we'll continue designing these. This is just a baby, it's just been born."

The violins have earned Yamashita national media attention in Japan, but it's difficult to say whether the dream of hammering one someday had encouraged anyone to apply there for a job. Tatsuto said that while the company is eager for fresh talent, he sets the bar high for new workers. Applicants have to demonstrate a real dedication to the craft of hammering. Decades ago, this might not have been as difficult as it is now. Japan's lifetime employment system has steadily eroded since a wave of corporate restructuring in the 1990s broke companies' reluctance to lay off workers. With the lack of a job-for-life guarantee, many young people have abandoned the fierce company loyalty of their parents and grandparents, opting instead for a freer, less materialistic, and much less work-oriented lifestyle.

So it's a tall order for Tatsuto to find 20-somethings committed enough to stick with a job he says will take a decade to master. At the same time, he can't risk spending the time and energy to train apprentices who will quit before they can perform craftsman-level work. When I talked to him, in midsummer of 2010, he'd interviewed 20 applicants so far that year and had hired just two.

"We have them hammer something. That's the first test," he said. "They have to have the feeling that they want to become an excellent craftsman like these old men. If they ask about salary and vacations from the beginning, then we just say good-bye."

"This is going to take 10 years," he said. "It's only the people who really want to get good at this that can make it."

Yamashita's place in the history of Japan's bullet trains is well-established. The company has worked on more than 300 shinkansen, and has crafted some two dozen types of trains. Things have changed over the years, of course. Manufacturers have resorted to machines to mold nose cones. For instance, machines are used for some of the N700 shinkansen, which went into service in 2007. But the hammer is still an essential ingredient in Japan's high-speed train world. Machines that mold nose cones are expensive and waste much of the metal. The number of nose cones of any given model is so low that it's still more economical to make them by hand. Tatsuto Yamashita says he has so many contracts lined up that he's already guaranteed work for years to come.

But until he's trained a cadre of younger craftsmen, the key to the future of Tatsuto's company is his older workers. Six of his 34 workers are 60 years old or older, and he's clearly not ready to let them go just yet. Kunimura and Fujii officially "retired" at the end of 2009, then went right back to work part-time at Yamashita as technical advisors—basically, to train younger craftsmen. They each work 16 days a month. Younger workers have taken over the main factory operations. When I visited again in the summer of 2012, they were still going strong.

"It's better to come to work than to just daydream at home," said Tatsuto. "There's work for them taking care of younger workers. There's always something useful they can do."

Kunimura has been a key to the training program, which is getting some domestic media exposure. A documentary by Japan's national broadcaster, NHK, showed him coaching a younger worker. The two were an odd couple, a trim Kunimura with a crew-cut next to a 20-something with long, orange-tinted hair, looking just as rough around the edges as the hammer men themselves looked in their black and white photos from the 1960s. As a mentor, Kunimura was stern, quietly competent, and gentle all at the same time. He let the younger worker experiment, finding his own way with the hammer. Then Kunimura would examine his handiwork, calmly shake his head, and hand the young man a fresh sheet to start over. With the cameras rolling, the frustration was clear on the apprentice's face. The following day, he called in sick. It looked as if he'd already soured on the job. But the following day he came back, this time determined to make some progress. Kunimura was there with him, feeding him fresh sheets of aluminum as the young man spent the entire day hammering.

Kato Manufacturing could easily be nothing more than a relic. The company was founded in 1888 as a forge, and has stayed in the same family for four generations. Just like Yamashita, the Kato factory, which makes a dizzying variety of steel products, such as fuel tanks for Boeing jetliners, car doors for Mitsubishi, hair-dryer parts, and even divider walls for highways, depends on human labor to operate its steel presses and molds and polishers.

The reliance on human capital could be a fatal flaw. The company sits on a hill overlooking part of the small central Japanese city of Nakatsugawa, the kind of place that young people flee as soon as they can for Nagoya, Tokyo, or Osaka for school and jobs. Those left behind mostly just get old, and Kato could have found itself stalled rather than expanding, as workers faded into retirement and few young people turned up to replace them. In 2002, current president Keiji Kato faced such a quandary: demand was strong, the Japanese economy appeared to be lifting from the 1990s doldrums, and he needed more workers. But he didn't have the people.

"We're a manufacturing plant, we operate 365 days a year," said Kato. "Our objective is profit, of course, so we need workers to operate the machines. We had 10 days of holidays and I thought that was a waste. Who could we depend on to work those days? We could use temporary workers, but we wanted people to work longer-term."

Kato found out the talent he needed sitting in his own backyard, waiting.

That year the city did a survey on "elderly awareness" that found most residents who were 60 or older wanted to work, but only 25 percent of them actually had jobs. So Kato went on an advertising campaign to encourage older folks to apply for jobs. He handed out flyers and posted adverts in local newspapers declaring

"Everyday is Monday!" The idea was that the Kato factory was going full-blast round the clock—and that retirees who had nothing to differentiate the workdays from the weekends could join the action on any day they chose. The response was strong: Kato got 100 applications for 15 positions. When I visited in 2010, roughly half the 100 workers at the factory were 60 or older. The retirement age is 65, but Kato rehires about 80 percent of his own retirees as part-timers.

The company, however, gets more than just a bunch of workers. The scheme also plays on some special circumstances in the Japanese system.

First is the flexibility built into the complex pension system, which consists of a basic national benefit plan open to all Japanese whether they were employed or not, and another benefit package on top of that which depends on earnings on the job. Back in 2002, pension benefits were pegged to the age of 60, the earliest companies could force workers to retire at the time. That meant that retirees who joined Kato at the time of his advertising campaign were already receiving some kind of benefit. The beauty of this is that pensioners in Japan, as in many places elsewhere, can still receive benefits even if they continue working, as long as they don't pass a threshold determined by pay and the number of hours worked each week.

How did that help Kato? Well, if a retiree came to him looking for a job, Kato didn't have to pay him full wages. In fact, many retirees don't want full wages, because that would lower their pension benefits. While he pays his own retirees fuller salaries, Kato pays elders coming from the outside about 800 or 900 yen an hour, less than $10. That's about the same that a 19-year-old working the cash register at a convenience store makes. The formula will face some challenges as the pension eligibility age creeps up. A 62-year-old who isn't receiving any pension benefits might not be amenable to working for the minimum wage. But for now, as we saw with the struggling salarymen at Tokyo Job Center, money isn't a top motivation for the silver job applicant.

"In our case, we kill three birds with one stone," says Kato. "Old people get to work. If they work, they can relax. The meaning of work is to be useful. It's not so much that they are healthy, so therefore they can work. It's more that, since they work, they get energetic and healthy. If they don't do anything, they go senile. They want to use their own skills and knowledge and be depended on."

One of the other birds, of course, is the benefit to the company. Hiring an older worker costs Kato one-third of what it costs to hire younger people. But his motivation extends beyond money. Seniors, with no kids at home to look after, have no trouble attending to deliveries and service on weekends or holidays, boosting the company's presence in a country where customers generally expect suppliers to be at their beck and call round the clock. And, Kato said, older workers are valuable as trainers for younger employees.

The third bird is providing a model for the region. Kato loves to rattle off the names of publications and universities who have sent reporters and researchers to study his operation. Since we met, he's written a book about hiring workers age 60 and older. He said hundreds of people had visited his plant to see what he's been doing.

He says that makes sense.

"Among the developed countries," he said, "the most advanced in terms of aging is Japan."

The domain of the hammer men seems as clean as an operating room. The rubber soles of my shoes squeak on the floor. Fresh paint gleams from the khaki green floor and the blue steel girders holding up a ceiling of corrugated steel. In the section closest to the administrative offices, workers man computerized machines that slice through sheet metal with a mechanical blow-torch, or stamp it into identical shapes the size of train armrest ashtrays. A young man sands the edges of a square of aluminum with a wire brush fixed on the end of a drill. The din of industry fills the air, the hissing and clanking and thumping of metal on metal.

In the next room, an older workman bends over a red steel frame, taking measurements. Another scans the blueprint for the new E5 bullet train, which was to debut the following spring, and speed along the rails at 320 kph.

Behind them, Susumu Okada, 62, works intently in a gray work uniform, white knit gloves, and a dark blue cap turned backwards on his head. His job that day is shaping the cockpit. A rust-red steel frame with waffle iron-like ridges sits in the middle of the room and he circles it, planning his work. He takes a formed sheet of aluminum and wedges it into place on the frame. He screws clamps on it to keep it in place, and taps it with a wooden mallet to make it conform more perfectly to the frame. He mumbles to himself when the piece doesn't fit perfectly, then taps it some more with the mallet. He fits more pieces around the structure, and it finally takes form, looking something like the front hood of a car. Above it is the window frame the drivers will sit behind, the control panels before them. With a mechanical wire brush, Okada smooths the edges of each piece.

Now that he knows it will more or less fit together, he takes it all apart and focuses on the first piece, hammering it a little, then straightening up to study his work, concentrating with gloved fingers to his chin. Then he bends again for a closer look, and some more hammering. I don't dare interrupt him. He mumbles a little to himself. Then he crouches to look at the fit from a different angle. Okada hammers again. I wander around him for 20 minutes, shooting photos silently. He never looks up.

At Yamashita's older workshop, the platypus-like nose cone of the E5 is in the early stages of construction. The marks of the hammer are scattered, whitish smudge-marks all over the hull, like the spots on a cheetah. Workmen have finished hammering and welding, and now are sanding their masterpiece for painting.

The other force keeping workers like Fujii and Kunimura on the job is the wish to continue developing their skills as hammer men.

"Sheet metal working is very deep. The more I do it, the more I learn about it," Kunimura says. He points to a photo of the nose cone of a bullet train. The front has sides that bulge out like jowls. This shape, he says, was especially tough.

"I'm going to be 66 and I'm still healthy. I have this skill, so I can keep going. Some people who have technique quit and go to China. That's a waste. Japanese technique goes to China, and they make the parts and we have to import them."

In a country beset by a spate of "silver divorces" between lifelong housewives and their recently retired husbands, Kunimura credits his job with helping to maintain his marriage.

"If I stay around at home, my wife would hate me, so I'm better off working," he says, laughing.

While some of this workers aren't as fast as they used to be, Yamashita has taken that as a price for keeping them around and capitalizing on their special skills. During production of the N700, the company was late getting parts to Hitachi, and the train maker had to produce some of the parts itself. Hitachi complained to Yamashita, but he has no regrets.

"It was just too bad," Yamashita says, "but my workers are getting older and they can't work 24 hours a day."

Just in the way that hammering lends itself unexpectedly to art, mastering this obscure craft also lends itself to philosophizing. For these graying workers, the decades-long process they've gone through to master their technique mirrors the way anything worth doing is achieved: years of hard work punctuated by moments of despair and moments of elation. Those years, one hopes, lead to a deepening of understanding and appreciation for their skills, and a proud satisfaction with a job well done, despite the odds.

The way they're being managed in the final years of their professional lives contributes strongly to that pride and contentment. Instead of being pushed out by early retirement or shunted off to inconsequential, low-prestige tasks, these men have been given senior workmen sage-like roles of authority. Tatsuto and the other workers treat them as true wisemen, and the respect is returned with loyalty to the company and a passion for training the next generation.

And a little bravado.

"Nobody can beat me at hammer work," Fujii said, loosened up by a couple of beers one night after work. "My skill has to be given life. This ability we have," he added, searching for the right words, "I feel it's like an art."

It's far from clear how successful Tatsuto's gambit will be. In a few years, Fujii and Kunimura will be 70, and no one knows whether the recruitment and training efforts will yield enough to keep the company on course. Missed deadlines could endanger their relationship with Hitachi, or the foul economy and burgeoning fiscal deficit could slow high-speed train development. Japan's bullet trains are well-made and have proven already they can run for decades; demand for new nose cones depends on expanding ridership and further investment in new routes and models. Japanese producers are scrambling to secure overseas markets, but profits—as evidenced by the revolt in several U.S. states against high-speed rail projects—are far from guaranteed.

And though Yamashita's survival is convincing proof that skillful hammering remains the most cost-effective way to build a high-speed nose cone, technology stops for no one. An advance in lightweight plastics or mechanical aluminum presses could suddenly send the hammer men in the direction of blacksmiths and other professionals of the past. The hammer men's work is already on display in museums. Someday, that may be the only place where it can be seen.

But Tatsuto is not ready to give up on the hammer yet. In Japan, it wasn't rare to run across men in manufacturing—small company presidents or factory managers—who said they would urge their sons to find better work, something with better pay or less wear and tear on the body. Something clean and steady, something that would never leave dirt under their fingernails. Tatsuto was different. He was already thinking about the next master hammer man: his four-year-old son.

The boy, Masato, once waddled out in front of a TV screen showing a video of his grandfather hammering a square yard of sheet metal, curving it over a block of iron.

The boy squealed with happiness, jumped up on his tippy-toes and started pounding his fist, gripping an imaginary hammer.

The story of Yamashita Kogyosho illustrates how possession of in-demand skills can turn older workers from a potential liability into a key to business survival.

But the hammer men live in a society where work is valued to a high degree, and that devotion is abetted by an economy and government structure that assumes citizens, when given the chance, will almost always choose work over leisure. To a large extent, the Hammer Men of Kudamatsu—like the "Leaf Women" of Kamikatsu in Chapter 1—teach us as much about Japanese culture and values as about developing work opportunities for older people in the developed world.

Now we turn to a country where heavy government investment—again, abetted by very different societal norms—forged an "early retirement" culture in the 1970s and 1980s. France's rapidly aging population now has outlived these policies, forcing the government to reverse course in hopes of encouraging workers long accustomed to the idea of quitting in their late 50s to stay on the job a few more years.

But old habits die hard.

This chapter was reported during two trips to Japan, in June–July 2010 and June–July 2012, in addition to knowledge of the country picked up during my two stints as a reporter for Associated Press in Tokyo in 1995–2001 and 2003–2008. All details and statistics were gleaned from interviews or materials provided by the companies and agencies involved unless otherwise noted.

Michel Wattree, 63, drives his school bus through villages near Vesoul, France, in June 2013.

7

The Old Continent Gets Older

BUCEY-LÉS-GY, *France*

Route 66.

Its asphalt ribbon unscrolls across the Midwest, from Chicago through St. Louis, across Missouri, Oklahoma, northern Texas, over the hardscrabble southwest to Los Angeles. It has carried transcontinental foot-runners east and migrants west. John Steinbeck's Okies escaped the Dust Bowl on "The Mother Road" to California in *Grapes of Wrath*; Jack Kerouac's wanderers in *On the Road* evoke the spirit and the route without ever mentioning it.

Route 66. No highway embodies more fully the American ideal of the open road, freedom, and boundless possibility.

And no road holds greater promise for Michel Wattree.

"That's the American dream in France," he said. "Everybody knows it."

Early every morning he hauls his paunchy 63-year-old body into a German-made MAN bus, and pulls out of Danh Tourisme in Bucey-lès-Gy, a village tucked among the undulating, cultivated hills and thick forests of eastern France, less than a two-hour drive from the Swiss border. The rolling landscape of the province of Franche-Comté has long been something of an independently minded frontierland. The Gauls, Franks, and Merovingians have all ruled here; later came Burgundy and the Hapsburgs. The place always put up a fight. The province didn't become permanently part of France until Louis the 14th pulled it into his kingdom, lost it briefly, and then conquered it for good in the late 1600s. The birthplace of Victor Hugo and Louis Pasteur, the province was one of the last areas in the country to surrender its serfs.

Wattree jokes about being royalty himself. Sort of.

"I'm king of the road, eh?" he shouted over the rumble of the bus.

Wattree's route, however, is hardly that of Kerouac's speed-addled heroes, or the adventurers forging their way into the American West. Compared to wanderers, rifle-wielding rouges, or land-seeking settlers, Wattree's cargo is relatively sedate: schoolchildren. He winds his 63-seater through rolling hills and villages, ferrying gaggles of fresh-faced kids from bus stops to schools in the morning, and back again in the afternoon. And while Americans love to think of their Route 66 as pointing the way to the optimism of the future, Wattree's frontier folds perpetually into the past, studded with centuries-old hamlets with origins rooted in hazily remembered fiefdoms. Some of that past is more recent. His morning run carries him past Combeau-Fontaine's Place 15 Juin 1940—marking a German attack on the town just days before France's surrender to the Nazis in World War II.

One morning in June 2012, Wattree made his usual first stop at Arbecey, a hamlet of a mere 250 inhabitants—and the bus erupted with the yelps of the children leaping on board with their backpacks and lunch boxes.

"Bonjour, chauffeur!" the children shouted as they bounded onto the bus. Wattree laughed in the tumult, greeting the kids and announcing over the din at every stop that an American journalist was on the bus with them today and urging them to talk to me in English.

He turned to me and smiled. Sure, the job provides him with pocket money and something to do for a few hours every day. But it wasn't Kerouac. It wasn't Will Rogers or the Wild West or the Blues. He wasn't at the wheel of a Corvette convertible.

"This," he said, gesturing toward the din in the back of the bus, "is not Route 66."

Life hadn't always been so domesticated for Wattree, or so unlike his dreams of the open road. He quit school at 16 and went into the French army. One day he sat down in a tattoo parlor and offered up his left forearm for the image of a scorpion—the venemous predator found on every continent but Antarctica. After earning every vehicle license he could think of under the auspices of the military, he finished up his service and started driving trucks full-time in 1970, hauling whatever what was offered to wherever it needed to go: Germany, the Netherlands, Poland, Hungary, the former Yugoslavia and Czechoslovakia, Spain, Italy.

He kept going for 39 years.

"I'm trained as a mechanic, but I just love to drive," he said. "It's a passion. I spent my whole career in transportation, and I wanted to keep doing a little even in retirement."

So after officially retiring, he started looking for a way to stay on the road, even if just locally. Happily for him, just around that time—2009, the year he turned 60—businesswoman Josette Duede and her husband Daniel were striking an accord with the staff at their Dahn Tourism company on the employment of older workers.

Making room for retirees made good business sense. Duede's largely rural corner of France is home to an older population, and many residents were eager to supplement farming income or pensions with part-time work. Driving a bus short distances is not a physically demanding task. Nearly all of her 200 buses and mini-buses work with the local school districts, transporting some 5,000 students a day. That translates into hours that suit retirees' lifestyles: drivers like Wattree work four or six hours a day, with plenty of breaks between runs. They enjoy holidays off and summer vacations.

"They have nothing to do," Duede said of retirees. "They're bored, so this gives them something to do."

Under the accord with her workers, Duede says she shifts schedules to suit drivers' needs or desires. Unlike the yellow school buses that roar between bus stops and schools across America, Duede's fleet features spiffy coaches with well-cushioned adjustable driver seats. The driver's cabin is fitted with a breathalyzer tube that blocks the ignition until the driver tests negative for alcohol.

The labor accord allows her to fill her ranks with part-time workers, most of them older. Of about 200 people on the payroll, less than two dozen are full-time. While the pact commits Danh to maintaining a workforce with at least 40 percent over 50 years old, the actual numbers come in much higher, at around 70 percent. The average age of male employees, for instance, was 56 in 2011, while the average overall was nearly 53 years old. And the action plan obliges the Duedes to train their older workforce: each year, they need to provide training to at least 15 percent of their workers aged 55 or older, while assessing the skill levels of at least 30 percent of them.

Duede says much of the training goes toward teaching drivers how to operate the computerized controls on the newer buses.

"They learn more slowly, maybe," she said. "But they learn very well."

In return, the company gains flexibility in employing workers only when they are needed. And the fact that many are already drawing pensions takes pressure off labor costs. When I visited, drivers like Wattree were making the French minimum wage, a little over 9 euros an hour, or about $12 per hour. He said the money is good enough for pocket cash on top of his 1,500 euro-a-month pension. And new retirement regulations under former president Nicolas Sarkozy allowed retirees to work longer hours and make more money, so Wattree can drive without losing pension benefits.

Still, those earnings wouldn't cut it for everyone. There's no way anyone could raise a family on that kind of salary. "It's not suitable for a young person who needs to work full-time," he said. "That's why there are so many older people working at Duede."

This is a familiar example of how business needs, government policy, and personal motivation can combine to provide more work for older people. The workers, thanks to pensions, are willing to work part-time for less pay. With a guaranteed income for life, they don't need a lot more extra money. This suits companies who only need workers during limited hours, and aren't willing or able to pay top-dollar with extensive benefits. Government policy encourages it all by removing disincentives, allowing workers to keep more of what they make.

The good news is that the arrangement works well for everyone involved. The bad news? It almost never happens in France.

It would be easy to dismiss Wattree's fascination with Route 66 as a quixotic dream—or delusion—when contrasted with the reality of yelping school children and postcard-perfect lanes he creeps along in a bus. But in France, the fact that he works at all at his age makes Wattree something of a revolutionary.

Across Europe, governments are scrambling to confront the aging of their populations. The "old continent," along with Japan, is on the front-line of the struggle of the world's most advanced economies to maintain—and, they hope, to grow—their industrial might while at the same time adjusting to the erosion of their working populations and the explosion of the ranks of the elderly. Europe has more than just economic production or employment statistics to defend. It also is struggling to defend an idea, born in the smoldering ashes of World War II: that former sworn enemies can live in peace, enjoy the political benefits of democracy, bask in the affluence of advanced market capitalism, AND guarantee their populations basic standards of health, education, and income—in a term, social justice—through an elaborate welfare state.

Now the fruits of that successfully attained affluence—longer lives, extended years of good health—are threatening to help undermine the engine that makes it all possible: the industrial economy. Governments are finding the only way to keep the juggernaut on course is to overhaul the prized welfare state and trim back some of its more princely benefits.

In a world of overpopulation, the first problem Europe faces is a lack of Europeans. As in other places, affluence in the postwar era brought with it an initial baby boom followed by sharply declining fertility rates, far below the rate of 2.1 children per woman needed to sustain the size of a population. A 2011 European Commission report on aging showed fertility for the 27-member European Union at 1.59 in 2010, down precipitously from 2.70 in 1960. Fertility rates are coming back somewhat: the European Commission has forecast an EU-wide increase to 1.64 by 2030 and further to 1.71 by 2060. But that still won't be enough to keep population steady on its own. And the fertility landscape takes on even more urgency when we look at Germany, which in this decade at least has been the continent's financial anchor and engine for economic growth. Here, fertility rates are among the lowest in the world: 1.36 in 2010, projected to rise only modestly to 1.54 by 2060. Germany, like the rest of Europe, will have to look beyond its own reproductive power to populate the labor force that will power its economy and replenish its tax coffers.

Immigration can help, and many European countries have opened their doors to refugees and migrant workers from the rest of the continent and beyond. But economists and demographers generally agree this is only a temporary solution. Immigrants, after all, get old too. Many bring their children, but not all, and they may or may not bring higher fertility rates with them. Those higher rates can also evaporate rather quickly in a generation or less as immigrants adjust to the norms and conditions of their host country. The other question mark hanging over any move to counterbalance declining fertility with immigrant workers is that the newcomers can often find themselves disadvantaged in the labor market, particularly when times are as hard as they've been in debt-crisis Europe. Some are wondering whether immigration policy should be modified to encourage the entry of more highly skilled workers that have better chances of contributing significantly to industry and tax revenues. Setting such conditions for newcomers, however, can conflict with the humanitarian mission of welcoming refugees no matter what their skill level or economic viability. So immigration can soothe some of the pain, but it's no panacea.

The European baby shortage has magnified the overflow of the elderly. Europeans live far longer these days than before, in some cases startlingly so. Babies being born in some countries—Germany, France, Italy, and others—can expect today to live 11 years or more beyond what could have been expected in 1960. This is a great achievement, but it changes conditions in the economy. Those additional years come at the very end of lifespans, as all additional years do. So instead of enjoying the benefits of 11 more years of productivity, tax generation, and child-bearing, societies are bearing the burdens of 11 more years of pension income, health care, and housing. For the EU at large, life expectancy at birth has increased from 66.9 for men and 72.2 for women in 1960, to 75.3 for men and 81.7 for women in 2009. Demographers disagree over to what extent life expectancy can expand further beyond the 80s, making meaningful forecasting difficult. Still, the EC report took a stab at it, forecasting that across the EU, life expectancy for men would soar from 76.7 years in 2008 to 84.6 in 2060, while women would gain 6.5 years from 82.5 to 89.1. Barring a sudden deterioration of health care, nutrition, and overall living standards in Europe, the aging process is going to continue.

For our purposes, the vital measurement is of how the double-effect of declining younger populations and the staying power of the older generations is driving up the average age of populations. In 2010, those aged 65 and over accounted for 17 percent of the population of the 27 nations of the European Union; that percentage is forecast to nearly double to 30 percent by 2060. Perhaps pointing to the massive resources that will be needed in health care in the future, the same projection shows the 80 and over crowd growing from 5 percent of the population today to 12 percent in 2060. I haven't seen anyone arguing seriously that working lives will extend that late. Who will pay to care for this burgeoning demographic? How will society come up with the funds for the nursing homes, the hospital stays, the home helpers, the age-adapted living spaces, the physical therapy, the transport assistance, the hospices and end-of-life care?

The answer, barring a sudden explosion of productivity that turns each individual into a massive and sustainable wealth machine, will depend on the size of the labor force (i.e., the working-age population). Here is where we run head-on into the European quandary—and the statistic that gives economists and demographers night-sweats. The segment of the population aged 15–64, the customary working-age span, is contracting, from 67 percent in 2010 to 56 percent in 2060. Demographers like to crunch these numbers to come up with what is known as the old-age dependency ratio. That number will shoot up sharply between now and 2060, from 26 percent in 2010 in the EU to 52.5 percent in 2050. That means that roughly four working-age people support one retired person these days; in 2060 there will only be two working-age people to care for that one elderly person. So either those workers will have to toil twice as productively or pay twice as much to keep that one retiree fed, housed, and cared for, or the retiree will have to scale down his or her expectations. The dependency ratio, the European report shows, will be higher in Europe than in pretty much anywhere else in the world—except, of course, in Japan, where the U.N. pegs it at over 70 percent by mid-century.

European nations, like most other governments facing this future, are addressing this by attempting to reduce the percentage of retirees and expand the working-age population by making working lives longer. That means raising retirement ages. Research so far has verified what would be dictated by common sense: making people wait longer to receive their pensions is a very effective way to get them to work later in life. This saves the system money by cutting the amount of time the state is required to pay out benefits. It also has a double effect: working people pay more taxes than those on a pension. So each additional year of work is not only one less year an individual is receiving pension benefits; it's also an additional year for that person to generate tax revenues for the state. So this powerful tool has become increasingly popular across Europe.

The debt crisis that roiled the Eurozone in 2009 has spurred frenetic action in parliaments across the continent to shore up finances by trimming back pension payouts. But that's nothing terribly new. The overhaul of pension policy has actually been gathering pace over the past decade.

Germany is the home of the pension: Otto von Bismarck first introduced the idea of a pension and retirement age in 1889, setting the cut-off age at 70. It was later lowered to 65 in 1916. In 2007, the government shifted this in reverse: over the next dozen years or so, the retirement age will be raised by one-month and then two-month intervals each year, ending the process at age 67 in 2031. Penalties for early retirement at age 63 will double over the period. The German example is typical: countries taking this route by and large use a gradual approach, attempting to ease their populations—and employers—into higher retirement ages over several years, rather than shocking them with a sudden jump. This method also minimizes the differences between different age groups, so the accident of being born in one year rather than the previous one is acceptable for most people.

Such programs are found across Europe. Spain abolished mandatory retirement in 2002, made further changes in 2007, and in 2011 set a gradual increase in the retirement age of 65 in 2013 to 67 in 2027. France will raise retirement with full pension benefits to 67 by 2023, and the government provoked riots when it raised the eligibility age for the lowest level of state pension benefits from 60 to 62 in 2010. Italy, where the European Commission's 2009 Ageing Report showed pension payments gobbled up a stunning 14 percent of gross domestic product in 2007, the highest rate in the EU, bureaucrats are busy turning the country from one of the industrialized world's earliest retirers to among its latest. Full retirement age will be 69 by mid-century, and the government is stopping up some of the avenues Italians have used for years to exit the workforce before retirement age. In the United Kingdom, the retirement age is rising for women from 60 to 65 by 2020; the age for both men and women for the state pension will rise from 65 to 68 between 2024 and 2046.

It's hard to overstate what a reversal such policies represent in Europe. Back in the 1970s and 1980s, country after country on the continent scrambled for ways to get older workers *out* of the labor force. On the one hand, the trend was part of the general expansion of the social welfare state growing out of *les trente glorieuses*—the three decades of spectacular economic growth between 1945 and 1973. As economies grew, so did the desire for a life of leisure, and so did the elite's willingness to pamper voters with benefits in good times. In France, as in other countries in Europe, access to the state largesse was increasingly seen as a citizen's right, the pursuit of freedom from work as the signature of European civilization. It was also a deliberate policy to, as the economy slowed in the 1970s, stem rising youth unemployment by driving older workers out of the labor force in hopes that employers would replace them with the young.

The early retirement policy, it seemed, had something for everyone. Labor unions loved it because it allowed them to claim victories for the working man, particularly once growth slowed and the economic pie stopped expanding. Companies loved it because they could clean out their highest-paid employees in amid increasing pressure to restructure. Workers loved it because it meant their month-long August vacation could now be extended year-round at state expense—at an age when they could still enjoy it in style.

So avenues for getting out of the workforce proliferated. You could take plain old early retirement on both state and private pensions. Some countries allowed workers to go onto unemployment insurance for a few years until they were eligible for pensions. In France, which became a leader in early exit from the labor force, jobless workers were no longer obliged to look for work in exchange for benefits once they turned 58. Around Europe, workers' compensation and disability rules were loosened to provide 50-somethings with enough to live on. The movement was particularly strong in the leading continental economies—France, Germany, Italy, and the Netherlands—but it affected nearly all of the Western industrialized world, and labor force participation rates for people from their mid-50s on fell sharply, despite an increase in women moving into the workworld.

In one respect, these policies were a blinding success. Workers age 50 and older left the workforce in droves, and companies freely downsized to adjust to tougher economic times. In France, participation rates for both sexes between the ages of 55 and 64 fell from some 55 percent in the early 1960s to a low of 31.4 percent in 1995. Other major European countries also dropped sharply.

The policy gave enterprises much greater flexibility when confronting boom-and-bust volatility since the 1970s. They could cut costs by pushing out higher-earning older workers knowing there was a comfortably feathered safety net waiting for them. But policymakers had also expected something in return— that corporations would fill their empty offices and factories with younger workers, solving Europe's burgeoning youth unemployment problem. But that never happened, at least to the extent that would have made a dent in rising numbers of jobless young people. Youth unemployment continued to be an enormous drag on economies and societies in Europe, and is—as we've seen elsewhere—an enduring argument against boosting labor force participation for older people.

Many economists argue employment policies of the 1970s and 1980s were based on what they call the "lump of labor" fallacy. The lump of labor theory is that the number of available jobs is fixed; all you have to do is move the older workers out of jobs and move the younger workers in. Many theorists these days, however, argue that this doesn't work for several reasons. One is that companies cannot easily replace an experience older worker with an unskilled younger one; the two cannot do the same jobs. Another reason, as pointed out by several researchers in an International Monetary Fund working paper in 2008, is that the causes of youth unemployment in Europe go much deeper than a simple lack of work. The authors took a close look at Belgium, a country with such a low level of labor force participation among older citizens it gives even France a reason to gloat. The paper found that such factors as unemployment insurance schemes for the young, minimum wages, mismatching between university education and the needs of the marketplace, and the lack of job-oriented internships were far more of a drag on youth employment than the presence of older people in the workplace. "We could not observe any positive link between early retirement and youth employment. On the contrary, we observe a negative link indicating that the activity rates of both young and elderly workers are sensitive to business cycles," the authors concluded.

Researchers looking at the United States have come to similar conclusions. Alicia H. Munnell and April Yanyuan Wu, researchers at the Center for Retirement Research at Boston College, have urged policymakers and employers to put the "lump of labor" theory to rest. "This horse has been beaten to death," they wrote in a 2012 paper. "An exhaustive search found no evidence to support the lump of labor theory in the United States."

Instead, early retirement engendered other changes in the workplace, eroding older employees' relevance on the job and setting the stage for the current uphill battle. First, early exit from the workplace pushed to ever-earlier ages a sort of "short-timer syndrome" that eats into a worker's productivity. As a person gets closer to retirement, the perceived value of training, skill-building, or taking on challenging, career-boosting projects declines. There's not much point in embarking on an overhaul of your IT skills at 53 if you expect to retire in two years. The same goes for your employer: there's not much sense in spending money and time on training you in forward-looking techniques if you could be out the door in just a few years. This common sense supposition plays out in the real world. Two researchers at Maastricht University in the Netherlands found in 2009 that, on average, older workers participated more in job training in European countries with later retirement ages.

This array of forces—the institutionalization of early exit from the labor force; structural biases against older workers; and an enduring, society-wide addiction to retirement—hit French president Nicolas Sarkozy head-on in 2010 when he pushed a modest proposal to raise France's retirement age through Parliament.

On paper, the legislation didn't look revolutionary: all Sarkozy wanted to do was raise the minimum age to receive a state pension from 60 to 62. After all, the French are among the earliest retirers in the world. With debt piling up, much of the world in the worst economic recession since World War II, and French society aging at a steady clip, the legislation seemed a prudent move to adjust—however modestly—to fiscal, demographic, and economic reality.

But this is France, and no one proposes scaling back a piece of the welfare state without paying a heavy price. Hundreds of thousands of French—including high school students who wouldn't be eligible for pensions until mid-century—stormed into the streets to protest the proposal, smashing storefronts, overturning cars, lighting trucks on fire, hurling stones at riot police, and miring air and train travel in delays. The mayhem triggered gasoline shortages. Striking sanitation workers left trash rotting in heaps in the streets. Acrid clouds of tear gas wafted down the boulevards of Paris, Lyon, and Marseilles. By the time Parliament finally passed the measure in October and Sarkozy signed it, his support ratings had sunk to a lowly 35 percent. He'd be out of office within two years, himself a victim of involuntary early retirement when he lost a re-election bid in 2012 at the young age of 57.

When successor Socialist François Hollande was sworn into office in May 2012, his first step was predictable enough: he rolled back part of the Sarkozy retirement reform, lowering the retirement age back to 60 for those who started working at 18 or younger.

The partial reversal for reform illustrated the quandary that France—the country that perhaps most has come to exemplify for the world the European joie de vivre—faces as it confronts the growing pains of an aging economic power.

France is far from any kind of political consensus over how to extend working lives or even whether it really needs to in the first place. Yet the country is conscious that it is undeniably aging: amid the changeover from Sarkozy to Hollande, *L'Express* magazine ran a special edition: "Invent Your Life at 50," featuring articles about work, study, leisure, family, and romance for the late middle-aged. French aristocrat Ines de la Fressange smiled gloriously on the cover: "At 50 years old, she becomes a model and falls in love."

Why is France so ambivalent? In the 1990s, the country was on par with the rest of Europe in its measures to keep its older workers on the job. But over the past 15 years, other countries—Sweden, Great Britain, Germany—have made sometimes dramatic strides in increasing labor force participation among older workers, particularly those aged 55 to 64 as France has stagnated. For Anne-Marie Guillemard, an aging worker specialist at University of Paris Descartes Sorbonne, the answer lies decades in the past when France embraced wholeheartedly—in her view, too wholeheartedly—the lump of labor theory.

"We used early exit schemes for 30 years very massively, probably more massively than any other European country," Guillemard said in an interview in her office in Paris in May 2012. "And this has been devaluating the older worker labor force, but also developing age discrimination in employment."

In the 1980s and 1990s, early retirement seemed a small price to pay for the sake of keeping society at peace and avoiding the kind of disorder Sarkozy faced a few years ago. Faced with punishingly high levels of youth unemployment—since 1975 it has surged from 5 percent to more than 26 percent in 2013—a powerful consensus between industry, labor, and individuals pushed the country deeper into a commitment to early exit from the workforce than just about any other European nation.

One measure of that commitment has been the dropping retirement age in France. The pension eligibility age was lowered to 60 during the late 1970s and early 1980s—and there it stayed until 2010. But the retirement age is just one part of the puzzle. France also created bureaucratic structures, workplace management habits, and widespread personal expectations now blocking the way to prolonging worklives. The deeply embedded addiction to retirement plays out in the country's labor statistics, particularly when compared to other leading nations in Europe. Many of France's neighbors hit their lowest average retirement ages in the 1990s before making efforts to reverse course. Britain bottomed out in 1998 and has been rising since; Germany has added more than 18 months to the average worklife since the mid-1990s. Even Italy has made progress since 1999. Yet the French have more or less resisted the global backlash against early retirement: as of 2011, on average the French were still retiring sooner than workers in any other major European power.

For Guillemard, author of 2010's *The Challenge of Aging: Age, Employment, Retirement, International Perspectives*, the early retirement push of the 1970s and

1980s severely disfigured the country's labor market, making the relative brevity of the French working life nearly impervious to a rising official retirement age.

First, making it so common for 50-somethings to retire has encouraged employers to discriminate against older workers. France has legislation against such bias, but Guillemard has conducted surveys that show human resource managers in France routinely hesitate to promote or provide training for anyone over 45 in private industry because of expectations they will soon be out the door. Increasingly, workers are seen as disposable, used for a short period and then discarded. As Guillemard and researcher Dominique Argoud pointed out in work published in 2004, the protections the French state put in place for laid-off workers in their 50s actually encouraged employers to fire older staffers guilt-free, knowing there was a generous safety net waiting for them.

Guillemard argues such policies, which were aimed at creating jobs for younger workers, are actually making it more difficult for them to get hired. The workplace is less and less a place for training and retraining. "This age discrimination in employment is not a concern only for older workers, but also it hit the youngest," she said. "If the elders are not efficient at work, the youngest are seen as not having enough experience to take a job."

The result is what Guillemard calls an "early exit culture." Employers consider you a "senior" from the age of 45, and you consider yourself a senior as well. The combination of youth unemployment and early exit has narrowed the scope of an individual's peak years of employability to a thin band of 20 years, roughly between 30 and 50. Compounding this concentration has been the 35-hour workweek introduced under Socialist prime minister Lionel Jospin in 2000. The idea behind it is essentially the same as the theory that drove European countries to push older workers out of the labor force: there is a fixed amount of work to be done and society has to ration it. Supporters said the shorter workweek—it had been 39 hours since the 1980s—would even out the difference between those working long hours and those with no job at all, forcing employers to spread the work around to more people.

But employers by and large did not go out and hire more people to do the work left undone by the shorter hours. Instead, critics say, they forced workers already on the job to squeeze 39 hours of work into the 35-hour week, thereby intensifying the work. Guillemard finds this deeply damaging. At a time when France needs to be adjusting the labor market to the abilities and limitations of older employees, she argues, the 35-hour week made the French workplace even more inhospitable to them. Yet the shortened workweek is now considered sacred in France. When Prime Minister Jean-Marc Ayrault suggested in October 2012 that he was open to discussing the merits of the law, he was immediately slapped down by labor leaders and other ministers in the cabinet. He quickly backtracked.

Not that the government has been at a complete standstill on aging workers. In fact, Paris has made a series of moves over the past two decades to reverse the decline in employment among people in their 50s and early 60s, though the effect so far has been minimal. As with the law pushed by Sarkozy in 2010, the main thrust of government policy has been to tinker with the pension system to increase the costs of early exit from the workplace.

The engine of change, as in most European countries, is fear of a fiscal melt-down. A series of reports in the late 1980s and early 1990s detailed how the combination of generous pensions, aging demographics, and low labor force par-ticipation rates for those over 55 meant that the country's "pay-as-you-go" system was headed for major trouble as more people retired and fewer people entered the workforce. One estimate forecast that aging by itself would trigger a deficit in the system of a full 8 percent of GDP by 2030. These reports made it plain that either benefits would have to be cut substantially or contributions would have to increase sharply if the system were to be kept solvent into the 21st century.

The power of the unions and the general popular support for the system, how-ever, have made raising retirement ages and restricting benefits perilous, severely restricting government action. Authorities started the reform process in the 1980s with the safest option of increasing contributions. When it was clear that wasn't going to be enough and rising payroll taxes would eventually eat into employ-ment, the government started tweaking the system to lengthen working lives. In 1993, for instance, the state increased the amount of time a person would have to contribute to the pension system in order to receive full benefits from 37.5 to 40 years, phased in over a decade.

As William Tompson, a senior economist at the OECD, has argued, a stum-bling block to progress has been the fragmentation of the pension system. Pension plans differ widely depending on employees' work—what they do and what union represents them. A move to increase pension ages, for instance, needs to be nego-tiated separately for the train workers, or school teachers, or sanitation employ-ees. The 1993 pact, for instance, only affected the private sector, leaving out the legions of public workers in France who had more lucrative pension plans. Wider action was politically treacherous: massive strikes shut down a 1995 attempt to reform the public system, helping to drive Prime Minister Alain Juppé from office. A series of government-commissioned reports issued in the late 1990s and early 2000s called for the further lengthening of the contribution period and implementation of gradual retirement, but these too were attacked by both the unions and employers.

Since 2003, the government has instituted a series of reforms based on a gradu-alist approach, attempting to bring pension plans for the public and private sec-tors in line with each other, while creating incentives to stay at work and penalties for leaving early. The process has been helped by moderation among some French labor unions in light of the long-term insustainability of the system. The 2003 reform was pivotal: it increased the number of years public workers have to pay into the system to receive a full pension, provided bonuses for contributing for more years beyond the minimum, raised the minimum mandatory retirement age from 60 to 65, and imposed penalties for contributing to the pension system for fewer than the required 40 years. In a successful bid to win the compliance of more moderate unions and avoid crippling strikes, the government left out the public sector transport, electrical, and gas workers; raised the guaranteed minimum pension; allowed early retirement for workers who started working at age 16 or earlier; and offered better pension benefits to certain types of workers. The irony was not unnoticed: while the government was urging private industry to hold onto older workers, it was allowing state workers to walk out the door just as early as before.

The 2003 reform has been followed over the years by smaller steps that by and large have imposed costs for quitting work early, increased the benefits for staying later on the job, and attempted to limit escape hatches for 50-somethings looking to retire. Following the Sarkozy reform of 2010, France is now on its way toward having a fairly typical pension regime for the continent, at least on its surface: eligibility for the lowest state pension level was set to increase to 62 by 2018, while the age for a full pension will increase to 67 by 2022. The number of years workers need to pay into the system to qualify for a pension is also steadily rising, headed toward 41 years and 4 months for those born in 1953 and 1954. The government has also made it illegal for a company to force an employee to retire before 70.

Still, keeping that system afloat in France is getting harder all the time, despite the decade-long effort to rein in costs. The French so far have turned up their noses at the defined contribution plans at work in other parts of Europe, notably Sweden, and the pay-as-you-go defined benefit model is running aground rather quickly. The system suffered a 14-billion euro ($19 billion) deficit in 2011. The main problem now seems to be the overall ineffectiveness in France of pension reform in lengthening worklives. A 2012 review of France's pension changes by the OECD concluded that the government had shut down many of the previous pathways to early retirement, though more work was needed to spread best practices for employing older workers in the public sector and to attract people over 50 to public jobs. Though the report acknowledged that the labor force participation rate for the 55–64 age group had grown since 2005, the slow pace of growth also highlighted the lack of effectiveness in the measures taken so far in France: the labor force participation rate for that age group was still 11.5 percentage points below the OECD average. Unemployment for older workers was higher—and of longer duration—in France. Older workers retire two or three years earlier, and French companies are far less successful in getting workers to stay on past 60.

The meager results from the steps taken so far have raised questions among some about the applicability of the standard model of raising work levels of older people to France. The common wisdom is that raising pension eligibility ages and closing off avenues to early exit from the workforce will naturally encourage people to work longer. Instead, what some policy experts see is a rise in unemployment among older workers who get squeezed out of the job market before they are eligible for bona fide retirement. The government in 2012 reported that the number of jobless workers age 55 and older surged 84 percent from early 2008 to late 2011, while the number of younger jobless rose 30 percent. At the end of 2011, 9.1 percent of the unemployed were aged 55 or more, against 6.7 percent in early 2008 and only 5 percent in 2000. And, as is the case elsewhere, older unemployed stay out of a job for longer periods. Three quarters of those aged 55 to 64 who reported being unemployed in 2010 were still out of work a year later. "The problem is that people actually do not necessarily work longer—they just (stay) unemployed longer," said Serge Volkoff, a statistician, ergonomist, and then-director of the Research and Study Center for Experience, Age and Populations at Work in Paris.

This has shifted some attention to the company side of the equation in recent years. The government began requiring companies to put in place by January 2010 so-called "plans of action" or to strike agreements with unions aimed at making more room for elders in the workplace. For some critics, like Guillemard, the decree simply foisted the responsibility for coming up with jobs for older workers onto the shoulders of the companies, while the government focused almost exclusively on reforming the pension system.

Overall, few seem to have taken the plans seriously, but there are exceptions. Volkoff co-authored a study in 2012 of more than a dozen French companies that had taken steps to adjust to an older workforce. Some companies instituted systems to figure out which tasks or postures were toughest for their workers, and then took steps to reduce the physical wear and tear, such as creating carts to carry heavy materials, or changing the configuration of work stations to reduce painful positions, repetitive motions, or the likelihood of accidents or injury. Some companies also attempted to "map" different positions according to their difficulty for older workers in hopes that they could then move individual employees through a succession of jobs as their physical capabilities changed over time. Others examined the workload on night shifts, and one considered taking steps such as allowing naps on the overnight shift to help workers avoid exhaustion. Companies were also negotiating phased reductions in worktime for older employees, reconfiguring workflow organization to suit the differing capabilities and preferences of older workers, and setting up an office culture that allowed seniors to act as mentors, work partners, and "spokesmen" for younger colleagues who hesitated to speak up at work meetings. Employers were even coming up with new positions well-suited to older workers.

Still, Volkoff conceded such practices were still quite rare in France. His study, he said, purposely focused on outlier companies taking action on this front. Most companies, meanwhile, have done little or nothing to address the issue.

One company that has made notable progress is Areva, the France-based energy conglomerate and world leader in the nuclear power business. The case illustrates how in Europe the largest companies are often the only ones with the resources and economies of scale to implement effective older worker programs.

The case of Areva also highlights a growing quandary for companies that rely on an aging cadre of engineers and other technicians with specialized knowledge.

Areva launched a full program to retain older workers in its labor force in 2008, offering training to workers over 50—a rarity in France—and setting up a program to transfer knowledge from more experienced staffers to newcomers. The 2003 pension reform, lamentably, phased out a growing practice of offering gradual retirement to older workers, but here, too, Areva somewhat bucks the trend: the company actively seeks out talented retirees and offers them part-time gigs of three days a week. When I visited the company's offices in downtown Paris in 2012, Areva had 80 such consultants at work.

"We want the workers who are 50 years old and older to be just like other employees," declared Philippe Thurat, Areva's director of diversity and equal opportunities.

It's clear why the company is interested in keeping its gray workers: there are so many of them. Of the company's 28,000 France-based employees, 33 percent of them are 50 or over, and 13 percent are 55 or older—a stand-out demographic in a country that hustles workers out the door so early in life. Only 15 percent of the company's workers are under 30. Like many companies dependent on the specialized knowledge of their workers, Areva is petrified at the thought of all its baby boomer engineers charging out the door on the permanent vacation of retirement.

The company not only aims to retain older talent—it is also busy recruiting it and keeping it up to date. While the average age of a new hire is around 30, Areva says 40 percent of its recruitment is aimed at workers who are already in mid-career. Naturally, this is a way to cash in on training done on a competitor's dime: mid-career hires who earned their stripes elsewhere typically need little orientation in a new company to get up to speed. But it also means the Areva is invested in making sure that a 45-year-old hire is going to stay more than 5 or 10 years. So the company is committed to something relatively rare in France: training. A union agreement requires 30 hours of training a year per employee. Thurat said Areva provides about 33 hours.

"It's indispensable," he told me. "The nuclear industry requires a special knowledge."

Areva woke up to the challenge of retaining its seniors in 2005 after realizing the benefits of having an age-diversified workforce: while older workers have institutional knowledge and experience, the younger ones come in with more extensive computer and IT training. The current policy was put into place in 2008, before the government required such programs. The company is also trying to spread that knowledge and experience around through a budding mentorship program. Areva had 1,200 people in an in-house "work-study" program in 2011, and has assigned each younger hire to an older mentor. In France, the company has about 1,000 mentors, of whom 400 are considered "seniors."

Despite such progress, overall the picture that emerges of action on older workers in France is one of stasis. After the 2003 reform, several companies started showing up in research papers with innovative "knowledge transfer" programs and policies aimed at keeping their older workers, but the economic crisis that started in 2007 largely put a stop to that action as companies focused on just staying afloat.

"Five years ago it was a hot topic, but then we moved on to unemployment," said Benedicte Gendron, a specialist in economics and human resources at University of Montpellier III in southern France. While there is some action at select larger companies, she said, smaller firms just don't have the money or inclination to make progress on older worker management.

"The priority is more like how to survive," she said.

That stasis is also reflected in a widespread skepticism in France about whether lengthening the worklife is feasible or even desirable. While critics like Guillemard and others bemoan the country's failure to get with the European program of boosting labor force participation rates among older workers, it's easy to find officials in France who scoff at those ringing the alarm bells. At DARES, the Labor, Employment and Health Ministry's statistics bureau, bureaucrats with offices overlooking the Seine just south of the Eiffel Tower insisted that France was making sufficient progress. I met three officials there who opened our meeting by launching into a defense of French policy. "I don't want you to have the impression that the rate of action in France is lower than other countries, because there has been a big change," said one official, who spoke to me on condition of anonymity.

In any case, time is on France's side, they argued. By 2035, the baby boomers—who form the bulge in population pyramids from Tokyo to Helsinki—will largely have exited the scene, leaving a more level, and fiscally sustainable, distribution of ages in their wake. In addition to that, France has a rather healthy fertility rate when compared to Germany or southern Europe: 2.0 children per woman in France, according to the World Bank, compared to 1.4 in Germany and Italy. "This could all be temporary," said a second official. "It all depends on the trend of productivity."

In other words, the combination of boomers dying off, plenty of babies, and increasing labor productivity could mean it's not that important to keep older people working after all.

Gerard Cornilleau, an economist at the Institut d'études politiques de Paris, known as Sciences Po, argues that it's perilous to decide which countries are ahead and which countries are behind in Europe simply by comparing labor force participation rates of older workers. Germany has made more progress in finding jobs for the aging, he says, because it has to. By 2050, the populations of Britain and France will have eclipsed Germany as Europe's most populous country. Germany, with its lower fertility rate, is under far more pressure to beef up its labor force with older people than France is. At the same time, the declining number of German children allows the state to move resources from education for young people to job training for the old. So Germany has both more incentive and more resources to make the transition to an aging workforce.

True, Cornilleau concedes, France needs to do more to provide work for its older people. But it has a substantial younger population as well. The French challenge, he argues, is to provide for growth across the board rather than concentrating the gains on one particular demographic segment. "If we have no growth, and (an) increase in employment rate of older people, we'll have more and more and more unemployed young," he argued. "And if we have growth without an increase in employment rate of older people, we'll have a problem for financing retirement, and so on. So we need to solve the two problems together."

And yet, the demographic and social realities in France are inescapable. People aged 65 or older are forecast to make up 18.6 percent of the population in 2015, and that percentage is projected to increase to 23.4 percent by 2030 and 26.2 percent by mid-century, with the strongest growth among those 75 or older—in other words, the French most in need of income and health support. So it seems short-sighted to shrug off the need to extend working lives in France just because the demographic challenge may be less severe than in Germany.

While it's easy—and perhaps satisfying in a particularly Anglo-Saxon way—to generalize about the French love affair with vacation and early retirement, it's clear that some older French are reconsidering the idea of finishing their lives with 30 years on the dole. And there are signs that, despite the strident efforts of labor and other interest groups to preserve the old system, support for some kind of change is building. In May 2013, the business paper *Les Échos* published a survey by pollster IPSOS that showed 63 percent of French want an in-depth reform of the pension system, 66 percent favored an extension of the number of years a person has to pay into the system to receive benefits, and 61 percent backed raising the retirement age.

Some companies are addressing the budding desire among retirement age French to work at least a few hours a week. On the high end of the market is Expertconnect, established in 2005 to bring together companies looking for experts—engineers and the like with specialized knowledge—for short-term projects and retirees with in-demand experience and skills.

Around the same time as Expertconnect got started, a 24-year-old Frenchman named Bertrand Favre was growing a bit restless working at an investment fund, buying up hotels and other properties in Miami. When he saw Americans of all skill levels seeking fulfillment—and an income—by working past retirement age, he wondered if France wasn't headed in the same direction. He quit the investment business and returned to Paris, co-founding his own employment service for older workers, BiTWiiN, in 2007. But with Expertconnect aiming at the executives and engineers, Favre set his sights on a different sector of the labor market: home improvement, handymen, and odd jobs. While workers signing up at the site are just as eager as the engineers to feel useful and stay active, they also typically enjoy far less generous pensions and have an incentive to supplement their income with part-time earnings.

The BiTWiiN website, http://www.bitwiin.com/, functions as a "help wanted" ad for older workers. It has entryways for individual workers, people looking for some work done at their home or other services, and companies. The site advertises jobs in babysitting, plumbing, driving, errand-running, aged care, and so on. The web-based company claims 15,000 subscribing workers and ties with some 4,000 clients.

"In the future I think we will see more and more retired people are working because they choose to do it," Favre, 29, told me in his Paris office.

"And," he added, "it's a way to get more money."

Michel Bocquet is one of those retired people. He was 60 when we met at the Dupont Café on the corner of Rue de la Convention and Rue de Vaugirard. The metal worker and journeyman fixer-upper started working in his teens and by 56 had accumulated enough years of labor to retire.

But he wasn't done yet. He took a year off, considered his options, and then in 2009, he ran across BiTWiiN on the Internet. Since then, he's been working part-time, doing metal work like installing iron railings in homes, assembling furniture, painting and other home improvements. Before he retired he made about 2,000 euros a month. As a retiree, his pension brings him 1,500 euros, so he supplements that with about 500 euros a month from part-time work two or three days a week.

"If I didn't do that, then no more car, no more Internet, no more house," he said. "I love what I do, and it's not too tough."

Bocquet, who describes himself on his business card as a "dynamic pensioner" who is "serious and well-groomed," doesn't take sides in the debate over retirement in Europe. After all, he could well understand how someone doing the work of a laborer for 40 years would want to—or need to—retire by the age of 60 or even earlier. For him, the system has worked well: he was able to bow out of compulsory work in his mid-50s, yet jobs arranged through BiTWiiN's website have given him the chance to use a lifetime of skills to make some money on the side— on his own terms. While his lifestyle isn't luxurious, but it does include scuba trips to the Mediterranean.

"If someone has been working all his life, he should be able to retire if he wants to—if he wants to," Bocquet said.

Still, he said, some people retire and they don't know what to do with themselves.

"The word 'retirement' means nothing to do," he said of some of his fellow French baby boomers. "But retirement isn't just for sleeping—it's for doing something, it doesn't matter what."

What do people like Bocquet and Wattree teach us? For one thing, they illustrate just how limited the choices are for would-be older workers in France. In a country where retirement—the sooner the better—is framed as a pillar of social justice, there is little room for public discussion of the merits of longer worklives. Longer romantic lives, yes, can be celebrated, but in the French context, work is hardly sexy. More often, work is associated with exploitation.

And yet, Bocquet and Wattree also show us how policy and individual determination can eventually trump tradition or cultural norms. The modifications in public policy over the past 15 years or so, for all their inconsistencies and loopholes, have created some spaces that workers and businesses—given the right incentives and circumstances—will willingly take advantage of.

Bocquet and Wattree also illustrated what I found in so many places: a very human attachment to our own work skills and abilities. This enduring search for usefulness is what makes the drive in Europe toward early retirement in the 1970s and 1980s such an anomaly, and in some ways so soul-defeating as well. Bocquet was a man who worked with his hands and his eyes. He was especially proud of his ability to measure the width of a piece of metal by sight. And he'd left evidence behind of his handiwork: the stairwells at the Gare de Lyon; the windows and furniture in countless apartments in Paris.

Wattree's skills, while less specialized, are more social. As we wound round the hills of eastern France, he kept a copy of *Trucks* magazine at his side, laughing with the kids as they boarded and then waved goodbye as they unloaded at school. After a lifetime of traveling across Europe, this seemed a good enough way to finish out his working days. In two years, he said, he'd retire at 65 and settle down in the country, chopping his own wood for heat.

At the end of the day, he dropped me off in Combeau-Fontaine, waving and joking that some day we'd meet somewhere between Chicago and Los Angeles.

"See you on Route 66," he said, before circling his bus in a giant U-turn and driving away.

The determination to work past traditional retirement age is a deeply personal choice, driven and influenced by financial need, existing work environment, and family considerations. Michel Wattree shows us how the charm he finds in his work—Route 66 and the dream of the open road—has encouraged him to stay economically active later in life.

One can see the transition charted in this book as one from an increasingly outdated dream of retirement to a new dream of work. True, dreams seldom are fully attained in real life. But they have the power to inspire us, motivate us, and spur us to action.

For decades, the image of retirement has held a dreamlike sway over the American middle class: the brilliantly green golf courses, the white sand beaches, the golden glasses of Chablis glinting in the sun. Most of all, retirement meant the freedom from work. For

our next chapter, we travel back to the United States to a place that has embodied that
dream to its fullest: Sarasota, Florida.

But what happens when a place like Sarasota starts to fill with people who are no
longer interested in the dream it has to sell?

This chapter is based on interviews and information gathered during a trip to France in May–June 2012. All the quotes and statistics quoted here were provided by interviewees or the companies and agencies they work for, unless otherwise noted.

James House, 79, works a milling machine at Sun Hydraulics in Sarasota, Florida, in December 2012.

8

Proteans in Paradise

Oh best of heroes, I have known some creatures
who have been changed but once, but then no more.
Others have been transfigured many times,
Like Proteus, who lives within the kingdom
Of that great sea whose arms encircle earth.
Oh Proteus, how many times your image
Comes to us as a young man from the sea,
Then as a lion, then a raving boar,
Or as a snake who many fear to touch!
Horns change you to a bull, or you might be
A sleeping stone, a tree, or water flowing,
Or fire that quarrels with water everywhere.
Ovid, "The Metamorphoses"

I met Julie Cotton at C'est La Vie, a cafe and restaurant that spills out onto the side-walk on Main St. in Sarasota's historical district. The restaurant's motto, a quote from Molière, seemed appropriate for the west coast of Florida, one of the great concentrations of elderly people in the world: "Man's greatest weakness is his love of life." I sat down to enjoy some coffee at an outside table, the morning sun to my back, watching tanned, silver-haired couples settle into breakfast, digging into crepe St. Tropez served with leafy salads and sipping cappucinos or Mighty Leaf Tea. Youth was here as well, but in frugally measured doses: a middle-aged guy in cyclist tights approached two 20-something women dining in the alcove entrance to the restaurant ("I noticed you sun-bathing" was his opening line). Julie showed up, walking down the sidewalk and then slowing at the entrance with that hesi-tant look people have when searching for someone they've never met. I got up and waved.

In a town built on its reputation as a sun-and-fun playground for well-off retir-ees, Cotton is something of an enigma: a campaigner for older people who still want to work. I contacted her after finding a report she co-authored that declared Sarasota—home of Siesta and Longboat keys and some 50 golf courses—to be "an ideal living laboratory to showcase the value of a mature workforce." The report could be taken as an advertisement for herself. At 65—"That sounds really old to me. I don't feel 65"—Cotton's resume is a yard long.

She also is a veteran of reinventing herself. Born at the beginning of the postwar baby boom in Framingham, outside of Boston, Cotton was not destined to live the life of an archetypal 1950s housewife, though she made sacrifices for the people she loved. Out of college and married, she worked for the U.S. Department of Defense at the height of the Vietnam War to help put her first husband through medical school. The job was not a good fit, ideologically speaking. On the inside of the building, she worked on civilian manpower management issues for the Navy. Outside the building, she marched against the war. She bristled at the disconnect between her personal and professional lives.

"It was horrible," she recalls. "The moment he finished medical school, I hustled out the door so fast."

Cotton had places to go. First she went back to school, earning a doctorate in education specializing in human development at Harvard. After getting her degree in the 70s, she taught behavioral science at University of Connecticut School of Medicine in Farmington, Connecticut. Her focus was on the behavior of doctors and worklife balance—something that as the wife of a doctor she certainly had the inside perspective on. In the 1970s and 1980s, Cotton's speciality was cutting edge, and she started giving seminars around the country. That morphed into a busy consulting career. She eventually left UConn and became a consultant for Aetna Insurance Co., where she helped build an in-house diversity program, including a project as the content designer for a video series on workforce diversity filmed by Hollywood producers.

There were struggles along the way. After having a daughter, she and her husband broke up in the early 1980s. Remarried a few years later, Cotton and her second husband had their eyes on California by the mid-1990s. Her daughter from her first marriage was in college, so the time was right. But this wasn't going to be a "wife gives up career, follows husband out west" scenario. If anything, Cotton says it was she who took the lead. It turned out there was no shortage of work for a human resources specialist.

"I was applying for jobs in what's called organizational development, organizational effectiveness, and at that time, there was such an abundance of those opportunities, it was amazing," she says. "I got a job offer everywhere I went. Never happened to me before or since." California was anything but boring. Over 10 years, Cotton went through a series of organizational development and HR jobs in Silicon Valley. She signed on with one supervisor who eventually disappointed her, then engineered her own lateral transfer to a more promising boss. At another job, she quit when the company started going down the tubes—and took her work team with her to yet another company.

That wasn't meant to last either.

"That company went essentially belly-up. It happens all the time, all the time. So that's when I said, 'OK, three corporate jobs out here. What's my true love? Working one on one with senior executives,'" she recalls. So she settled in with an outfit called Mariposa Leadership as a career coach for executives, taking on the midlife crises of the movers and shakers. And there she stayed for a decade, building a client base.

And then came Sarasota. How does a woman who at 65 says, "I have a wonderful sense of emerging opportunity" move to a part of the world that is so much of an institutionalized way-station on the path to inactivity and death that it's known as "God's waiting room"?

For an answer, we have to go back one generation.

A sailor and a nurse kiss at the entrance to Sarasota.

Cast in aluminum, the couple stretches 26 feet high on the city's bayfront at a crossroads, in full view of those coming in off the keys across the John Ringling Causeway bridge into downtown, or those driving north or south along U.S. 41. Titled "Unconditional Surrender," the statue copies one of the iconic photographs of World War II, shot during celebrations in Times Square after Japan's defeat in August 1945.

Like pretty much everything else in this town, the statue—in place since 2005—is a target of discussion and controversy. Detractors say the statue is cheesy "copy" art in a place that produces plenty of its own original creative work; supporters argue it's an apt honor for the "greatest generation" that fought and won World War II, came back home, fathered the baby boom, and built the most powerful nation on Earth.

And then retired to places like Sarasota.

Men like Julie Cotton's father.

Sarasota grew as an elderly mecca in the golden age of American retirement, when—in the popular imagination at least—gold watches and defined benefit pensions marked the full-stop end of a career and the beginning of a life of leisure. Sarasota, for the growing numbers who could afford it, offered perfect, suncast skies, palm-lined coastlines, and a thriving arts and light sports scene. People didn't come to Sarasota to find challenging work or encore careers in their 60s. They came here in search of the perfect antidote to work, a place to cruise out the rest of one's days warm and relaxed, sipping Pinot after a day on the links, watching the sun slowly sink into the Gulf of Mexico.

That was the course Cotton's parents followed. Her father came back from the South Pacific after the war and became the owner of a group of outdoor clothing and equipment shops in Massachusetts with his brother and a third associate. Years went by. When the shop he ran burned down, destroying a cellar full of inventory, he rejected his brother's proposal to respond to adversity by expanding the business, preferring instead to down-shift to manager of one of the existing shops. When an opportunity came to build a home in the Sarasota area and retire, he—like many in his generation—took the chance to stop working entirely.

"Out the door and never wanted to work again" was how Cotton described her father's retirement.

Thus began Julie Cotton's 30-year relationship with Florida. Her parents stayed put for years. They aged. First her father died, and then her mother passed on in 2001. By then Julie and her husband had developed a fondness for the place. She inherited some money from her mother and invested in a house in the area, and they traveled back and forth between there and San Francisco. Eventually they sold the Florida home—and bought another house in Sarasota. By 2008, Julie said, the traveling back and forth was getting old, the kids were all on the East Coast, the economy was tanking and owning two houses was looking increasingly like a bad idea. The only home they could make money on was the one in California, so they sold it. In 2009, they made the big move to Florida.

And then Julie's second marriage, one that had lasted 27 years, unraveled. By 2012, she was divorced in her mid-60s and on her own. Far from her daughter. Far from her stepchildren. Very far from siblings (one was in Oregon, the other in Germany). She has a set response when people start talking about getting together with family for the holidays: "Please, let's just have a different conversation right now."

Work, too, was a challenge. Despite the sprawling real-time connections of the Internet, Julie was just too far from clients in California to keep her coaching business thriving. And while there were plenty of retired CEOs in Sarasota, not many were in the hard-driving stage of life in which they would need someone like Julie to coach them on to greater professional conquests or help them balance the needs of career and family.

Clients were in short supply, but some things she had plenty of. Energy. Ideas. Ideas about contributing to the community. About building opportunities for boomers like herself who wanted to keep active in the world of work. And, finally, about channeling some of her experiences—including painful ones, like the end of her marriage—into a new adventure of writing.

For this, she turned to the Internet.

"A few months ago I moved into a new house and have been busily turning it into my new home," she wrote in her first blog post in January 2013, a month after we met. "As I'm renovating parts of this house I am very aware that I am also reinventing parts of me."

In a part of the world that her parents sought out as the best place for an ending, Julie Cotton was determined to build a new beginning.

Google "boomers," "retirement" and "work" and see what you get. Here's a random sample from August 6, 2013:

_ Despite reaching retirement age, baby boomers stay on the job—*Boston Globe*
_ Boomers: Get job recruiters on your side—MarketWatch.com
_ Many boomers delay retirement, take on more work—*Kane County Chronicle* (Illinois)
_ The oldest baby boomers launch their retirement—Money.USnews.com
_ Is baby boomer retirement behind the drop in the July unemployment rate?—PBS.org/NewsHour
_ Boomers—Will they shun retirement?—HuffingtonPost.com
_ Employment Assistance—Retirement Jobs—Boomer Jobs—Retiredbrains.com

The effect of the baby boomers on retirement—and the effect of retirement on baby boomers—is getting an ever-closer look as Julie Cotton and her cohorts move into their mid-60s. The troubles of Ron Dziuda and Rita Hall illustrated the financial challenges wrought by the Great Recession on those in their 50s and 60s. We've seen how those in the health, education, and other sectors of the economy can sometimes count on innovative company policies to extend their worklives. In this final chapter, we'll look at how the generation that came of age in the era of Vietnam, Woodstock, and Watergate is arriving in a place like Sarasota with different expectations of what this stage of life means.

We'll also see how, true to form, the boomers are changing the rules of the game.

By and large, the consensus of academics and other observers is that many healthy, well-educated, career-oriented boomers are more determined to work until later in life than previous generations. It's not only because they need the money, though money can be a prime motivator. The generation that made "Get It While You Can" a cultural value is not known for pinching pennies for the sake of their savings accounts, an attitude many are paying for now. But folks sipping breakfast cappuccinos at C'est La Vie usually don't list money as their primary motivation. Instead, they say they are after personal fulfillment.

Of course, life is not always as pretty as Main St. in Sarasota on a sunny December morning. Sure, fulfilling work is nice if you have it, but a lot of people out there just need an income. Maybe those workers would rather be lying on the beach on Longboat Key rather than stuck in an office in Akron—or a Target in Plainfield. And, as AARP economist Sara Rix points out in the Huffington Post article mentioned earlier, those who are at work at 65 are still in the minority. Many boomers are taking early retirement just like their parents did. They're just not skipping out as early as the previous generation. The changing gender mix of the work world is also playing a significant role: much of the increase in labor force participation among 65-year-olds overall is due to the influx of women like Julie Cotton into the job market over the past generation.

Still, the boomers who could retire if they wanted to but are choosing to work *for the sake of it* are drawing significant attention. As the media headlines above attest, the image of the still-vibrant senior is by now fully anchored in the evolving definition of the boomer generation. Indeed, opining, studying, and prognosticating about the fate of the boomers, the more than 70 million souls born between 1946 and 1964, has over the past 15 years or so become its own industry, with branches in academia, trade publishing, film, and the lecture circuit. And, for better or for worse, the ideas of the "work in retirement = fulfillment" gurus are burrowing their way into breakfast conversations in places like C'est La Vie.

One of the more useful ways to describe the motivations and the methodologies of Julie Cotton and her cohorts in Sarasota and other cities across the country would be "protean." The term derives from Proteus, the Old Man of the Sea in Greek and Roman mythology, the heavenly servant of Poseidon who was a great seer and trickster embued with the supernatural power to change his appearance. In 1976, Douglas T. Hall, an expert in organizational behavior, used the phrase "protean" to describe a still-rare brand of career that was managed and propelled by the individual, rather than by an employer or company. Motivations were also different for these proteans. Instead of chasing promotions and raises, these new-age careerists sought "psychological success"—fulfillment on their own terms, driven by continuous learning and identity change.

Hall's ideas came well before their time. In subsequent writings he's described the 1980s as the heyday of the organizational career. But by the 1990s, the idea resurfaced with his *The Career Is Dead, Long Live the Career*, and it undergirds some of the increasingly popular theories about how boomers can renovate and recharge their careers as they approach the age when their parents were planning for retirement. The protean concept also promises to guide workers as they confront the erosion of the retirement system and companies' ability or willingness to marshal employees through their careers or provide for them beyond their years of peak productivity.

One of the leading public voices behind this new type of career, particularly when it comes to boomers, is Marc Freedman, founder and CEO of Encore, Inc. As the name of his operation suggests, Freedman's chief rallying cry is that of the "encore" career—a work endeavor that blossoms in late middle age and leads the individual in a new direction that can fill out the final decade or two of a working life. Typical encore candidates have achieved some level of success by their mid-50s, yet are frazzled by out-of-control working hours and drained of the passions and energies of their 25-year-old selves who started on this path. Whereas in the past, such people perhaps could turn to early retirement to deliver them to a place like Sarasota, these days such options are drying up, and finances are such that boomers are increasingly worried they will outlive their nest eggs. Whether money is an issue or not, Freedman argues that shunting boomers off to the golf course is a waste of resources that could be deployed in the interests of their own personal fulfillment and society at large.

So instead of the permanent vacation of retirement, Freedman counsels a "sabbatical"—a period lasting months or years that allow our frazzled boomer to rest, recharge, and reconnect with unquenched interests of the past.

Ideally, these interests would have a community service component. Freedman's books—including *Prime Time: How Baby Boomers Will Revolutionize Retirement and Transform America* (1999), *Encore: Finding Work That Matters in the Second Half of Life* (2007), and *The Big Shift: Navigating the New Stage Beyond Midlife* (2011)—are populated by insurance agents who end up working with the homeless and truant officers who become critical care nurses. The interest in community service has been a constant in his work. In one of his early writings, a 1994 report for The Commonwealth Fund's Americans over 55 at Work Program, Freedman recommended substantial expansions of existing volunteer and job-placement programs for older workers, including the program Rita Hall participates in, the Senior Community Service Employment Program.

For Freedman, the aging of the boomer generation offers an unprecedented opportunity for American society: a bountiful, healthy, imaginative, experienced, and highly educated crop of civic-minded volunteers, entrepreneurs, and innovators with—thanks to the modern institution of retirement—loads of time on their hands. Citing the work of groups like Experience Corps, which deploys some 2,000 volunteer tutors aged 50 and older in 19 cities around the United States, Freedman backs a fulfillment of a 1960s-era proposal pushed hard by Robert F. Kennedy of a national corps of older Americans to perform vitally needed public services.

In the years since his first book, as the economy and the country's finances have worsened, Freedman's focus has shifted in growing favor of work rather than pure volunteerism. So, rather than the earlier vision of people retiring in their 60s to throw themselves into pro bono education or health care for the underserved, by 2007's *Encore*, Freedman was looking forward to a future in which boomers shifted to "work with meaning" in their late 50s or early 60s, postponing withdrawal from the labor force until their mid-70s or even later. He also finds greater room for lower-income boomers, who—thanks to "enlightened public policy"—take a year or two off to build new skills that open the door to higher incomes in the last third of their worklives.

"We now know that baby boomers are going to work longer than their parents did, whether they have to or want to, or most likely of all, are propelled to extended working lives by some combination of the two," he wrote in *Encore*.

"The movement of millions of these individuals into a new phase of work constitutes one of the most significant transformations of work this country has witnessed since millions of women broke through to new roles in the labor market," he argued.

In 2011's *Big Shift*, Freedman pushes for a series of public policies to open up space in the labor market and give older workers the means to retool for a new career, including college programs aimed at mature students, a national volunteer program like Peace Corps for 50-plus Americans, HR policies that help employees move into new careers, the creation of tax-free savings accounts and other financial aid to help people manage midlife transitions, and an "Encore Bill"—essentially a GI Bill to train boomers for community service. Freedman also calls for reforming Social Security, but not in the way you'd expect, as in raising the eligibility age. Instead, he wants to let people dip into benefits earlier than their 60s to finance the transition to an encore career or take that sabbatical to rethink things.

Another leading active aging guru is gerontologist Ken Dychtwald. In addition to a raft of books including 1989's *Age Wave: The Challenges and Opportunities of an Aging America*, Dychtwald is founder and CEO of a company called—predictably enough—Age Wave, which churns out aging-related research and helps other companies develop products for and market to boomers. He's a common presence on the lecture circuit—a 2005 *Fortune* magazine profile quoted his speaking fee at $50,000.

Dychtwald's focus is somewhat wider than Freedman's: he casts a net that covers many of the implications of the movement of the boomer generation into old age. He sees several factors that have promoted a new concept of aging, including increasing longevity, the widening quest for meaning in these extra years, and the decline of the company pension. Similarly, he unpacks the process people these days go through as they approach and enter into retirement: the dreams of happiness and leisure, the sense of liberation, and the slow realization that there's got to be more to existence than the typical retirement life.

This is where work enters the picture for Dychtwald. Boomers, he argues, want to work, but on their own terms. In a talk at the 2013 American Society on Aging conference in Chicago, he pointed to his own survey of 50,000 boomers that showed some 70 percent of them wanted to work in retirement. But not full-time. Respondents show a preference for part-time work, mentorship roles, charity work—and most of them want to do something other than what they've done in their careers.

"So I think there's a new definition of retirement emerging," he told the audience at ASA. "I think we've seen enough retirees who are just adrift, and people want to be more connected. College towns I think are in a boom. You're gonna see people trying to reinvent themselves: Who can I be next? But what people would really like would be a little more freedom, freedom to reflect, freedom to sleep, freedom to play, freedom to write, freedom to read, and freedom to maybe work."

Dychtwald and Freedman are admitted popularizers, and they are riffing off of reams of research into boomers in retirement that otherwise rarely make it over the walls of academia into the popular media. And that research widely supports the thesis that boomers intend—either for financial or personal fulfillment reasons—to keep working beyond the age when their parents collected their gold watches from the company and moved off to Sun City or Century Village.

For instance, research by Nicole Maestas, a senior economist at the RAND Corporation, has compared baby boomers, so-called war babies born in the early 1940s, and children of the Great Depression. She found that boomers are better educated and wealthier than earlier generations and intend to retire later as well. Financial problems loom for the boomers, however. On average they are wealthier than their parents, but their greater longevity means they might not have enough money to last them for all the time they have left. Still, Maestas argues financial considerations don't account for all of boomers' greater attachment to work.

Filling in the picture, she argues, is a desire to keep working.

"Our findings . . . suggest that the greater labor force attachment of the Early Boomers may be driven in part by noneconomic factors such as stronger preferences for work or perhaps even a stronger work ethic," she wrote in a piece published in 2007.

Boomer brains are partly to blame. The postwar era witnessed explosive growth in the number of college students, partially because of population growth, but also because public colleges expanded dramatically as higher education was increasingly seen as the pathway to social mobility and higher income. Enrollment surged 49 percent in the 1950s, an astounding 120 percent in the 1960s and 45 percent in the 1970s. These baby boomers have poured into the workplace, into careers and families and child-raising—and now, retirement—with more years of schooling than any generation before them. The Julie Cottons of the world pride themselves on their ability to work with their minds, to marshal their education and experience and intelligence in the pursuit of a goal. In the process, many people end up defining themselves—and their all-important intellects—by their careers. After all, what lesson do we learn in academia more than the life of the mind matters most? For many of us, the life of the mind gets its most extensive workout on the job, whether it's reassembling a motorcycle engine or designing the next iPhone. That sense of self does not magically disappear once the calendar announces you're 65 years old.

Mentality is also a factor. After all, the boomers are the generation that stoked America's fascination with youth culture. Examples of codgers performing stunts once reserved for the young—playing professional sports or wailing on a guitar in front of arenas filled with aging fans—are legion. The boomers have shown a determination to ascribe youth and vigor to whatever stage of life they happen to be in, wrinkles be damned. The Who's "I hope I die before I get old" has over the decades slowly morphed into "60 is the new 40." One popular, tongue-in-cheek calculation for "elderly" is to take your own age and add 15 years. The phenomenon is writ large in a place like Sarasota, where the 60-year-olds are the kids, and some refuse to be painted with the same brush as the "true elderly," the plentiful 90-year-olds nodding off in the air-conditioned Senior Friendship Center. And then, one can imagine, there are the still-vigorous octogenarians turning away their whispy-haired heads in horror at the comatose 100-year-olds.

Health is a wild card. Will boomers be healthier than the "Depression generation" in old age? Are our "healthy years" really increasing? Will the boomers' higher obesity rates do them in? The evidence is mixed, in part because much of the research depends on self-assessments of health, so analysts are left to puzzle out the meaning of answers to slippery questions such as "Is your health better, worse or the same as five years ago?" A MetLife survey of baby boomers at 65 published in April 2012 reported that most respondents rated their health as excellent to very good, and 68 percent claimed their health had not changed in the previous three years. While common sense might dictate that longer lifespans of today mean better health, some studies suggest boomers are reporting higher rates of obesity and hypertension, and a more pessimistic view of their own health than their elders. A study by researchers from the West Virginia University School of Medicine and the Medical University of South Carolina made headlines in February 2013 by concluding that 50-somethings reported significantly lower "overall health status" than in a study two decades earlier. "Despite their longer life expectancy over previous generations, U.S. baby boomers have higher rates of chronic disease, more disability, and lower self-rated health than members of the previous generation at the same age," the study concluded.

At least two factors have mitigated the impact of health on the workplace so far. One is that boomers are still young enough—in their 60s—to have avoided the most debilitating effects of chronic illness to some extent. They are also able to avail themselves of more advanced medical treatments than earlier generations, provided they have health insurance. So even if they do suffer more medical problems, more advanced techniques and treatment are available to put them back on the Stairmaster. At the same time, work is increasingly seen as a way to stay physically, psychologically, and mentally healthy, meaning some may see work as an essential ingredient in their healthy aging plan. But the bottom line is: it's too soon to tell.

It's clear that Julie Cotton and people like her are on the frontier of a new stage in aging lifestyles, and that new stage will involve employment in their 60s and 70s to an extent that has not been seen in the United States since World War II. Cotton's generation is certainly used to being on the cusp: they embodied the youth counterculture of the 1960s, the so-called "Me Generation" of the 1970s; they led the technological revolution of the 1980s and 1990s. Dychtwald likes to say that boomers transformed each era they participated in. But it is perhaps more precise to see it as a dialectic between the boomers and their world. After all, the history of the past 50 years has been driven by much more than the simple presence and action of boomers. At each stage, they walked into conditions created in the vortex of politics and economy and technology. And demographics. After all, the boomers didn't create themselves: they were engendered by their parents, born into a world that was already transforming at an unprecedented speed. The postwar economic boom in the United States and Europe bankrolled their 1960s fantasies and the media machine that turned their culture into a worldwide phenomenon. The Cold War and Vietnam gave them their darkest moments and their most glorious rallying cries.

And now, the confluence of medical technology, the Internet, and economic trends—much of it by now of their own making—is giving them long lives and F. Scott Fitzgerald's long-elusive second chapter.

And so what happens when boomers like Cotton show up in a place like Sarasota, bursting with energy, ideas, and a desire to do real work?

For many, the answer is: not enough.

There's plenty of money in Sarasota.

Just look at the housing market. About 6 percent of the owner-occupied homes in the city are worth over $1 million—over 900 of them, and well over the state level of 1.7 percent, according to Census Reporter, a database based on U.S. Census numbers. The percentage of homes between $500,000 and $1 million, 13 percent, is more than double the state rate. Household income isn't so shabby either: 4.3 percent of households make more than $200,000 a year, well above the state rate of 3.5.

So where is all that money coming from for those nice condos and palm-ringed homes? Apparently from somewhere else. Median household income is about $40,370, about 10 percent below the state level. And income is weighted at the extremes—there are higher percentages of rich people in Sarasota, and higher percentages of poor people. So while about 54 percent of Florida households have income of less than $50,000 a year, nearly 60 percent do in Sarasota. The poverty rate in Florida is 16.8 percent—in Sarasota it's 22.3 percent. Sarasota also has a higher percentage of owner-occupied homes worth less than $100,000.

The numbers paint a picture of a typical service economy, made up of the rich folks who come to get served, and the low-paid folks who serve them. And not as many of the well-paying high-tech, finance, and manufacturing jobs in between.

"There is a lot of money, but it's not generated here because we don't generate anything here," says Tim Dutton, former executive director of Sarasota County Openly Plans for Excellence (SCOPE), a community organizing non-profit.

Dutton, age 61 when I first talked to him at the end of 2012, ought to know. He showed up in Florida in the mid-1990s after a career in hospital administration that had taken him from his home in Ohio all the way to Haiti, where he worked for three years. What he found in Sarasota was a community custom-built for retirees who want to bask in the sun or play tennis and golf during the day and take in *Carmen* at the Sarasota Opera or check out exhibitions like the World War II photography collection at the John and Mable Ringling Museum of Art in the evening.

Dutton's 89-year-old father was one of them.

"This is a great place for people that age because there's a lot to do. He goes to a lecture series every winter for three months," Dutton told me when we met at a Starbucks. "You could do that around various topics five days a week. It's pretty cool."

But for some, Dutton among them, this isn't quite enough. He asks questions that reflect the ethos of the era in which he came of age, the 1960s, and the proclamations of gurus like Freedman and Dychtwald:

"It's just about self-indulgent to only be mentally active," he said. "I know that's important and it's a good thing from a health standpoint, but the other thing that I think matters a lot . . . is being engaged in activities that matter. The self-indulgent part is: 'I know more, I'm smarter, I'm staying intellectually engaged.' But so what?"

The "so what" doesn't have to be work. The answer for many who don't especially need money is volunteerism. And on that score, Sarasota delivers. Dutton said there were some 2,000 non-profits in the area working on everything from literacy to homelessness to aging. The practice of volunteerism is embedded in the community, where there are opportunities in line with just about any interest, including children and youth and health and medicine. A random search in the Sarasota-Bradenton area turns up groups looking for drivers, receptionists, volunteer coordinators, breast cancer-research donation collectors, exchange student hosts, and dozens of other opportunities. Nearly all the retirement-age people I spoke to in Sarasota were involved in some kind of volunteer or community-oriented activity.

The one thing that Sarasota doesn't have a lot of is challenging work for older residents. Sure, there is light, part-time work in the area. In the city there are more than a dozen Publix supermarkets and nearly as many CVS stores, both of which make a point of hiring retirees to bag groceries or stock shelves, matching a large chunk of their clientele. And the work, where it can be had, fits the bill for folks who need the money, are going stir crazy at home, or are looking for an undemanding, low-stress boost to a Social Security check. If you sit down with someone like Paul Anderson, who has his fingers firmly on the pulse of the labor market as president of Suncoast Jobs, an Internet job-search agency active in Sarasota, Tampa, and Naples, and ask him about jobs for older workers, greeter positions are what it's all about.

"I can't remember the last time I went into a Walmart and saw a greeter below the age of 60 or 70," he says. "They just love the interaction, the engagement of people, that sense of being back in the workforce and having the sense of work, to be out of the house doing stuff."

But for boomers like Cotton and Dutton, a job at Publix isn't going to satisfy the need for "work that matters." Julie had a taste of that kind of light, largely unchallenging activity when she volunteered at a hospital distributing supplies one day a week. She lasted six months. It would take a personal financial meltdown for her to seek a job stocking shelves at CVS.

"I think I am more of sort of a classic baby boomer in that I'm looking for more, looking for something and it just translates into: 'Does this engage my brain in any way?'" she told me one day over lunch.

"The only part I liked was hanging out with the high school students," she said of the hospital job. "They were fun. Otherwise I have to admit it felt somewhat demeaning. Other people could do that with great pride. But I'm like, 'I've got so much more to offer than this.'"

Julie isn't alone. Sarasota is stocked with former CEOs, entrepreneurs, and company presidents; people who up north were high-powered executives, long-accustomed to running things, commanding offices and companies, leading dozens or hundreds—or thousands—of employees. The culture clash that awaits them in Sarasota can be jarring, says Bob Carter, the president and CEO of Senior Friendship Centers. Carter presides over a network of community facilities offering a buffet table of services for the aged and their families on the west coast of Florida, from ballroom dancing and bingo to day-care and volunteer medical services for the elderly.

I met Carter as he was planning for a "senior economic summit" the following month to look for ways of developing work and volunteer opportunities for the talented labor pool in the area. A 65-year-old Army vet who has spent his life working in the government and non-profit sector, he chuckled about a retired executive he met once who was so surrounded by escorting minions during his career that he had gone years without so much as pressing the buttons in an elevator. Bigwigs show up in Sarasota with a lifetime of credentials and prestige, yet have to pick between manning the drive-thru at McDonald's or volunteering for no pay, Carter says. That can be a tough sell for people accustomed to measuring their self-worth by the figures on their paychecks.

Carter knows what he's talking about. He's faced it himself, albeit on a smaller scale. When he came down to Florida from Massachusetts in the late 1980s intent on making the shift to non-profits, he was offered a job as a financial manager—at $15,000 a year, a considerable cut from what he was making up north.

"There was enough money set aside and I was married at the time, so I could pull this off at 15. But I had to get my head around that I was earning this much then, and now I'm going to earn this much, and am I devalued now?" he said. "So my mind-game was, I'm working for pay two days a week and I'm volunteering three days a week."

Two decades later, Carter is on the market for any innovation that will help him handle the tide of overqualified, A-personality retirees looking for something to do. A few years ago the centers started offering so-called workateer positions as a way of cajoling someone who could charge $150 an hour on the open market for consulting services into doing the same work at the Centers for $25 an hour. "There were some folks that just couldn't come to volunteering, they still felt there needed to be a price tag on their efforts," Carter says. "For them to accept it, we came up with this term of workateer: 'Yeah, I'm a workateer.'"

But the bottom line is that Sarasota just isn't the kind of place with much opportunity for seniors looking for paid work.

"A decade-plus ago, people were calling up and saying, you know, I need to do something, I need to volunteer," Carter says. "I'm getting more calls now, 'I'm looking for a part-time job. Do you know of anything?' "

The past few years seem littered with efforts aimed at spurring challenging work opportunities for retirement-aged boomers in Sarasota—efforts that for one reason or another haven't gone very far.

Julie Cotton, for instance, channeled her frustrations into a "white paper" co-authored with two other writers—Sandra Kassalow, president of a management consulting firm, and Jane Paquette, head of a business consulting firm—published in February 2012 aimed at drawing attention to the untapped talent pool in the area.

The paper, which appeared on a local website, made a straightforward argument: (1) For a variety of reasons, including increased longevity, higher education levels, and financial difficulties stemming from the Great Recession, older workers are increasingly interested in staying on the job; (2) Sarasota, as one of the oldest areas in the country, has an abundance of talented 55+ residents with many decades of valuable experience; (3) As a bellwether for the rest of an aging nation, Sarasota is well-positioned to become a leading innovator in attracting and retaining mature workers and creating the multi-generational labor force of the future.

The report highlighted two locally based companies that had had some success in building age-diverse workforces: Sun Hydraulics, a valve design and manufacturing firm, and FCCI Insurance Group. The authors concluded by urging area businesses to recognize the mature talent pool in their own backyard and overcome simplistic stereotypes of older workers. The paper called on businesses to restructure workplaces to take full advantage of the mature demographic, implement creative recruiting and employment programs to draw 55+ Sarasotans to the workplace, reach out to older employees already on the payroll to assess what they need to stay on the job, and develop training opportunities to these older workers to keep their skills current.

"Sustained focus and commitment will be critical to making a real difference, especially with Sarasota's tough economic and employment picture," the authors wrote.

The paper came out at a rocky time for the area's economy. Sarasota is hugely dependent on tourism, retail, and construction. In the 2000s, the housing boom in the area reached alarming proportions. Houses and apartments moved in droves into the real estate "flipping" market of buying and selling properties for unheard-of profits. Anderson, the employment agency head, said he bought a house around 2005, threw a new welcome mat at the front door and sold it in less than two months for 70 percent profit. "I didn't do anything," he said. "I think my whole investment in upgrades was $70 at Target." The lure of spectacular profits drew developers and fueled boom-town construction. Then came the bust in 2007. Unemployment in Sarasota County rocketed from 3.4 percent in 2005 to over 11.9 percent in 2010.

The area has recovered somewhat in recent years, with joblessness dropping to under 7.5 percent, but the wounds are still fresh. With so many companies in do-or-die survival mode, not many employers in 2012 and 2013 were interested in finding innovative ways of attracting older workers. And with so many younger workers out of a job, government agencies and public opinion at large were unlikely to take older workers as a priority. Even by the time Cotton and her partners released their report, the economy hadn't improved enough to earn their findings or recommendations much of an audience.

"We wanted to do a sort of a road show with it, we wanted the Chamber of Commerce, we wanted the Economic Development Council, we wanted local employers, we wanted anyone and everyone who touches the job market to pay attention," she told me. Cotton had hoped that the paper would generate interest among employers and perhaps she and her partners could move in as consultants.

That didn't happen.

"I'd like it to translate into some kind of consulting firm, quite honestly, we're not going to spend a lot of time," she said. "It was more work than we expected and didn't really gain any traction."

Part of the problem was ambivalence about whether to embrace Sarasota's increasingly aged future, or work to avoid it. Dutton says that for a long time area companies and county leaders nursed hopes of drawing a younger demographic to the area and building the economy on that, rather than working with the one thing the area has in abundance: old people.

"There was this real sense that this is bad news to label us as a place that's old. It will mean our decline. We want to grab our high school graduates and college graduates and make sure they stay here, be an attractive space like Boston is for young people around the country," Dutton told me. "And I said, 'That isn't gonna happen. What is gonna happen is we're old and we're gonna get a lot older.'"

The attitude, however, is slowly changing as the reality of the Great Recession's effect on the area sinks in, Dutton says. The slowdown stalled in-migration, prompting a dip in population in 2007–2008. The recession proved more than ever that Sarasota had to treat its aging demograph as an asset rather than a liability.

"This is our comparative advantage," he says. "Sarasota is in a position to be ahead of the thought process and the ideation and the innovation about aging."

Dutton, as head of SCOPE, was behind one of most significant efforts in Sarasota to make that happen: the Institute of the Ages.

The original idea grew out of a 2006 SCOPE report calling for the area to capitalize on its aging demographic by becoming an incubator for companies producing products and services for the elderly. Three years later, the project was enshrined in Sarasota County's five-year economic development plan as a proposed institute acting as "a focal point and aggregator for markets and industries." Dutton, who by then was leading SCOPE, said his organization raised some $250,000 for the idea from donors and enlisted RTI International, a researcher in North Carolina that services governments and companies in 75 countries, to assess the feasibility of the project and help design it.

The hope was—and is—that the Institute would help turn Sarasota into a laboratory of older living, as a hub of commercial and research activity centered on catering to, studying, and improving life in an aging society. Promoters argue that Sarasota should use the Institute to put itself at the frontier of an aging nation and world, drawing products, researchers—and money and jobs—to the area.

The project, however, was marked early on by a lack of consensus about what its main purpose and effect would be. The Institute turned to Sarasota County for a further injection of start-up money, armed with an estimate that it could generate up to 800 jobs and $155 million in economic activity within its first 10 years of operation. The county, using a different methodology, estimated those figures were far too optimistic, coming up with an estimate of 99 new jobs and a $17.8 million output. Still, Dutton and other backers prevailed, winning $1.2 million from the county and pledges of some $900,000 more from other sources by 2011.

The Institute then mounted a search for a leader. In April 2012, Tom Esselman—who made his mark by developing the singing greeting card at Hallmark—was chosen as a business-savvy promoter, and the Institute was formally launched in the fall of that year.

One of its first projects has been the test-marketing of in-home tracking devices that would allow distant relatives—typically adult children—to monitor their elderly parents' movements. The selection of a product being tested by a far-away company—in this case, Silicon Valley—has disappointed some Sarasotans who fear the Institute will fall short on its promise of creating jobs, and instead turn out to be a front for companies intent on using the elderly as guinea pigs for new products. The Institute is also building a registry of area residents, complete with detailed demographic data, that could be used to create focus groups for marketers.

"There was this disconnect because the community thought it was going to be some sort of breakthrough for part-term gigs, flexible, meaningful employment," says Kathy Black, a social work professor at University of South Florida, Sarasota-Manatee and an expert on aging and work.

"Instead, what is happening is it's being used as a test-bed," she said, citing the tracking monitor and registry projects. "We can find a hundred places to try a product—that's not what people wanted. I'd say it has to be for the community and they'd say it's going to be for the community, but that's not the way it's turning out."

Esselman called for patience and understanding, saying the opening projects were just first steps in a process that would build funding and lead to wider benefits for Sarasota, converting the area into what he called "a Silicon Valley for innovative aging." He sees Sarasota making contributions to knowledge in how aging intersects with retirement, health care, financial planning, elder abuse, and employment. "And the fun stuff too," he added, "such as music and dancing and fitness, Zumba classes."

But Esselman voiced frustration at what he suggested were misperceptions of the Institute's intents.

"It's like pulling teeth to get people to understand we're not here to market to them," he said. "The only way we're going to get there is to have them be willing participants."

Nancy Schlossburg, professor emerita at University of Maryland and expert and author on lifetime transitions, worked with Dutton in the early days of the Institute and conceded that the concept had changed over the years from a body that would serve older people to one that would focus on their roles as consumers. She didn't seem to mind that much.

"We didn't feel we needed direct service because there's the Senior Friendship Center, there's Jewish Services, there are a lot of organizations that are doing direct service," says Schlossburg, who has lived in Sarasota for more than a decade. The Institute, she said, will not only be helping companies to test products, but will also be "taking the lead in some thinking about what's happening."

But that doesn't mean that Schlossburg, a member with Marc Freedman on the Institute's advisory board, is eager to have her children install sensors in her house to monitor her movements. The Silicon Valley company working with the Institute called to ask if she wanted to be in the study, and her answer was clear: Absolutely not.

"You think I want my adult children tracking me? And these young people didn't understand. I said listen, you are categorizing all old people. I'm a sensible old person," she told me one morning over breakfast. "I don't need to be tracked, I don't need my kids tracking me. I won't let them check on me. I have my own life and my own privacy, just like they have theirs."

She shook her head.

"You're categorizing all old people as frail," she continued. "I am not frail. When and if I become frail, then I will rethink it."

In the meantime, Schlossburg was busy building a post-retirement career well into her 80s, studying and writing about the ways seniors succeed or fail at their own protean chapters.

This was the good life.

The retirees lived in a run-down trailer park in sunny Cortez, north of Sarasota. Every morning the men packed up their gear and went fishing with their buddies.

The women got together and ambled around the local shopping mall. What could be better than that?

No loudly voiced angst-ridden quests for meaning. No frustration at the lack of challenging opportunities, tantalizing new adventures, or a glorious two-decade "encore" after the first 65 years of life.

Instead, what these folks felt was very simple: contentment.

Schlossberg, who was interviewing them in 2003 for a book about retirement, was flabbergasted. So flabbergasted, in fact, that she went back for more interviews just to be sure—and her subjects kept telling her the same thing.

"When I drove in the first time, the grass was like that false carpeting, and no trees around the pool area, and I thought, 'Oh my god, this must be horrible,'" she recalled. "And I started my first interview, and these were the happiest people I had interviewed!"

"They never expected a second home, so their life was better than expected," she says. "This is hideous and they're loving it."

At the other end of the spectrum among Schlossberg's subjects was a former CFO of alcohol giant Seagram's. He had every reason to be happy in retirement: a lifetime of achievement and wealth, prestige and status, topped off with a $1 million-plus pension.

There was, of course, one thing he didn't have any more: power. And that made him miserable.

Retirement, he told Schlossberg, is hollow.

"So the contrast between this one person and the other, a lot has to do with expectations," explains Schlossberg. "For the working-class people, if you have a pension then you're in a very different situation than if you don't."

Schlossberg has studied life transitions—not only retirement, but also going to college or adjusting to a divorce—for decades, developing a theory that still shows up in doctoral dissertations and academic journals. Her life's work has been a search for an answer to a very simple question: why do some people like the guys at the grubby trailer park in Cortez manage successful transitions in life, while others like the wealthy booze exec struggle?

To help tease out an answer, Schlossberg breaks transitions down into three categories that seem to operate differently. One category is the transition you expect to make, the changes that are planned: the well-mapped engagement and marriage, the on-time graduation from college. Next are those that are unplanned, such as the failed marriage, the sudden death of a loved one. Finally, she points to what she calls "non-event" transitions: the marriage that never happens, the career that never quite gels.

Then she looks at what all transitions have in common. One, they change roles, relationships, routines, and assumptions. The birth of a child is a good example: it turns wives and husbands into mothers and fathers, alters family dynamics, and certainly up-ends routines and ideas about the world, humanity, and oneself.

Second, transitions take time, and different changes could take vastly different amounts of time to adjust to, just as people have different adjustment times.

Finally, Schlossberg came up with what she calls the "4 S System" for coping with transitions. One "S" is self: the personal strengths and weaknesses we bring to the table. A second is situation, the conditions we find ourselves in at the time of a major change. For instance, a successful transition to retirement or to life after the death of a spouse can take considerable effort and care. But going through those two life-changing events simultaneously can have a serious impact on the success of dealing with either one. Another "S" is supports, referring to the network available for help—family, friends, agencies, or groups—during the transition. More is better. Finally, there are strategies for coping. Schlossberg says the best evidence indicates there is no one magic path through a transition. People need an array of strategies—talking to friends, counseling, exercise, hobbies, meditation, whatever—to draw on as they plow through life's challenges. Again, the more, the better.

Schlossberg argues this model can help people decide how to time those transitions they can control. An example she uses is a move across the country. Do I bring a resilient self to this change, or am I on the verge of a nervous breakdown? Is my situation—financial or otherwise—stable and strong, or is it weak and uncertain? Will I have a support network, or will I be isolated and on my own? Do I have a variety of ways I can cope with this? The model can also help an individual deal with an unanticipated change by examining all the parts needed for a successful transition and strengthening those that require the most attention.

It all makes perfect sense on paper. When she retired and moved to Sarasota, Schlossberg put the theory to the test in her own life.

It started with a business card.

In 1998, Schlossberg retired after 24 years from the University of Maryland and moved down to Sarasota with her husband, Stephen Schlossberg, a former general counsel of the United Automobile Workers and top Labor Department official.

So she was launching one of those major life transitions that she had spent so many years thinking, writing, and speaking about, and she figured a good place to start on her new self was her business card. The one she retired with was much too ornate. As she's said in speeches, she was now a professor emerita, but so what? No—now she'd have to get back to basics.

So she made a card with just her name on it. No professional affiliations, no titles, no big institution backing her up. Just Nancy Schlossberg.

"Because I have no identity, nobody cares who I was," she says of that time. "Then after a while I thought, 'If I ever publish a book, then I'll get another card.'"

Schlossberg's transition, like many of them, took time. She joined an arts board—and then realized that wasn't for her. She's not a fundraiser. So, she gravitated back to the concerns that have always fascinated her: transitions. Only this time, her focus would be on retirement. And it would be for a general audience.

Then came a stream of trade self-help books—*Retire Smart, Retire Happy: Finding Your True Path in Life; Overwhelmed: Coping with Life's Ups and Downs;* and *Revitalizing Retirement: Reshaping Your Identity, Relationships, and Purpose.* She joined Dutton on SCOPE. She's on the advisory board at the Institute for the Ages. She writes blogs that run on the *Psychology Today* website, she pens columns for the *Sarasota Herald-Tribune*, she manages her own website, TransitionsThroughLife. com. She's co-president of a consulting group, TransitionWorks. And she has continued an active speaking schedule well into her 80s. When we met, she was readying for a talk in February 2013 at Southern Methodist University titled, "Aging with Panache: Our Love-Hate Relationship with Age."

"I actually open up talking to the mirror and I ask the mirror if I'm the fairest of them all," she says of the lecture. "And guess what? I'm not! The mirror tells me I'm not, and that gets me into my whole thing on aging."

Schlossberg has encountered trouble along the way. Her husband died in 2011 at the age of 90 after an illness for which he required care around the clock. But when we spoke, Nancy didn't spend a lot of time dwelling on it—only to note that the road into aging is different for everyone. She is thankful that she's been able to remain active this late in life, and that she is in a place where it's possible.

"As my daughter says: 'The only thing retired about you is your paycheck.' So I see a lot of people coming down who want to do golf and bridge that's just not my world," she says. "So they say you're gonna flunk retirement."

Schlossberg still has a business card with just her name—it's bold red with her name in white letters. But these days, it's not her only one. She says she's had about six since she moved to Sarasota.

"Now," she says, "you tell me what this means."

James House doesn't know Nancy Schlossberg but he knows what she means. Not that he spends much time thinking about it.

Instead, he works.

Right now a beige fishing hat sits on his head. Goggles shield his eyes, and a blue smock covers his 6-foot-plus frame from his chest down past the knees. Orange plugs guard his ears from the whirr and scream of the machine.

House turns to a tray stacked with aluminum blocks, each numbered and tagged. He grabs one, reads the specs, and punches the data into a computer terminal with his white-gloved hands.

He leans over to me in the high-pitched grind and echo of the factory.

"This way they know I've done my part," he shouts.

House then bends to the milling machine, a steel gray console of levers and buttons and shafts. He blows out the silvery curls and splinters of shavings from the center, fits the block of aluminum about the size of a pint carton of milk into the feed between two clamps. Then he twists the lever to tighten the jaws.

He punches a few more buttons to get the measurings right, then presses a green button that moves the block into the mouth of the mill between two spinning heads. Filaments of aluminum scatter across the top of the machine. House then takes the newly sized block, turns to the belt sander and gently files down the rough edges, twists, puts it back in the tray, and grabs another.

And so on. For eight hours. House could very well be one of Schlossberg's "happy campers," as she calls them, living out his days sipping Bud in a trailer park. He certainly is old enough: when I went to visit him in December 2012 he was a month short of 79. He doesn't spend a lot of time talking about fulfilling his destiny or performing an "encore" career. And this son of a steelmill worker isn't one to turn his nose up at fake grass carpeting.

And yet, for any, all, or none of the various reasons he throws out—he doesn't trust Social Security, it doesn't pay enough, his aging body needs the workout, he just likes seeing the guys at work—he comes to the "saw and mill" section of the Sun Hydraulics factory on the northern edge of Sarasota two days a week at 4 a.m. to stand at the hunk of steel known on the factory floor as "Pops's Mill" and shave blocks of aluminum down to size.

Another reason he's still working at Sun is because they let him. House started there in 1992. When he "retired" from full-time work after a decade at Sun— about a year before we met—he considered the state of the economy and figured he ought to keep on the job part-time. So he went to the guy in charge at HR.

It didn't take much.

"I asked them on a Friday, and Monday they put me to work," House says. He started at three days a week, and after a while he downshifted to two 8-hour days a week. He gets $15.50 an hour.

It's rare enough for a company to allow its workers to stay on the job until their 70s, never mind take them back as part-timers as they near their 80s. But since its founding in 1970, Sun Hydraulics has built a reputation on doing things a bit differently from the rest.

The company's founder, Bob Koski, started Sun—which makes cartridges and manifolds for liquid hydraulic systems in machines like cranes, forklifts, and airplanes—as an experiment in what he called "horizontal management." That meant no lofty titles, job descriptions, or hierarchical organizational charts.

The plan was to avoid the personnel problems he'd seen in other companies where the most articulate workers rose to the top while the less articulate—but perhaps more knowledgeable—languished in the lower ranks and eventually left the company in bitterness and frustration. One of Koski's goals was to retain talent, rather than drive it out to make room for newcomers.

While Koski's original vision sounds idealistic, Sun has been successful, drawing attention from places such as *Fortune, Bloomberg BusinessWeek, Forbes,* and even Harvard Business School, which has conducted a series of studies about the company. Sun was also one of two companies cited in Julie Cotton's report as Sarasota's most innovative employers of older workers.

Glenn Glass, who seems to be the main HR official in the company, though his business card just has his name under Sun Hydraulics, said the company has naturally turned to middle-aged and older machinists coming down from the Midwest and Northeast, since there is a dearth of people with that kind of experience in Florida.

And then Sun keeps people like House for as long as they want to work and can do the job. Glass estimates about a quarter of Sun's 750 employees are 50 or older.

"Most of our senior workforce at Sun is really senior because they've been here for forever," said Glass, who is originally from the Pittsburgh area. "Florida is very transient, people come and go all the time, but really Sun is not that way. Our goal is for a long-term relationship, so we have a lot of people who have been here 5, 10, 25, 30 years."

House's journey to the 4 a.m. shift at Sun has been a long one, with more chapters and changes than he can keep track of.

He grew up in a home that was familiar with hard work. His father started working at the age of nine at the local steel mill, Ingersoll in Newcastle, Indiana, where he would spend the rest of his working days.

"You know what they done? They unloaded coal cars," House says of his father and his elementary school-age workmates. "I though, 'Jeez, pop.' But that's just the way it was."

House laughs.

"He didn't care. He done what he had to do to make it."

James House seems to have the same attitude. He, too, started working part-time at 9 years old, after school at a bowling alley, setting pins from after dinner until 11:30, then running home in the dark along the railroad tracks that drove past his house. He was up the next morning for school.

By the time he hit his teens, he grew restless. The world stretched far beyond his town in the cornfields between Indianapolis and the Ohio border, and he wanted to get out and see it. So just before his senior year of high school, House says he forged his father's signature and went into the Army. The Korean War was on and he was itching to get a piece of the action. He got his high school equivalency through the military and was about to ship out to Europe—despite his requests to go to Korea—when he got the news: the elder House had figured out his signature had been faked and lobbied to get his son out of the Army.

"Wouldn't you know they put me out on my birthday," House says. "I was 18 years old."

From then on, House became a journeyman. A protean for life. He worked at a Chrysler plant for several years, then drove trailer trucks for more than a decade. Got married, had kids. When his in-laws moved down to Florida, he helped them take their stuff down and had a look around.

House says his wife was the one who really wanted to move.

"I figured she wanted to come down here and I didn't know nothing about Florida, and I thought, well, you work down there just like you do up here," he laughs. "But that ain't right. You work here for a lot less."

Then began another long series of jobs. He drove a cement truck. He was a welder. He tended bar. He installed ceramic tile for many years. Then one day, he had a look at Sun. It was clean; a buddy he knew liked his job there.

"Hey, why don't you get me a job there?"

"Well," his buddy said. "Why don't you come on over?"

"So I come on over," House recalls, "and . . . they put me to work. And I been here ever since."

The loose structure at Sun and the expectation that workers should take responsibility for their own tasks without constant supervision are a solid fit for a man who has spent a life moving from job to job, building up a wide variety of skills—and a strong sense of independence along the way. House says he can take a break when he feels like it. When he has a bad day, there's always someone to help.

Times are changing, however, even at Sun.

Koski died in 2008. In recent years, the company has grown rapidly, and now has operations in several countries, including some places—such as South Korea—where the local culture has trouble adapting to the idea of an office without job titles or a hierarchy. Profits are strong and the company has been able to hire dozens of people, even in 2011 and in the first half of 2012. That growth has slowly pushed the average age of the employees down as younger people join. Glass said that when he came aboard around 2000, the average Sun employee was in his 50s; now that number has declined to lower 40s.

Still, Glass expects the age of the overall labor force at Sun will start to increase, as the population itself ages, and fewer people feel confident enough in their investments and savings to retire early.

House can't say how long he'll stay at it.

True, he doesn't talk in terms of "second acts" or the personal fulfillment through a career. But one thing he does have in common with the college-educated boomer professionals filing through the Starbucks in downtown Sarasota is an ardent wish to postpone the deterioration of old age. And he associates work with the effort.

Take muscle mass. House is a big man, but there's no hiding he's in his 70s. He says he's lost most of the muscle in his arms since he retired, and he fears the downslide would only accelerate if he stopped working entirely. Especially, he says, when he goes to the health clinic and sees other elderly "draggin' around."

House says his wife has found a gym for them to go to and they planned to start working out there in January, "so the next time you see me, I'll be even bigger." He has some vague investments that haven't paid off yet. When they do, he says he'll quit and spend the money.

In the meantime, he'll stick around the workplace that a fellow older worker and he call their "retirement home." His only health scare lately was an aneurysm in his aorta that required an operation.

"I had to have that fixed, so maybe they put in new parts. That's what's lasting, keep me going so long," he says. "I hope they didn't skimp on the parts."

The aluminum tray full of pulled pork was ready. The CDs were burned, the inflatable dolphins were inflated, and the kids' speeches—about the battle to desegregate the Sarasota beaches nearly 60 years before—were written. So Tim Dutton packed his pickup truck, a half-dozen kids on the inside, as many inflatable dolphins in the back, and headed to the beach, blowing his horn the whole way.

The "Beach Caravan," which on this day involved five carloads of children and a few adults, has become an annual rite with Dutton since he and his live-in partner, child psychologist Alison Pinto, launched the Sarasota Community Studio in a cement-floored space at a former lumberyard.

I went to watch the Studio in action in September 2013 and found Dutton, on the verge of turning 62, in the thick of a new chapter in his life.

The aim of the Studio, in Newtown, a traditionally African-American neighborhood just north of Sarasota's downtown, is to attack the area's problems—joblessness, lack of education, substandard housing—by engaging the neighborhood kids.

"It's really about community change," said Dutton, who lives with Pinto in a house in the area. "We're trying to shift the nature of who makes the decisions from someone on the outside to someone on the inside."

Much of the work is discovery of the assets of their immediate neighborhood, a 47-block area called Central-Cocoanut. Specially designed maps adorn the walls of the studio, and the children go on "scavenger hunts" over the summer to build their sense of what the community encompasses and what its needs are. Dutton and Pinto encourage the children—he says more than 100 have participated in the studio's activities since it started—to identify problems and propose solutions.

The evidence of their efforts is all over the studio. On one wall, a series of posters describe what Dutton and Pinto believe are the attributes that make children natural leaders and decision-makers: playfulness, curiosity, their abilities as storytellers and boundary-crossers, among others. A white board across the room is covered with notes taken during a group discussion on what the kids saw as a lack of reading skills in the neighborhood, along with various ways of overcoming that, such as reading groups and reading to younger kids in the area.

And then there are the maps. One shows varying reading levels of Sarasota children by neighborhood. Another features housing data showing which lots are boarded, vacant, or occupied.

It's an exciting, ambitious—if idealistic—project, but Dutton says there's one crucial ingredient missing: money.

Dutton says his own finances are a problem. The year before, he had quit SCOPE to concentrate on the Institute of the Ages. But then Esselman settled in to lead the Institute and Dutton was "let go"—he says without an explanation. By the time of the 2013 Caravan, he'd gone almost a year without a paycheck.

On top of that, the Studio had failed to draw any significant investors. Dutton and Pinto launched the project officially in January with an event attended by the Sarasota mayor and other local luminaries. The couple figured they could finance the thing for six months on their own, until deep-pocketed donors came in with some money to keep it going.

It didn't happen that way. Dutton says he and Pinto have financed the Studio—including $500-a-month rent for the space at the former lumberyard—with their own savings and donations of a few thousand dollars from his family. But that's as far as it's gone. Dutton says he's drawn some interest from outside Sarasota, but no deep pockets have opened up for the Studio yet.

"It's hard to get people to invest in communities of low income," he said as he showed me around the Studio.

One problem is the length of time it can take for an organization to receive nonprofit status from the federal government. Dutton made his application in 2012 and it still had not been reviewed when I visited more than a year later, though it did finally come through in December 2013. Another issue, Dutton said, is that the methodology the Studio uses—"asset-based" community development—may be too innovative to convince investors it's worth their money.

"We don't have enough proof to say it really makes a difference," he said.

With the future so uncertain in 2013, Dutton launched a serious job search. After many months of false starts, he landed a job as executive director of Suncoast Community Capital, a non-profit that aims to bolster low-income areas by providing business coaching, micro-loans, job training, and other services. He started just a week before the Caravan. On top of that, he was doing consulting work for RTI International, the think-tank in North Carolina that helped launch the Institute of the Ages. He also does work for the local Area Agency on Aging.

"It's not an easy row to hoe to find a job as an older adult," he said.

If Dutton's past is any guide, he isn't the type to pick the easy way out.

Dutton's father was a hospital administrator in Ohio and his French-born mother was a retail clothes buyer. The couple met in Alsace-Lorraine in eastern France during World War II, when the elder Dutton was a truck driver for the

Army, and his future wife's family ran an inn. Dutton was the middle of three brothers; one works in business in Vermont, and the other is an architect. Dutton says they're very successful financially.

That's a skill he says he has yet to master. After earning degrees in 17th-century British history and social and applied economics, Dutton found himself following his father into the health field. He worked for the city of Dayton in the health planning agency, and ended up running a hospital in Shelby, Ohio. But by the early 1990s, he was getting restless—and impatient with the traditional life formula of career and promotion.

So he made a protean move: he traveled to Haiti, decided he liked it, and applied for a job at Albert Schweitzer Hospital. Dutton moved to rural Haiti with his second wife and their two adopted daughters in 1991 as the hospital administrator.

"We didn't think that the normal life in the United States of career changes and stepping up the ladder was satisfying," he told an Associated Press reporter in Haiti in 1994. "There was an element of us needing . . . to make a difference. For our daughters, we wanted them to see that the world was a bigger place, and there were problems and pains."

Haiti had more than enough problems and pains. The hospital had electricity only a couple of hours a day, and the nearest telephone was a three-hour journey away. During Dutton's time there, military rule and economic sanctions nearly crippled operations at the hospital, which was chronically short on supplies. The impoverished patients struggled with AIDS and tuberculosis.

And yet Dutton says he found the work and the focus on survival invigorating.

"It was the coolest job—it was almost like being in the Peace Corps," he told me. "It was very tangible and very visceral."

After meeting his commitment of three years, Dutton came back to the United States, entering the world of Sarasota non-profits and moving through several positions until the formation of SCOPE in 2001 with Dutton as director. "It seems like I've had a lot of jobs," he said. "But that's because I'm old."

A lot of jobs, but not necessarily a lot of money for retirement, which explains Dutton's concern about income even as he approaches an age when many people in Sarasota are sipping martinis beside a pool. He took a 75 percent pay cut to move to Haiti and make $20,000 a year—not a bad living in a low-cost country like Haiti, but far short of the kind of income that generates a substantial nest egg.

Still, like many of his generation, he's adamant about how he wants to spend his time and labor.

"I don't care about money," Dutton told me one night, sipping the house white at Tommy Bahama's bar on Sarasota's Lido Key. "If I can't do something where I can feel I'm engaged in change, then I'm not interested."

The kids filtered into the parking lot at Payne Chapel A.M.E. Church, several at a time, a bunch in Allison Pinto's white Prius, a few in Dutton's turquoise

Toyota pickup. A couple of the children handed out balloons and a CD of their favorite songs that they burned at the Studio. Some of the children had written little speeches to mark the occasion.

"Okay, you ready?" Dutton, dressed for the beach in orange swimming shorts and a blue cap, asked the first girl to speak. "Why don't you stand over here so you can look at everybody." He turned to the other kids: "Okay, give her your attention!"

"Do you know," the girl started, "back in the day when Newtown got together and went to the beach to change the laws so everybody could come together in one big family at the beach?"

After a few speeches about the importance of the Civil Rights Era campaign to desegregate the beaches, the kids loaded up into the cars and the Caravan began, winding down the streets of Newtown, horns honking, balloons bobbing from the windows. People out on their lawns cheered. One man shouted, "Hats off! Way to go!" waving a baseball cap. They drove through a Publix complex, past the "No Surrender" statue at the waterfront and across the bridge to Lido Beach.

Once out on the sand, the crew set up a flip chart board with a sign reading, "Sarasota Community Studio Neighborhood Beach Caravan: TODAY."

Then everyone pulled out goggles and diving masks and inflated dolphins and ran for the water.

Dutton, Cotton, Schlossberg, and House—two of them boomers, two of them born in the Depression. But all of them embody in their various ways a knack for reinvention that has sustained them despite the difficulties of "hoeing that row" later in life. They have moved to where jobs or fate lured them, adjusted to sometimes jarring changes in life, and—more often than not—have landed on their feet. Some have relied on savings or education to get them through the rough patches, others on their willingness to live without the frills. And they all, in their own way, defy the image of Sarasota as a laborless paradise for the old and wealthy.

And like Proteus, that Old Man of the Sea, they all were looking forward to some new stage in life: Cotton was working on her writing, planning a memoir; House was ready to start going to the gym with his wife to hold onto his "muscle mass."

Dutton, of course, had his new job to dive into. And there were new decisions to face: while he'd been looking for a job, he'd applied for the Peace Corps, and now it was a real possibility he'd be offered a position the following year. "Should I do this or not?" he asked later that night at Tommy Bahama's. "That's the question I'm really wrestling with."

But that afternoon at the beach, he was content to splash in the waves of the Gulf of Mexico with the kids. After a while he pulled himself away and came back up on the sand for a moment.

He squinted in the sun.

"From now, I just make sure nobody drowns," he said, dripping wet. "Which is funny, since I'm not that good of a swimmer."

This chapter is based on interviews and reporting conducted in December 2012 and September 2013, a telephone interview with Tom Esselman in January 2013, and additional phone conversations with Julie Cotton, Tim Dutton, and Bob Carter.

Hirohisa Matsumoto, 84, sits in his fishing boat at the dock on Okikamuro Island, Japan, in June 2010.

Epilogue

Galapagos: Islands of the Old

Drink your fill when the jar is first opened, and when it is nearly done, but be sparing when it is half-empty; it's a poor saving when you come to the dregs.
—Hesiod

A man in a fedora stands alone outside the locked factory gates. Wet, silent streets. Gray sky. Turning away, he walks into town to an employment agency. At the door are scrawled announcements for farmhands, short-order cooks "young," construction workers "20 to 50 years." Forlorn, he holds a thin jacket against the cold as he trudges to a grocery store where he picks up two cans of baked beans, then roots in a shopping cart for a loaf of day-old bread at half-price. At home, he and his wife sit wordlessly at the kitchen table. The meager meal is barely touched. He hangs his head, running his hands through his gray hair, while his wife rubs one of his hands, nods her head, and gazes at him with warm, worried eyes.

The narrator's voice intones: "You've just seen a fine and decent citizen doing penance for his sins. His sins are many. Item: He is over 50 years old, but with years to go before Social Security. Item: He is unemployed through no fault of his own. Item: The skills which gave him work the past 30 years are now out of date. He is, in short, broke, out of work, and desperate."

The scenario could fit any of the millions of older workers who have struggled through the past few years of economic dislocation across the developed world. It could describe Ron Dziuda of Plainfield or Kjell-Åke Ericsson of Stockholm. It could tell the story of any of the people crowding into Mature Services offices in Akron, the Silver Human Resource Centers in Tokyo, or BiTWiiN in Paris in search of help finding a job. Or, sadly, its dismal narrative could fit the millions more to come as the economic and political crises of the moment distract us from this and other leading long-term problems of our time.

But it's not about any of them. The scenario is from "The Wise Years Wasted," a documentary produced by the U.S. Department of Labor in 1965, when most of the older workers in this book were children or young adults, looking ahead to a bright future in a thriving economy. Narrated by Chet Huntley, the work describes the pilot programs launched under the Kennedy and Johnson administrations aimed at developing work opportunities for older Americans. The need for an expansion of such programs is urgent, Huntley tells us, because millions of aging workers will be desperate for employment by 1970. "You will have a problem of national magnitude: the gray ghosts of the Great Society," he tells us. Near the end of the program, Geneva Mathiason, the head of the National Council on the Aging, tells us: "None of this is easy, but the alternative is unthinkable. No American community can afford to have men and women able-bodied in their 50s and early 60s, anxious, willing and needing to work, live out their lives in idleness and drift into dependency."

We've come a long way since 1965. Many of our problems have been solved with money, the unprecedented affluence produced by the greatest economy on earth. We expanded Social Security. We created Medicare. The spread of company pensions and buyouts and the American Dream of Retirement eased the transition for the middle and upper classes from the workplace to the shuffleboard court. In Europe, the welfare state marshalled its forces to pay those in their 50s and 60s in return for their idleness. Elderly poverty plunged across the developed world.

But if the Great Recession has taught us anything, it's that the party is ending. For many of us, it's just as well. (We defeated in large part the dependency that Mathiason warned us about 50 years ago, but we never beat the idleness. We can no longer afford either of them.) It really is about time we made good on the promises of the 1960s, when the advances of the modern industrial economy made so apparent the mismatch between our evolving model of work and the needs and capabilities of our aging bodies. As Johani Ilmarinen argues, we need to give more thought to reforming the workplace to accommodate humans, rather than distort humans to accommodate the workpace. Surely it is easier to alter an artifice of our own making, the workplace, than it is to alter the body of a human, which has evolved over the millennia.

Taken to its extreme, such a vision is radical. Since the invention of the first tool, we have enhanced and abetted and distorted the human body to accommodate the task at hand. By now, our machines and computers are completely beyond the average person's comprehension. Thus the appeal and beauty of the hammer, that most elemental of tools. The mystery of the hammer men of Kudamatsu lies not in the tool, but in the skill these men carry in their minds and bodies. One might argue that even a craft is a matter of manipulating the human character to accommodate a task. So our line of reasoning must be refined. From our earliest beginnings, humans have honed their skills, the craft of living in the world. Where is the dividing line in the continuum between this craft and distortion, between the art of the hammer men of Kudamatsu and the terrifying slapstick of Chaplin in *Modern Times*?

So is aging the new frontier, the region where we find that line, the place where our bodies finally reject the contortions of the workplace? I believe accommodating our older workers will help us humanize our workplaces. Take the 12-hour nursing shifts at Scripps Health. If such a shift is just too exhausting for a 60-year-old nurse, then perhaps such a shift is a bad fit for everyone: its abolition would benefit nurses across the board. This may be why, in places as different as La Jolla and Stockholm, we find that employment practices and pro-job policies that accommodate older workers benefit everyone and vice versa. Modern science has given us longer lives and given old age the look of a new invention, but in the end the new era of old age may teach us what it means to be human.

At the outset of this journey, I posited Kamikatsu as a possible destination, a possible vision of the future. There are such places all over the globe, including America. In Needham, Massachusetts, for instance, in what is perhaps the most celebrated instance of an elderly workforce in the country, aged employees toil at Vita Needle, churning out syringes, pins, and other products. "60 Minutes" has been here. The *New York Times* has been here. German documentary-makers have been here. Caitrin Lynch, an anthropologist at Olin College of Engineering, spent a year working at Vita Needle for a 2012 book, *Retirement on the Line: Age, Work, and Value in an American Factory*.

Vita Needle has received all the attention for good reason: it's a remarkable place. The average age of its workers is the mid-70s. Former waitress Rosa Finnegan, the oldest employee at the time of a *PBS Newshour* piece on the factory in early 2013, was on the verge of turning 101. "I think coming here keeps me going," she told PBS reporter Paul Solman. Across the workfloor, wooden tables stand in rows and gray-haired workers bend to their tasks, doing the light labor that has powered the company to record profits despite economic hard times. "I'm never gonna quit working," said the second-oldest employee, Bill Ferson, 94.

The factory illustrates all the positive aspects of employment for older workers: employees are satisfied with their work, thankful for physical and mental activity, and happy to escape boredom and idleness. They feel useful, make some extra money, and believe the job helps them stave off decline and senility. Their employment suits the owner, Fred Hartman, as well. He's built record profits in part because of benefits his workers receive from the government. His older workers are already on Social Security, so he doesn't have to buy their loyalty with high pay. Hourly wages fall between $10 and $20. And these elderly part-timers don't get full-time benefits; instead, they're on Medicare. Above all, they're good workers: "Attention to detail, attention to quality, loyalty," Hartman says.

Like Kamikatsu, Vita Needle is a wonderful example, a Galapagos of aged worklife. We can learn so much about what working arrangements—pay structures, work conditions, schedules, and so on—that can contribute to successful employment for older people. But it also suffers from the limits of the Galapagos analogy: it's unique. Lynch, who has studied the place for years, says she knows of no other place like it in the United States. Vita Needle and Irodori are happy accidents, fortuitous black swans that have sprouted into existence thanks to coincidences of geography and history, economics and personality. Attempting to replicate them on a broad scale does not seem feasible. Their uniqueness makes them great objects of study, but it also limits their reproduction.

Indeed, why should older people be relegated to companies where only older people are employed? If they are valued as employees—and the evidence shows that they are, or ought to be—then why limit their benefits to a few select companies? Instead, what we want is to effect a wider proliferation of knowledge, techniques, and practices that will open up spaces in the workplace for older people. The key is engendering diversity in workplaces across the board, in the interests of generating the labor of a much larger number of older people. Irodori and Vita Needle may have changed the dynamics of their respective corners of the world, but those corners are tiny. Sprawling industries like health care and country-wide systems like the jobs councils in Sweden, in contrast, have the capacity to change thousands of lives.

So I'd like to take time here to explore some of the lessons and avenues forward suggested by the stories in the preceding pages. The narratives in this book are an infinitesimal slice of life, but they—like the narrative of any individual's life— have the capacity to speak larger truths. What might some of those be?

1. The Great Recession has made confronting aging and work more urgent than it has been in decades

The recession has accomplished this in several ways. First, the stock market crash and collapse in housing prices liquidated boomer nest eggs meant to sustain them in retirement. True, the stock market has bounced back and made impressive gains, and as of this writing, in April 2014, unemployment in the United States has fallen to 6.7 percent. But the relative stagnation of recent years has denied those near retirement of several years of expected asset growth. Panic sellers in 2008 and early 2009 locked in their losses and missed the gains. Many people with money to spend have spurned stocks out of fear of instability, meaning they haven't enjoyed the resurgence in equity prices. These people will need or want to work more years to make up what they lost and save enough for retirement. Rock-bottom interest rates have also hurt the growth of savings.

Second, many working men and women have lost their jobs in their 50s, too young to start receiving pension or Social Security benefits, but too old to compete successfully in a job market biased against them. This lost generation of workers was forced, like Ron Dziuda, to burn off savings and 401 (k) plans and go into debt to maintain homes, put children through college, or just survive. These workers, too, locked in their losses, forced to sell at the bottom of the market. Those worst off are still looking for work or have given up, or may have reached 62 and are taking reduced retirement benefits. They will want or need to work at least part-time to supplement their meager Social Security checks, never mind dream of working full-time to postpone retirement long enough to receive higher benefits.

Those who have gotten jobs are better off, but may still struggle. They are starting over at 55 or 60, and many will have to pay off debts before they can even think of rebuilding decimated savings accounts. They will toil in the shadow of illness, injury, economic instability, or the whims of an employer—all factors that could cut their working lives short before they have liquidated their debt or rebuilt a nest egg or even reached eligibility for retirement benefits. This is made all the more bitter by the fact that typical re-entrants to the working world are paying the price for readmission in lower salaries compared to the jobs they lost in the recession. For someone like Ron Dziuda, working until age 70 would be a gift.

Finally, whatever confidence workers had before 2007 has been shattered. They were reluctant about stocks, so they lost out on equity gains. A home no longer is the investment it once appeared to be. If jobs ever could be taken for granted, they no longer can, even for older workers with seniority and experience. In a world in which the rug can be pulled out from us at any moment, we will want to earn as much as we can for as long as we can.

2. Retraining and career services for older Americans must be higher priorities for government

"The Wise Years Wasted" pointed out three major factors that made retraining older workers a necessity: the high pace of technological change, automation that was quickly eroding the role and value of manual labor, and the overall expansion of human knowledge, which made the classroom lessons of the 1920s increasingly obsolete.

The pace of change in the workplace in 1965 seems quaint compared to the digital revolution now taking place. The computerization of the workplace, the explosion of the Internet, and the blinding speed with which social media have invaded every facet of our lives have been deeply disorienting for many older workers. In a training office in Joliet, Illinois, I saw an older man pound a computer table in frustration and anger as he struggled to find his way into an Internet job site. It's the stuff of jokes, the old and outdated baffled by what young people see as the simplest of technologies. But we will all be there one day without the proper training.

It's clear that our 50- and 60-something workers are in many cases sadly ill-equipped to adjust to the high-tech workplace of the present or the future. Even looking for a job requires a digital savvy beyond the reach many of them, particularly those lacking higher education or on-the-job experience with technology. The lessons of 1965 are still valid today. It was out of that environment that the Senior Community Service Employment Program grew. But as the story of Rita Hall illustrates, the program is severely limited: the income limit restricts services to only the poorest of older Americans, and present funding is only enough for the program to handle 1 percent of eligible participants. And the training itself, while valuable, is rarely the kind that will greatly expand the horizons of its beneficiaries. One can't help but be struck by the difference when one walks into one of Sweden's well-funded job councils, where laid-off workers have counselors who shepherd them into a network of training agencies to ready them over the course of months for re-entry to the labor market.

Governments across the board are using later eligibility ages for retirement benefits as a lever to force older workers to stay on the job. There are benefits to the policy: it's easy to understand, it saves the state money, and it forces individuals to think in terms of longer worklives. It can appear to be the only solution in an era of tightened government budgets and fierce political opposition to deficit spending on so-called entitlements. Our societies are no longer as flush with cash as they were in the 1960s. Raising retirement ages, however, does raise important questions of fairness. What about those who work in physically demanding jobs? Should they be required to work as long as literature professors? As economist Paul Krugman asks: Should we stop janitors from retiring because lawyers live longer? And what about segments of the population who on average live shorter lives and therefore enjoy shorter retirements? In these pages, we have seen how working longer can yield important benefits for individuals, companies, and society. However, retirement policy should not be used as a cudgel.

As much as France's largely foiled efforts to extend worklives invite ridicule from critics, the government's determination to allow certain groups to retire earlier, such as those who started working in their teens or those in tough occupations, acknowledges the great diversity in the older population. One size will fit this demographic even less than others. Success will be measured by how much we can design a system under which extra years of work will benefit the individual as well as state coffers. The fulfilment of an individual's role in society is the center of this book, not government finances.

America already has a training infrastructure, but it isn't being used in a coordinated manner—or with a steady enough stream of money—to make a real impact. Research shows the U.S. job training system to be a welter of disjointed and underfunded initiatives and pilot programs. In 2012, labor market expert Maria Heidkamp of the John J. Heldrich Center for Workforce Development at Rutgers University called for "new legislation that establishes a more flexible, more robust lifelong learning, education, and training delivery system in alignment with the country's postsecondary education institutions and local/regional economic development efforts." In other words, a seamless national workforce development strategy that goes far beyond what is offered by SCSEP or the 1998 Workforce Investment Act.

There are foreign examples that deserve a closer look. One is Sweden's system of job councils. These organizations provide many of the functions Heidkamp recommends for an American system: firm links with educational and training institutions, provision of income support for laid-off workers, and an emphasis on use of digital technology for both job searches and training. Another foreign model that could be expanded upon is the way the Japanese government spreads best practices for employing older workers. The system helps encourage companies to think outside the box, and then recruits managers as advisors for other companies struggling with the same issues.

This brings us to our next area: what companies can do.

3. Companies can do a much better job of profiting from the value of older workers and defeating negative stereotypes

The degree to which American companies have ignored the role of the older worker in their enterprises is astonishing. Despite the drumbeat of news and academic reports about the aging of society, survey after survey illustrate how rarely companies assess the demographics of their own workforces to figure out who is retiring when and what skills they might be taking with them when they leave. It's understandable: in the environment of the past few years, survival is the leading short-term priority, and additional long-term tasks such as assessing the demographics of a workforce will always take a backseat if employers see them as "extras" rather than essentials.

That's why programs such as the Best Employers at AARP are so valuable—they highlight the importance of older workers in businesses and help publicize the best innovations among companies who employ them. So far, the leaders are companies in growing industries that are reliant on the rare skills and technical knowledge of their older workers, such as Scripps Health. While many managers see using older workers as a potential cost rather than a benefit, companies such as Scripps are excellent examples of how creating an older worker-friendly workplace and earning profits can co-exist. For these companies, holding onto their talented and experienced older workers is a matter of survival. As the middle and late waves of boomers move within range of retirement, this will be the case for a great many more businesses.

The tools are already largely in place. A wealth of innovation and research has already gone into aging and work, and companies around the world are using techniques with good results. Models abound. Enterprises like Irodori have been built from the ground up to suit the employment needs of older workers. Companies like Vita Needle have discovered an elderly employment "sweet spot"—and are saving on labor costs—by hiring older workers to do undemanding work, subsidized by state retirement benefits. Outfits around the world are using a now-familiar set of tools: flex-time, ergonomic workplaces, mentoring, staged retirement, retraining, and employment subsidies. Researchers are at work developing a comprehensive "age management" approach that would guide companies in mapping out career trajectories that meet the needs and circumstances of workers at different ages.

Age bias is a persistent drag on progress. Lawsuits are up: 22,857 people filed age-related complaints in 2012 with the U.S. Equal Employment Opportunity Commission. That's an increase from 16,548 in 2006. The trend peaked at the height of the recession in 2008, but has remained stubbornly above 22,000 in the years since. Age-related complaints are now 23 percent of complaints filed with the EEOC, up from 19.6 percent in 2006. Lawsuits can be a double-edged sword: while rising numbers suggest a more vocal backlash against bias, they also can inhibit employers from hiring older workers for fear of facing legal action if things don't work out. Developing a solution for a problem so deeply ingrained in our culture is beyond the scope of this book, but the proliferation of positive examples of older employment will go a long way toward dispelling the outdated notions behind such bias.

A useful analogy could be the struggle to win women an equal role in the workplace. While we are far from successful in achieving that goal, certainly we have progressed far from the world of "The Wise Years Wasted" of 1965, when employment was cast as an exclusively male concern.

4. Individuals will need to prepare early for longer working lives

To a large extent, this comes down to individual action. This means developing the expectation both that we will have to work longer in life and that we will have to prepare for it ourselves.

First comes the preservation of the physical self. Diversity in health and capabilities increases as we age; at 65, one can be fit and alert or slow and hobbled. Nobody plans to fall apart at 55 or 60, and health can be as unpredictable as anything else in life. But so much of modern life seems designed to destroy our bodies before their time, from a suicidal preference for heart-clogging fast foods to the design of communities that discourage walking or riding a bicycle in favor of driving. Never before has the quest for comfort led to so much discomfort. The necessity to work until, say, 70, would require us to take better care of ourselves and plan for the long haul.

Our careers will also have to be planned more carefully. The work of Marc Freedman and Ken Dychtwald is useful here. An ideal would be a mid-career sabbatical built into our worklives in the same way, say, maternity leave has been, to give the individual an opportunity to assess the long term. Will I be able to continue doing what I'm doing now until 70? What additional skills or training should I acquire now to extend my worklife? What opportunities do I have to access that training? What can I do now to remake my career for the long run?

That's the ideal. The reality is that it is getting harder and harder to stay relevant in the workplace. Annual performance reviews are switching to quarterly, the reasoning being that the demands of the economy change so rapidly that what was needed in December may have changed by March. So we need to develop our careers for the short term and the long term. We not only need to plan for employability from 60 to 70; we also have to make sure we'll be employable next month or next year.

Retirement planning is key here, as well. The company pension is disappearing and the 401 (k) system has floundered on the twin shoals of insufficient savings and market volatility. No one can seriously plan to subsist in retirement solely on Social Security benefits, which in time will either be postponed until even later in life, reduced, or both. A more realistic vision of what we need to retire will better inform our career decisions. How much longer do I need to work? Career extension management could help us get to the comfortable retirement the postwar American dream has long promised.

In the meantime, life goes on for the older workers and would-be workers in this book. Rita Hall was still at Mature Services as of April 2014 after deciding that, amid her health problems, all she really could handle anymore was part-time work. "Whenever my Heavenly Father wants me to work, he'll find me a job," she said. Julie Cotton worked in 2013 on a potential book about the unraveling of her marriage, but set aside that heavy material the following year to turn to her other activities, including leadership of a "lean-in circle" patterned after Sheryl Sandberg's bestseller *Lean In: Women, Work, and the Will to Lead*. She was feeling hopeful about Sarasota's transformation into a dynamic center for elder culture. "I think it's going to become an even more robust community," she said.

Tim Dutton was on the verge of another adventurous change in his life. When I last talked to him he was a few weeks away from traveling to the Kyrgyz Republic, or Kyrgyzstan, to work for the Peace Corps. The Community Studio was still going strong now that it had non-profit status, and so was his relationship with Alison. Somehow, he hoped, it would all work out. But he was focused on the next chapter in Central Asia. "I'm still working," he said, "so I haven't had a lot of time for studying the language." By the end of April, he'd be gone.

Decline, of course, waits for no one. Those of us lucky enough to live long will know obsolescence by the end. Time will pass us all by. Our sphere of relevance, however wide we imagine it to be in middle and late middle age, will for most of us have narrowed to those we love the most by the end. Perhaps that is all that matters. The struggle described in these pages is to extend our relevance, our places in the world, for a little longer.

For some in this book, signs of decline grew more apparent over the course of my research.

I went back to visit Sun Hydraulics in September 2013. I needed to look more closely at the machine James House worked for a very prosaic reason: I didn't know the names of its parts. Pops's Mill, a 50-year-old confabulation of parts from different machines, was still there. But Pops wasn't. The degenerating discs in his back—an injury he hadn't told me about before—had sidelined him. His step-son, Kevin Fougerousse, 52, who also worked at Sun, said his dad could barely get around on his own.

"He can't even hardly walk," Kevin told me, shaking his head. But the old man still wanted to work. His idea, Kevin said, was that maybe he could come back to Sun, but for a sitting job, of which there were a few around the shop—a job that didn't involve the twisting he did when he reached for aluminum blocks on a tray behind him and tightened them into the vice on the machine in front of him. House was going on 80, but he still had some living left, and keeping a job would help him do it. "He's not ready to give up," Kevin said. "By him working a couple of days a week, that gives him the money to go camping."

Still, places where old people are welcome to keep at it as long as they're able, places like Sun or Yamashita Kogyosho or Vita Needle, are rare. They are quixotic Galapagos-like locations that look quaint, idealistic, or old-fashioned, but actually can tell us our future.

One of the most remarkable islands of the old I've come across in this decade-long journey among aging workers is an actual island, three-mile-long Okikamuro, in the Seto Inland Sea, southwestern Japan. It is perhaps the grayest corner in one of the world's most rapidly aging countries.

The morning clouds had burned off and the sky stretched blue across the sea when we climbed aboard the fishing boat *Sho Un Maru*—*Bright Destiny*—and set out in search of horse mackerel and shrimp. It was June 2010. My wife Kyoko had smartly brought along a black parasol; I was in short sleeves with no sunscreen, working on the fierce sunburn I'd regret for a week.

At the helm was Hirohisa Matsumoto, at 84, Okikamuro's oldest active fisher-man. He was a bit threadbare: I recognized the shirt he wore from the day before, and the day before that, marked by what looked like a coffee stain on his chest. The brim of the straw hat that protected him from the sun was eaten away in one corner.

But his body and mind were in fine shape. I'd been stalking him for a few days, trying to find out when he was going fishing so we could go along with him. During that time, he'd hardly stopped talking. He explained the computerized navigation system on his boat, told me about his fame as the last man in Japan to make his own fish hooks by hand, and chronicled his many years of life. He'd grown up on Okikamuro when it held thousands of residents. Then came World

War II and his two near-misses with death on the mainland in the relentless Allied bombing in the final year of the war.

Matsumoto had a skill found among many older workers: he always landed on his feet. Injured in an accident near the end of the war, he spent a year in a hospital and met a clockmaker who taught him how to repair watches. Back on Okikamuro, now flooded with soldiers returned from the war, he made a living fixing timepieces and just about anything else. "I can do all sorts of things," he liked to say. But eventually digital watches put him out of business, and as he aged he returned to the essential occupation of an islander of the Inland Sea: fishing.

Matsumoto stuck with it longer than anyone else.

As he aged, so did the island. These days, Okikamuro is literally at the end of the road. Visitors must drive from the mainland over one bridge to an island called Suo-Oshima, drive over a small mountain, and then travel over a thin bridge to Okikamuro. From a population of thousands, the island has withered over the years. Young people took off for the cities, and nobody of child-bearing age replaced them. The last school here closed in 1989. It became an island of the old, peopled by long-timers or prodigal sons and daughters who returned after retiring from careers in the cities. By the time we showed up, there were only 150 Okikamurans left. The average age was 67, but that made the place sound younger than it really was: the presence of one 30-something couple with very young children skewed the statistics. The two largest age groups are those in their 70s and 80s. They subsist on government pensions, supplemented by tending vegetable gardens or fishing. Today, the island's most enduring landmark is the sprawling hillside graveyard that overlooks the harbor.

It took some coaxing to get the old man to take us out onto his boat. The first day we met, he mumbled vaguely about going out later in the week, but it wasn't clear whether he would take us with him. Then it rained for several days in a row—Japan's June monsoon season. Finally one morning, the sun peeked out of the clouds. The old man came out of his house and sniffed at the breeze over the harbor. "It's still high tide. It'll take an hour, an hour and a half to let out." He looked up at some low-lying clouds coming over the mountain. "Since it's so clear, I don't suppose it'll get windy. Those clouds are moving pretty slowly." Encouraged by this forecast, I ran to get Kyoko. An hour later, we were boarding the *Bright Destiny*.

On Matsumoto's boat, Rule No. 1 was wordlessly clear: stay out of the way. His frame—wiry and muscled, slightly bent at the upper back—moved methodically and efficiently over the deck, pulling the tie-line off the dock, gripping the rudder with one hand and the throttle with the other. He had the routine down. When we got out to his nets, he hauled them up from the water with no fuss, disgorging their contents—shimp and crabs, some squid—into the watery hold. He'd told me he'd keep fishing as long as his legs could move. The way he pulled those nets up with barely a grunt, it didn't seem like that time would come anytime soon.

"There's no retirement for me," he said. "Not until I die."

Two years later we came back for another visit. Matsumoto was in strapping form. He was immediately familiar when we met him at the bed and breakfast his son runs on the island, launching into an old story—one we'd heard before—about how he'd been injured in the war. There was a break in the conversation, and then the old man started up again. "There was this time I got hurt in the war…" he began. Kyoko and I looked at each other. Was Matsumoto okay? His son, Shouji, shrugged. On Okikamuro, this kind of thing was normal. The old man was still going out on his boat, still living by himself in his 90-year-old house, still making his own fish hooks from piano wire. His son wasn't about to get in his way, no matter how forgetful he became.

"A lot of the children, they tell the old people don't do this and don't do that, or they come and take away their boats," Shouji told us one night. "But not me. If he died out on his boat, he'd be happy, right?" I had to agree. It would be cruel, wouldn't it, to deny anyone that old the chance to spend his last day drifting in silence over the calm tides of the Inland Sea on a boat called the *Bright Destiny*.

When his granddaughter got married a few years ago, Matsumoto sang a song called "Senri no Michi" at her wedding. The title means "The Road of a Thousand Ri," *ri* being a traditional measurement of length in Japan. "It's a song," the old man told me, "about how in a long life, there are sufferings but also fun times as well." But he didn't just show up at the wedding and sing it off the cuff—he practiced at home for a week on his home karaoke system. "The sound," he said, "is tremendous."

I would love to have stood in the alley outside his cluttered, rambling house on Okikamuro, listening to him croak the verses over and over, alone in his upstairs room, until they rang for him just right.

Notes

Introduction

page 1 "The transition so far has been messy": Alfred Lubrano, "Steep Rise Seen in Deep Poverty among Elderly," *Philadelphia Inquirer* (Oct. 11, 2013).

page 2 "That had increased to nearly 810 million": United Nations Population Fund, "Ageing in the Twenty-First Century: A Celebration and a Challenge," Executive Summary (2012), p. 4.

page 2 "Women gained even more, increasing from 61.2 to 73.3": *The Lancet*, "Global Burden of Disease Study 2010" (Dec. 13, 2012). http://www.thelancet.com/themed/global-burden-of-disease (Accessed Oct. 29, 2013).

page 3 "Global fertility has dropped 14 percent": U.S. Department of Commerce, United States Census Bureau, "International Programs." http://www.census.gov/population/international/data/idb/region.php?N=%20Results%20&T=13&A=aggregate&RT=0&Y=2013&R=1&C= (Accessed Oct. 29, 2013).

page 3 "Japan currently is the only country": U.N. Population Fund, *Ageing in the Twenty-First Century*, p. 7.

page 3 "It appears the last thing we want to do": Richard Dobbs, Anu Madgavkar, Dominic Barton, Eric Labaye, James Manyika, Charles Roxburgh, Susan Lund, and Siddarth Madhav, "The World at Work: Jobs, Pay, and Skills for 3.5 Billion People," McKinsey & Co. (June 2012) http://www.mckinsey.com/insights/employment_and_growth/the_world_at_work

page 3 "Social Security is estimated to be flush enough to pay": Stephen C. Goss, *U.S. Social Security Administration Office of Retirement and Disability Report, The Future Financial Status of the Social Security Program*, Social Security Bulletin, vol. 70, no. 3, 2010. http://www.ssa.gov/policy/docs/ssb/v70n3/v70n3p111.html

page 4 "Some have estimated that the single step of raising the minimum retirement age to 70": Congressional Budget Office, *Choices for Deficit Reduction, Congress of the United States* (November 2012). http://www.cbo.gov/sites/default/files/cbofiles/attachments/43692-DeficitReduction_print.pdf

page 4 "By 2005, the proportion of those with traditional pensions": Ilana Boivie, *Issue Brief: Who Killed the Private Sector DB Plan*. National Institute on Retirement Security, March 2011. http://www.nirsonline.org/storage/nirs/documents/Who%20Killed%20DBs/final-_who_killed_the_private_sector_db_plan.pdf

page 4 "The 2012 National Study of Employers": Kenneth Matos and Ellen Galinsky, *2012 National Study of Employers*, Families and Work Institute (2012), p. 36. http://familiesand-work.org/site/research/reports/NSE_2012.pdf

page 4 "Employees preoccupied with paying today's bills": David McHugh, Elaine Kurtenbach, and Paul Wiseman, "AP IMPACT: The World Braces for Retirement Crisis," *Associated Press*, Dec. 29, 2013. http://bigstory.ap.org/article/unprepared-world-braces-retirement-crisis-0

page 4 "By 2012, that percentage had increased": Bureau of Labor Statistics, *Employment Projections*, December 2013. http://www.bls.gov/emp/ep_table_303.htm

Chapter 1

page 21 "In 10 years, annual sales soared to 170 million yen": Masahisa Fujita, "Economic Development Capitalizing on Brand Agriculture: Turning Development Strategy on Its Head," *Institute of Developing Economies*, Discussion Paper No. 76, November 2006. http://ir.ide.go.jp/dspace/bitstream/2344/312/3/ARRIDE_Discussion_No.76_fujita.pdf

Chapter 2

page 26 "Companies now are finding they can hold onto valuable older workers": Alicia H. Munnell and Steven A. Sass, *Working Longer: The Solution to the Retirement Income Challenge.* Brookings Institution Press, Washington, DC, 2008, pp. 121–130. Note: Elsewhere in their book, Munnell and Sass raise some serious reservations about the efficacy of staged retirement, and certainly it doesn't work in every instance. Society will need older Americans to work full-time longer, they argue, and working part-time doesn't help fill that gap. In addition, they say, only certain employees—educated, highly skilled, and working in occupations where part-time shifts make sense—will be able to take advantage of these opportunities, while others will not. I am not offering staged retirement here as a panacea for all that ails the labor market, but as one potential tool in the arsenal that companies have at their disposal in their efforts to encourage workers to delay their exits from the workforce.
page 26 "Young workers face a familiar Catch-22": Peter Cappelli and Bill Novelli, *Managing the Older Worker: How to Prepare for the New Organizational Order*, Harvard Business Review Press, Boston, Massachusetts, 2010, p. 57.
page 26 "Young workers face a familiar Catch-22": Paul Davidson, "Companies Training Cuts Add to Jobless Woes," *USA Today*, August 9, 2012. http://usatoday30.usatoday.com/money/workplace/story/2012-08-09/job-training/56922438/1
page 27 "The health profession gives us perhaps our fullest picture": AARP Best Employers for Workers over 50. http://www.aarp.org/work/employee-benefits/best_employers/
page 34 "The top choice, NIH, funds more than 300,000 researchers": About NIH, National Institutes of Health webpage: http://www.nih.gov/about/
page 35 "And part of that meant putting employees": R.J. Ignelzi, "Ex-cop Enforces Change at Scripps Health," *San Diego Union-Tribune*, July 31, 2011. http://www.utsandiego.com/news/2011/Jul/31/ex-cop-enforces-change-growth-at-scripps-health/2/?#article-copy
page 36 "The company is also doing an above-average job": E-mails with Lisa Ohmstede, Scripps Health public relations manager, September 2013.
page 37 "There are more than 3 million registered nurses": U.S. Department of Health and Human Services Health Resources and Services Administration, *The Registered Nurse Population: Findings from the 2008 National Sample Survey of Registered Nurses*, September 2010.
page 38 "Registered nursing is often listed as a top occupation": The 30 occupations with the largest projected employment growth, 2010–20, Bureau of Labor Statistics, February 1, 2012. http://www.bls.gov/news.release/ecopro.t06.htm
page 41 "Now the looming retirements of the World War II": David W. DeLong, *Lost Knowledge: Confronting the Threat of an Aging Workforce*, Oxford University Press, New York, 2004.
page 42 "In the long term, you cannot compete effectively": Ibid., p. 25.
page 42 "And that giant sucking sound you will hear": Ibid., p. 13.
page 42 "The same for dentists: in 2001": Laurie Harrington and Maria Heidkamp, *The Aging Workforce: Challenges for the Health Care Industry Workforce*, National Technical Assistance and Research Leadership Center (NTAR), March 2013. http://www.dol.gov/odep/pdf/NTAR-AgingWorkforceHealthCare.pdf

page 42 "The needs are spread across the board": Ibid.

page 43 "The report also suggested retaining older workers": Institute of Medicine of the National Academies, *Retooling for an Aging America: Building the Health Care Workforce*, April 11, 2008. http://www.iom.edu/Reports/2008/Retooling-for-an-aging-America-Building-the-Health-Care-Workforce.aspx

page 218 "This is interesting because it suggests": The Sloan Center on Aging and Work at Boston College, *Talent Pressures and the Aging Workforce: Responsive Action Steps for the Health Care & Social Assistance Sector*, June 2010, p. 31.

page 43 "The health care sector will be one of the leading sources": Harrington, p. 8.

Chapter 3

page 52 "The SCSEP, overseen by the Department of Labor": The Obama administration proposed moving SCSEP to the Department of Health and Human Services in its 2013 budget. That transfer had not happened at the time of this writing.

page 52 "The government reports the program gets nearly half its clients": Numbers on SCSEP budget and participation, and percentage of people getting jobs.

page 55 "For several years the sluggish and jerky development": Gunnar Myrdal, *Challenge to Affluence* (Random House, New York, 1963).

page 55 "It is no longer possible, as it once may have been expedient": The U.S. Senate Subcommittee on the Problems of the Aged and Aging, *The Aged and Aging in the United States: A National Problem*, 1960.

page 55 "It's easy to see the reason for the concern": The National Bureau of Economic Research, *Social Security and Elderly Poverty* (2004). http://www.nber.org/bah/summer04/w10466.html (Accessed Jan. 7, 2014).

page 56 "Taken together, they constitute a section": Michael Harrington, *The Other America: Poverty in the United States* (The Macmillan Company, New York, 1962), p. 102.

page 56 "America tends to make its people miserable": Ibid., 102.

page 56 "Those who could not were left to fend": Howard N. Fullerton Jr., "Labor Force Participation: 75 Years of Change, 1950–98 and 1998–2025," *Bureau of Labor Statistics, Monthly Labor News* (December 1999), p. 4. http://www.bls.gov/mlr/1999/12/art1full.pdf

page 57 "Circumstances were ripe for government action": Population by Age and Sex for the United States: 1900 to 2000, Part A. Number, Hobbs, Frank and Nicole Stoops, U.S. Census Bureau, Census 2000 Special Reports, Series CENSR-4, Demographic Trends in the 20th Century, 2002; Projections of the Population by Age and Sex for the United States: 2010 to 2050 (NP2008-T12), Population Division, U.S. Census Bureau; Release Date: August 14, 2008.

page 57 "No economy can reach its maximum productivity": John F. Kennedy, *Special Message to the Congress on the Needs of the Nation's Senior Citizens*, February 21, 1963. http://www.presidency.ucsb.edu/ws/?pid=9572 (Accessed Jan. 7, 2014).

page 58 "They are not shunted aside": United States Senate, "Increasing Employment Opportunities for the Elderly," Hearings before the Subcommittee on Employment and Retirement Incomes of the Special Committee on Aging, U.S. Government Printing Office (Washington, DC 1964). The hearings were held in Washington on December 19, 1963; in Los Angeles on January 10, 1964; and San Francisco on January 13, 1964.

page 58 "The good times kept coming": Larry Ledebur and Jill Taylor, "Restoring Prosperity Case Study, Akron, OH," Metropolitan Policy Program at Brookings (Washington, DC, Sept. 2008), p. 44. http://www.brookings.edu/research/papers/2008/09/17-akron-taylor-ledebur (Accessed Jan. 7, 2014).

page 60 "Akron had become a typical Rust Belt has-been": Brookings.

page 61 "Another common thread between 50 years ago and today": United States Senate, 21.

page 62 "Randolph seemed to recognize": Ibid., 85.

page 64 "Losing the income was one thing": Cheryl Powell, "Doctors to Take over Majority Ownership of Cuyahoga Falls Hospital this Month," *Akron Beacon Journal* (June 12, 2009).

page 65 "A bump in the road": Elise Gould and David Cooper, *Financial Security of Elderly Americans at Risk*. The Economic Policy Institute (June 6, 2013). http://www.epi.org/publication/economic-security-elderly-americans-risk/. (Accessed Jan. 7, 2014).

page 66 "The following year, the government created 100 new Mainstream projects": Dale W. Berry, Nancy Sandusky, Steven van Dresser, *National Evaluation of Operation Mainstream Phase I: The Green Thumb-Green Light Program* (Kirschner Associates, Inc., Albuquerque, New Mexico, January 1971). An early focus of the program was rural. Here, too, the program earned high marks. In 1971, the Albuquerque-based auditing firm Kirschner Associates published an evaluation of Operation Mainstream's first pilot project aimed at older workers, called the "Green Thumb-Green Light" program, which DOL had contracted with the National Farmers Union. The pilot enrolled some 2,300 people in programs in about 180 counties around the country. The program provided work allowing enrollees to use already developed skills, for the most part as farmers, while at the same time serving the needs of the community, particularly the aged, poor, and handicapped. Activities included clearing brush and weeds, planting trees and bushes, building maintenance, and light construction work (p. 9). The program was open to people aged 55 and older, but most participants were 65 or older, more than half of them with farmwork experience. Enrollees worked three days a week, and earnings were meager: up to $1,600 a year (Older Workers: Operation Mainstream Can Help—pamphlet by DOL, 1972). A survey showed that enrollees were high satisfied with their jobs, and communities were satisfied with their work.

One of the guiding principles of the program was that by illustrating the effectiveness of older workers, it would gradually bolster senior employees' image in the business world. Still, even early evaluations show the difficulties the program had as employers still clung to their notion of older workers as inflexible, out-of-date, and liable to quit at any time, and showed no signs of embracing aging employees. Indeed, some of the problems cited 40 years ago still plague the program: limited job opportunities in areas targeted by the program, bias against older workers, and acknowledgement among nearly all participating employers that they would be unable to pay participants without federal funds.

Despite these issues, the study concluded that the programs were at least serving their intended populations, were successfully providing work that enrollees found interesting, and were improving the living standard of participants. As an additional plus, the program was also influencing agencies to provide expanded services to the poor. A concluding study on the entire Operation Mainstream program by Kirschner in December 1971 said the program could be expanded to several times its current size without being significantly reorganized.

At the time, the government was using Operation Mainstream to trumpet its efforts to help the poor elderly. A pamphlet from 1972 says that funds and job opportunities for workers 55 and older were doubled over the previous year "as a result of President Nixon's promise to the White House Conference on Aging." (Older Workers, page 2). "Through Operation Mainstream," the pamphlet says, "older people who once faced a bleak future have founding meaningful work and better lives."

page 67 "Senator Edward Kennedy, a driving force behind these efforts": Congressional Record, Senate, U.S. Government Printing Office (Washington, DC, March 18, 1970), p. 7805.

page 67 "Appropriations grew from $10 million in 1974": *The Senior Community Service Employment Program: Its History and Evolution*. A report by the National Council on the Aging to the Chairman of the Select Committee on Aging, House of Representatives (December 1988).

page 67 "Older Americans are enthusiastic": Ibid., p. III.

page 67 "The rationale was that the organizations": Congress of the United States, Congressional Budget Office, "Reducing the Deficit: Spending and Revenue Options" (March 2011), p. 118.

page 68 "The department has bolstered performance assessment": Code of Federal Regulations, "What Performance Measures/Indicators Apply to SCSEP Grantees?" cited by the Legal Information Institute, Cornell University Law School. http://www.law.cornell.edu/cfr/text/20/641.700 (Accessed Jan. 7, 2014).

Chapter 4

page 81 "In May 2012, the unemployment rate for workers": True, in some ways aging Americans weren't so bad off. Younger workers suffered more unemployment: 7.1 percent for the main body of the labor force, aged 25–54, and 16.1 percent for youth aged 16–25.

page 81 "For older Americans, the search for work": United States Government Accountability Office, Report to the Chairman, Special Committee on Aging, U.S. Senate, *Unemployed Older Workers: Many Experience Challenges Regaining Employment and Face Reduced Retirement Security* (April 2012). http://www.gao.gov/assets/600/590408.pdf (Accessed Jan. 7, 2014).

page 81 "An AARP analysis of April 2014": Carole Fleck, "Unemployment for Older Workers a Little Bit Better," AARP Blog (May 2, 2014). http://blog.aarp.org/2014/05/02/unemployment-for-older-workers-a-little-bit-better/

page 81 "The group started with cold calls": The account of Dziuda's history with Misumi is based on interviews with him and his wife. Misumi HR officials would verify Dziuda's dates of employment, but refused to comment on anything else, including his dismissal, citing company policy.

page 88 "Dossat was 55 at the time": Steve Green, "Las Vegas Man Wins $1.868 Million in Employment Age, Retaliation Suit," *Las Vegas Sun* (March 18, 2012).

page 88 "More than half the unemployed respondents": Colette Thayer, "Protecting Older Workers against Discrimination Act (POWADA) Public Opinion Report," *AARP* (May 2012). The telephone survey was conducted for AARP by GS Strategy Group with a random sample of older registered voters.

page 96 "And when older industries decline": Robert D. Atkinson, Luke A. Stewart, Scott M. Andes, and Stephen Ezell, *Worse than the Great Depression: What the Experts Are Missing about American Manufacturing Decline*, The Information Technology & Innovation Foundation (March 19, 2012).

page 96 "Or they feel lucky to score a part-time $13-an-hour job": The National Employment Law Project, *The Low-Wage Recovery and Growing Inequality* (August 2012).

page 97 "An Urban Institute study in 2012": Richard W. Johnson and Barbara Butrica, *Age Disparities in Unemployment and Reemployment during the Great Recession and Recovery*, Urban Institute (May 15, 2012). http://www.urban.org/retirement_policy/url.cfm?ID=412574 (Accessed Jan. 7, 2014).

page 100 "These numbers make sense when one considers": AARP survey, p. 50.

Chapter 5

page 105 "Unemployment for that age group in 2013": Arbetsförmedlingen, Statistics Sweden. Handed out during interview.

page 106 "Union membership in the United States": Bureau of Labor Statistics, United States Department of Labor, Union Members Summary (Jan. 23, 2013).

page 109 "According to statistics compiled by Ola Bergström": Andreas Diedrich and Ola Berström, *The Job Security Councils in Sweden*. School of Business, Economics, and Law, Gothenburg University and Institute of Management of Innovation and Technology (Oct. 5, 2006).

page 111 "So Swedes in their 60s": Arbetsförmedlingen, Statistics Sweden.

page 111 "Average life expectancy in Sweden is 82": Organisation for Economic Cooperation and Development, OECD Better Life Index, http://www.oecdbetterlifeindex.org/countries/united-states/ (Accessed Jan. 7, 2014).

page 112 "This report called for, among other things": Retirement Commission, *Measures for Working Longer* (English Summary), Swedish Ministry of Health and Social Affairs (April 9, 2013). Sweden has tinkered with its 100-year-old pension system before. In the 1990s, in reaction to its worst economic crisis in the postwar period, the government divided the system into three tiers. The state-funded "guarantee pension" is the base that provides a minimum income to workers with lower earnings. On top of that is the "income pension," which is financed by a 16 percent payroll tax, firmly tying a worker's benefits to pre-retirement income. In essence, the more you made on the job, the better your pension. The third, most innovative piece is called a "premium pension." For this pension, a 2.5 percent payroll tax goes into a fund that operates much like a 401 (k), but is supervised by a government agency. Investors are free to choose from a wide variety of funds.

page 114 "Reinfeldt argued that 50-somethings": Mats Öhlén, "Prime Minister Fredrik Reinfeldt Opens Up for Retirement Age at 75," *Stockholm News*, February 7, 2012. http://www.stockholmnews.com/more.aspx?NID=8385 (Accessed Jan. 7, 2014).

page 116 "That's still not bad comparatively": OECD, "An Overview of Growing Income Inequalities in OECD Countries: Main Findings" (2011). http://www.oecd.org/els/soc/49499779.pdf (Accessed Jan. 7, 2014).

page 116 "The potential to develop work": Juhani Ilmarinen, *An Essay on Longer Working Life*. Retirement Commission, Swedish Ministry Health and Social Affairs (2013), p. 10. "If the solution is to change working people to help them better fit into the global economy, it is the wrong and the slow way; it will take a long time before the aging process has changed to follow the track of the money-driven working life. The better and more sustainable solution would be to have working life be better adapted to the human aging process. The nature of work must move with much longer strides towards people, rather than the other way around. The potential to develop work to become more age-friendly or age-adapted is much greater than the potential to change the aging process. It should also be observed that working life is designed by people; those in charge of designing work, so that every generation can be productive, need a new competence to do so. This competence is called 'age management.'" http://www.sou.gov.se/content/1/c6/21/38/65/3654af6c.pdf (Accessed Jan. 7, 2014).

page 118 "The results: productivity on the line increased 7 percent": Isabelle De Pommereau, "How BMW Reinvents the Factory for Older Workers," *Christian Science Monitor*, September 2, 2012. http://www.csmonitor.com/World/Europe/2012/0902/How-BMW-reinvents-the-factory-for-older-workers (Accessed Jan. 7, 2014).

Also: Michael Millar, "How Old Age Technology Could Help Stop a Demographic Time Bomb," BBC News, February 25, 2013. http://www.bbc.co.uk/news/business-21535772?print=true (Accessed Jan. 7, 2014).

page 118 "A study by researchers": Reidar J. Mykletun and Trude Furunes, "The Ageing Workforce Management Programme in Vattenfall AB Nordic, Sweden." *Older Workers in a Sustainable Society*, Ed. Richard Ennals and Robert H. Salomon, Frankfurt am Main: Peter Lang, 2011: 93–105.

Chapter 6

page 125 "Around the world, bullet train nose cones": For a detailed description of the use of composites in nose cone design in the early 2000s, read Karen Mason, "Composites Aboard High-Speed Trains," *Composites World*, December 2004. http://www.compositesworld.com/articles/composites-aboard-high-speed-trains

page 126 "They hammer bullet train nose cones": For labor force participation rates in Japan, see Ministry of Internal Affairs and Communications, Statistics Bureau. International comparisons abound, including U.S. Bureau of Labor Statistics, Charting International Labor Comparisons, September 2012, which shows Japan with a higher rate for 65 and older than other Group of Eight advanced economies. Please note countries with high poverty rates or a lack of universal pension systems, such as the Philippines or Brazil, have higher rates. South Korea, whose government reported the rate was 28.9 percent in 2011, is one outlier that deserves special mention, though its economy is 20 percent the size of Japan's. Also, labor force participation rates for those age 65 and older will be less and less useful statistically, as countries start amassing greater populations of 80- and 90-year-olds far beyond the reach of the labor market. Perhaps comparing the 65 to75 age group is growing more meaningful.

page 127 "Seen on a graph": National Institute of Population and Social Security Research, *Population Projections for Japan (January 2012): 2011 to 2060*, offers a detailed forecast, including high-fertility and low-fertility scenarios. http://www.ipss.go.jp/site-ad/index_english/esuikei/ppfj2012.pdf

page 127 "The face of Japan": Much of the English-language coverage of Japan's demographic challenge is unmittingly grim, for some good reasons. One more balanced account is John W. Traphagan's "Japan's Demographic Disaster," *The Diplomat*, February 3, 2012. http://the-diplomat.com/2013/02/japans-demographic-disaster/

page 128 "In 2005, the country's total population": I covered this for the Associated Press in a story about the Irodori cooperative detailed in Chapter 1: "Japan Faces Aging, Declining Population," *Associated Press*, July 1, 2006. http://www.washingtonpost.com/wp-dyn/content/article/2006/07/01/AR2006070100420_pf.html

page 128 "By one estimate by the government": Joseph Coleman, "As Birth Rate Plummets, Japan Awaits Era of the Setting Son," *Associated Press*, August 23, 1998. http://articles.latimes.com/1998/aug/23/news/mn-15697

page 128 "In 2008, a group of lawmakers": Joseph Coleman, "As Population Declines, Japan Considers Importing Foreign Workers—Then Thinks Again," *Associated Press*, January 20, 2007. http://legacy.utsandiego.com/news/world/20070120-1022-japan-importingforeigners.html

page 130 "The workload seemed a bit overwhelming": JEED has information in English on its website: Japan Organization for Employment of the Elderly, Persons with Disabilities and Job Seekers, Support for Promoting Employment of the Elderly. http://www.jeed.or.jp/english/support_for_emp_eld.html

page 132 "Chimneys and industrial blocks rose up": Hikari has a monument marking the location of the Hikari Base. http://www.kamikazeimages.net/monuments/hikari/index.htm

page 134 "My father made the face of that train": For a useful summary of the history of the bullet train in Japan, see Japanese Bullet Trains—40 Years at the Forefront at Railway-Technology. com. http://www.railway-technology.com/features/feature1216/

page 135 "Kiyoto was proof enough": For a summary of the award, see: http://www.monodzu-kuri.meti.go.jp/english/introduction.html

Chapter 7

page 156 "A 2011 European Commission report": European Commission, *The 2012 Ageing Report: Economic and Budgetary Projections for the 27 EU Member States (2010–2060)*, Directorate-General for Economic and Financial Affairs of the European Commission, European Union, 2012. http://ec.europa.eu/economy_finance/publications/european_economy/2012/pdf/ee-2012-2_en.pdf (Accessed Jan. 8, 2014).

page 157 "So instead of enjoying the benefits": As explained elsewhere, younger people impose costs as well: they need to be housed and educated. Yet this is seen as an investment in a future of productivity. Caring for the elderly, aside from the demands of human decency, is largely a payback for past productivity.

page 157 "Still, the EC report took a stab at it": European Commission, p. 25.

page 157 "Perhaps pointing to the massive resources": Ibid., p. 26.

page 158 "So this powerful tool has become": For further discussion of this, see Jonathan Gruber and David A. Wise, "Social Security Programs and Retirement around the World: Micro Estimation," NBER Working Papers 9407, National Bureau of Economic Research, 2002.

page 159 "In the United Kingdom, the retirement age is rising": Cobbled together from several sources: European Commission; CESifo Group Munich, "Pension Reforms: 67—or Higher—Is Becoming the New 65," *CESifo DICE Report*, April 2012; Ariana Eunjung Cha, "Europe Looks to Pension Reforms to Ease Economic Crisis," *Washington Post*, July 10,

2012; Towers Watson, "Italy: Major Social Security Pension Reform Introduces Austerity Measures—August 2012," Towers Watson, Aug. 13, 2012.

page 160 "The movement was particularly strong": For details, see Bernhard Ebbinghaus, *Reforming Early Retirement in Europe, Japan and the USA* (New York: Oxford University Press, 2006).

page 160 "In France, participation rates for both sexes": For pre-1981 figures, see Constance Sorrentino, "International Comparisons of Labor Force Participation,1960–81," Monthly Labor Review, Bureau of Labor Statistics, February 1983, http://stat.bls.gov/opub/mlr/1983/02/art3full.pdf (Accessed Jan. 8, 2014); for later dates, see OECD's statistical database, OECD.StatExtracts, http://stats.oecd.org/Index.aspx?DatasetCode=LFS_SEXAGE_I_R# (Accessed Jan. 8, 2014).

page 160 "Other major European countries": In Germany, that number dropped from nearly 52 percent to bottom out at 42.9 percent in 2000. Italy was at 45.6 percent for both sexes in the early 1960s and at 73.5 percent for men. By 1999, only 29 percent of workers that age were in the labor force, though men were higher at 43.3 percent participation. Average retirement ages dropped across the board, according to the OECD. The French retired on average at 67.7 in 1970; that had dropped to 58.4 by 2006. In the UK, retirement age dropped from 67.7 in 1970 to a low of 61.7 in 1998. The Dutch dropped out of the workforce at 66.6 years old in 1970; by 1990, that was down to 59.7.

page 160 "On the contrary, we observe a negative link": Adain Jousten, Mathieu Lefèbvre, Sergio Perelman, and Pierre Pestieau, IMF Working Paper, "The Effects of Early Retirement on Youth Unemployment: The Case of Belgium." International Monetary Fund (2008).

page 160 "An exhaustive search": Alicia H. Munnell, and April Yanyuan Wu, "Are Aging Baby Boomers Squeezing Young Workers Out of Jobs?" Center for Retirement Research at Boston College, October 2012, p. 5.

page 161 "Two researchers at Maastricht University": Didier Fouarge and Trudie Schils, "The Effect of Early Retirement Incentives on the Training Participation of Older Workers," LABOUR 23 (Special Issue): 85–109. Fondazione Giacomo Brodolini and Blackwell Publishing Ltd. (2009).

page 162 "Yet the French have more or less": OECD, "Statistics on Average Effective Age and Official Age of Retirement in OECD Countries. OECD, 2012.

page 163 "As Guillemard and researcher Dominique Argoud": Anne-Marie Guillemard, and Dominique Argoud, "France: A Country with a Deep Early Exit Culture," in *Aging and the Transition to Retirement, a Comparative Analysis of European Welfare States*, ed. Tony Maltby, Bert de Vroom, Maria-Luisa Mirabile, and Einer Overbye, Aldershot, UK: Ashgate, pp. 165–85. The writers point out the protections the French state put in place for laid-off workers in their 50s actually encouraged employers to fire older staffers guilt-free, knowing there was a generous safety net waiting for them.

page 163 "When Prime Minister Jean-Marc Ayrault suggested": France 24, Une petite phrase d'Ayrault relance le débat sur les 35 heures, France 24, October. 30, 2012. http://www.france24.com/fr/20121030-france-couac-ayrault-35-heures-premier-ministre-temps-de-travail-gouvernement-cope-parisot (Accessed Jan. 8, 2014).

page 164 "One estimate forecast": William Tompson, "France: The 2003 Pension Reform," in *The Political Economy of Reform: Lessons from Pensions, Product Markets and Labour Markets in Ten OECD Countries*. Paris: OECD Publishing (2009), p. 8.

page 164 "Wider action was politically treacherous": In addition to Tompson, see Annie Jolivet, *Employment and Labour Market Policies for an Ageing Workforce and Initiatives at the Workplace: National Overview Report: France*. Dublin: European Foundation for the Improvement of Living and Working Conditions, 2007, p. 5.

page 165 "In a successful bid to win": Tompson.

page 165 "Unemployment for older workers": OECD, "OECD Thematic Follow-up Review of Policies to Improve Labour Market Prospects for Older Workers, France." OECD, 2012.

page 168 "While there is some action at select larger companies": Even the larger companies are letting their initiatives lie fallow. A few years ago, Gendron published her work on Cedilac, a milk sterilization factory and subsidiary of leading French dairy producer Sodiaal, maker of Yoplait yogurt. Gendron found about half of the factory's 200 employees were 45 or older, and management had implemented a successful program of transferring knowledge from older workers to younger ones by building a database of best practices. Yet when I contacted the company in 2012, officials said the program had stalled with the departure of a key human resources official.

page 169 "People aged 65 or older": Nathalie Blanpain and Olivier Chardon, "Projections de population à l'horizon 2060," Paris: National Institute of Statistics and Economic Studies, October 2010. http://www.insee.fr/fr/themes/document.asp?ref_id=ip1320

page 169 "While it's easy—and perhaps satisfying": I rented an apartment in the 15th arrondissement in June 2012 from a restauranteur who was preparing to sell his eatery. When I asked what he was going to do, he just shrugged and said, "The long vacation."

page 169 "In May 2013, the business paper *Les Echos*": Agence France-Presse, "Retraites: 63% des Français veulent une réforme en profondeur," *Les Échos*, May 2, 2013. http://www.lesechos.fr/02/05/2013/lesechos.fr/0202743102032_retraites---63---des-francais-veulent-une-reforme---en-profondeur--.htm (Accessed Jan. 8, 2014).

page 169 "On the high end of the market": Experconnect, with headquarters just blocks from the Champs Élysses in the capital's tony 8th arrondissement, caters to companies in energy, rail, defense, aviation, and other industries on the lookout for highly educated and trained workers. The agency advertises its seniors as uninterested in promotion, office politics, or high pay—telegraphing to potential clients that this could be a way to get some high-level performers at a discount and at minimum hassle.

Chapter 8

page 178 "As I'm renovating parts of this house": Julie Cotton, Julie Cotton's Blog, *Sarasota Patch*, January 6, 2013. http://sarasota.patch.com/groups/julie-cottons-blog/p/bp--a-new-toilet. Other blogs by Julie: http://wisewomennow.com/2013/09/14/as-the-seasons-turn-a-celebration-of-september/ and http://wisewomennow.com/2014/03/27/up-and-boom/#more-5046

page 179 "And, as AARP economist Sara Rix": Sara Rix, "Boomers—Will They Shun Retirement?" *Huffington Post*, June 20, 2013. http://www.huffingtonpost.com/sara-rix/retirement-work-longer_b_3442301.html

page 180 "Motivations were also different": Douglas T. Hall, *Careers in Organizations*, Dallas: Scott Foresman & Co., 1976.

page 180 "The protean concept also promises": Douglas T. Hall, et al., *The Career Is Dead – Long Live the Career: A Relational Approach to Careers*, San Francisco: Jossey-Bass Publishers, 1996.

page 180 "The interest in community service": Marc Freedman, *The Big Shift: Navigating the New Stage Beyond Midlife*, New York: Public Affairs, 2011; *Prime Time: How Baby Boomers Will Revolutionize Retirement and Transform America*, New York: Public Affairs, 2002.

page 181 "The movement of millions of these individuals": Marc Freedman, *Encore: Finding Work That Matters in the Second Half of Life*, New York: Public Affairs, p. 9.

page 182 "He's a common presence on the lecture": Nicholas Barchaver, "Pitchman for the Gray Revolution," *Fortune*, July 11, 2005. http://money.cnn.com/magazines/fortune/fortune_archive/2005/07/11/8265244/ (Accessed Jan. 7, 2014).

page 182 "But what people would really like": Age Wave, "Ken Dychtwald at American Society on Aging 2013," *YouTube*, April 8, 2013. http://www.youtube.com/watch?v=bEDW8hSuJio (Accessed Jan. 8, 2014).

page 183 "Our findings . . . suggest": Nicole Maestas, "Cohort Differences in Retirement Expectations and Realizations," in *Redefining Retirement: How Will Boomers Fare?* Ed. Brigitte Madrian, Olivia S. Mitchell, and Beth J. Soldo, Oxford: Oxford University Press, 2007, pp. 13–35.

page 183 "These baby boomers": The National Center for Education Statistics, *120 Years of American Education: A Statistical Portrait*, U.S. Department of Education, 1993, p. 66.

page 184 "A MetLife survey of baby boomers": GfK Custom Research North America, *Transitioning into Retirement: The MetLife Study of Baby Boomers at 65*, MetLife Mature Market Institute, April 2012. The same survey found respondents on average said they'd have to be 79 years old to be considered "old." https://www.metlife.com/assets/cao/mmi/publications/studies/2012/studies/mmi-transitioning-retirement.pdf (Accessed Jan. 8, 2014).

page 184 "Despite their longer life expectancy": Dana E. King, Eric Matheson, Svetlana Chirina, Anoop Shankar, Jordan Broman-Fulks, "The Status of Baby Boomers' Health in the United States: The Healthiest Generation?" American Medical Association, published online, February 4, 2013. http://trends.psc.isr.umich.edu/pdf/pubs/baby-boomer-health-united-states-2013.pdf (Accessed Jan. 8, 2014).

page 185 "Household income isn't so shabby either": These figures come from Census Reporter, a Knight News Challenge-funded project. Statistics are U.S. Census data. Census Reporter has a margin of error of 10 percent. http://censusreporter.org/profiles/16000US1264175/ (Accessed Jan. 8, 2014).

page 186 "Nearly all the retirement-age people": Volunteer Match is one such website. http://www.volunteermatch.org/search/index.jsp?r=msa&l=34295 (Accessed Jan. 8, 2014).

page 188 "Julie Cotton, for instance, channelled her frustrations": Link to Julie Cotton's white paper: http://www.suncoastjobs.com/workplace_gold.pdf (Accessed Jan. 8, 2014).

page 188 "Sustained focus and commitment": Ibid., p. 11.

page 189 "Unemployment in Sarasota County": Sarasota County Planning Services, "Sarasota County: How Are We Employed?" 2012. https://www.scgov.net/PlanningServices/Demographic%20Profiles/How%20are%20we%20employed.pdf (Accessed Jan. 8, 2014).

page 190 "The original idea grew out": Barbara Peters-Smith, "Sarasota Institute on Aging Gets $25,000 Gift," *Herald-Tribune*, July 26, 2011. http://www.heraldtribune.com/article/20110726/article/110729672#gsc.tab=0 (Accessed Jan. 8, 2014).

page 190 "Three years later, the project was enshrined": Scriggs & Associates, LLC, and IronWolf Community Resources and RTI International, "Sarasota County Five Year Economic Development Strategic Plan: A Roadmap to a Robust and Agile Economy, Sarasota County," April 2009. http://static.edcsarasotacounty.com/docs/user/executivesummary.pdf (Accessed Jan. 8, 2014).

page 190 "Still, Dutton and other backers prevailed": Barbara, Peters-Smith, "Esselman to lead Sarasota Institute for the Ages," *Herald-Tribune*, April 26, 2012. http://www.heraldtribune.com/article/20120426/ARTICLE/120429652?p=1&tc=pg (Accessed Jan. 8, 2014).

page 190 "The model can also help": Nancy K. Schlossberg, "Transitions: Theory and Application." Paper presented to IAEVG-NCDA Symposium, June 2004.

page 193 "Then came a stream of trade self-help books": Schlossberg, *Retire Smart, Retire Happy: Finding Your True Path in Life*, Washington: American Psychological Association, September 1, 2003; *Overwhelmed: Coping with Life's Ups and Downs*, Lexington Books, 1999; and *Revitalizing Retirement: Reshaping Your Identity, Relationships, and Purpose*, Washington: American Psychological Association, January 1, 2009.

page 194 "She writes blogs": Schlossberg, *Transitions through Life: How to Survive According to Nancy K. Schlossberg* blog: http://www.transitionsthroughlife.com/ (Accessed Jan. 8, 2014).

page 195 "The company's founder, Bob Koski": Louis B. Barnes and Colleen Kaftan, *Sun Hydraulics Corp (A)*, Harvard Business School, April 17, 1985. A follow-up was published in 1991, and the company still hears from researchers at Harvard periodically.

page 200 "For our daughters": David Beard, "Famous Haiti Hospital Clings to Life," *Associated Press*, August 28, 1994.

Epilogue

page 206 "No American community": Department of Labor, *The Wise Years Wasted, 1965*, National Archives and Records Administration, 1965.

page 207 "Caitrin Lynch, an anthropologist": Caitrin Lynch , *Retirement on the Line: Age, Work, and Value in an American Factory*, Ithaca, NY: Cornell University Press (2012).

page 207 "Vita Needle has received all the attention": "Manufacturer Vita Needle Finds Investment in Older Workers Turns a Big Profit," *PBS Newshour*, Jan. 2, 2013.

page 210 "As economist Paul Krugman asks": Paul Krugman, "Expanding Social Security," *New York Times*, Nov. 21, 2013. http://www.nytimes.com/2013/11/22/opinion/ krugman-expanding-social-security.html (Accessed Jan. 7, 2014).

page 210 "In 2012, labor market expert Maria Heidkamp": Maria Heidkamp, "Older Workers, Rising Skill Requirements, and the Need for a Re-envisioning of the Public Workforce System," Council for Adult and Experiential Learning (CAEL), 2012. Heidkamp, of the John J. Heldrich Center for Workforce Development at Rutgers University, called for "new legisla-tion that establishes a more flexible, more robust lifelong learning, education, and training delivery system in alignment with the country's postsecondary education institutions and local/regional economic development efforts" (p. 12). http://www.cael.org/pdfs/TMT_ Reenvision_Public_Workforce_System (Accessed Jan. 9, 2014).

page 212 "The trend peaked at the height": U.S. Equal Employment Opportunity Commission, Charge Statistics FY 1997 through FY 2012. http://eeoc.gov/eeoc/statistics/enforce-ment/charges.cfm (Accessed Jan. 9, 2014).

page 214 "It is perhaps the grayest corner": I visited Okikamuro in June 2010 and June 2012.

Bibliography

AARP Best Employers for Workers over 50. http://www.aarp.org/work/employee benefits/best_employers/

Action for Older Americans, 1964 Annual Report of the President's Council on Aging. N.p., 1965.

Agence France-Presse, "Retraites: 63% des Français veulent une réforme en profondeur," *Les Echos*, May 2, 2013. http://www.lesechos.fr/02/05/2013/lesechos.fr/0202743102032_retraites---63---des-francais-veulent-une-reforme---en-profondeur--.htm (Accessed Jan. 8, 2014).

Age Wave, Ken Dychtwald at American Society on Aging 2013. *YouTube*, April 8, 2013. http://www.youtube.com/watch?v=bEDW8hSuJio (Accessed Jan. 8, 2014).

Atkinson, Robert D., and Luke A. Stewart, Scott M. Andes, and Stephen Ezell, *Worse than the Great Depression: What the Experts Are Missing about American Manufacturing Decline*. The Information Technology & Innovation Foundation (March 19, 2012).

Barchaver, Nicholas, "Pitchman for the Gray Revolution," *Fortune*, July 11, 2005. http://money.cnn.com/magazines/fortune/fortune_archive/2005/07/11/8265244/ (Accessed Jan. 7, 2014).

Barnes, Louis B., Colleen Kaftan, *Sun Hydraulics Corp (A)*, Harvard Business School, April 17, 1985. A follow-up was published in 1991, and the company still hears from researchers at Harvard periodically.

Beard, David, "Famous Haiti Hospital Clings to Life," *The Associated Press*, August 28, 1994.

Berry, Dale W., and Nancy Sandusky, Steven van Dresser, *National Evaluation of Operation Mainstream Phase I: The Green Thumb-Green Light Program*. Kirschner Associates, Inc. (Albuquerque, New Mexico, January 1971).

Blanpain, Nathalie, and Olivier Chardon, "Projections de population à l'horizon 2060," Paris: National Institute of Statistics and Economic Studies, October 2010. http://www.insee.fr/fr/themes/document.asp?ref_id=ip1320

Boivie, Ilana, *Issue Brief: Who Killed the Private Sector DB Plan*. National Institute on Retirement Security, March 2011. http://www.nirsonline.org/storage/nirs/documents/Who%20Killed%20DBs/final-_who_killed_the_private_sector_db_plan.pdf

Bureau of Labor Statistics, *Employment Projections*. December 2013. http://www.bls.gov/emp/ep_table_303.htm

Bureau of Labor Statistics, United States Department of Labor, Union Members Summary (Jan. 23, 2013).

Cappelli, Peter, and Bill Novelli, *Managing the Older Worker: How to Prepare for the New Organizational Order*. Boston: Harvard Business Review Press, 2010, p. 57.

Cha, Ariana Eunjung, "Europe Looks to Pension Reforms to Ease Economic Crisis," *Washington Post*, July 10, 2012.

Chiva, Anthony, and Jill Manthorpe, *Older Workers in Europe*. Maidenhead: Open UP, 2009.

Clark, Robert L., and Olivia S. Mitchell, *Reinventing the Retirement Paradigm*. Oxford: Oxford University Press, 2005.

Code of Federal Regulations, "What Performance Measures/Indicators Apply to SCSEP Grantees?" Cited by the Legal Information Institute, Cornell University Law School. http://www.law.cornell.edu/cfr/text/20/641.700

Coleman, Joseph, "As Birth Rate Plummets, Japan Awaits Era of the Setting Son," *Associated Press*, August 23, 1998. http://articles.latimes.com/1998/aug/23/news/mn-15697

Coleman, Joseph, "Japan Faces Aging, Declining Population," *Associated Press*, July 1, 2006. http://www.washingtonpost.com/wp-dyn/content/article/2006/07/01/AR2006070100420_pf.html

Coleman, Joseph, "As Population Declines, Japan Considers Importing Foreign Workers— Then Thinks Again," *Associated Press*, Jan. 20, 2007. http://legacy.utsandiego.com/news/world/20070120-1022-japan-importingforeigners.html

Congress of the United States Congressional Budget Office, "Reducing the Deficit: Spending and Revenue Options" (March 2011, p. 118).

Congress of the United States Congressional Budget Office, *Choices for Deficit Reduction, Congress of the United States* (November 2012). http://www.cbo.gov/sites/default/files/cbofiles/attachments/43692-DeficitReduction_print.pdf

Congressional Record, Senate, U.S. Government Printing Office (Washington, DC, March 18, 1970), p. 7805.

Cotton, Julie, Julie Cotton's Blog, *Sarasota Patch*, January 6, 2013. http://sarasota.patch.com/groups/julie-cottons-blog/p/bp--a-new-toilet

Cotton, Julie P., Sandra K. Kassalow, and Jane A. Paquette, "Mining Silver for Workplace Gold: Sarasota County's Experienced Workers Add Value During Tough Times," published online: http://www.suncoastjobs.com/workplace_gold.pdf (Accessed Jan. 8, 2014).

Coulmas, Florian, *The Demographic Challenge: A Handbook about Japan*. Leiden: Brill, 2008.

Coulmas, Florian, *Population Decline and Ageing in Japan: The Social Consequences*. London: Routledge, 2007.

Davidson, Paul, "Companies Training Cuts Add to Jobless Woes," *USA Today*, August 9, 2012. http://usatoday30.usatoday.com/money/workplace/story/2012-08-09/jobtraining/56922438/1

DeLong, David W., *Lost Knowledge: Confronting the Threat of an Aging Workforce*. New York: Oxford University Press, 2004.

Department of Labor, *The Wise Years Wasted, 1965*, National Archives and Records Administration, 1965.

De Pommereau, Isabelle, "How BMW Reinvents the Factory for Older Workers," *Christian Science Monitor*, September 2, 2012. http://www.csmonitor.com/World/Europe/2012/0902/How-BMW-reinvents-the-factory-for-older-workers/%28page%29/2

Diedrich, Andreas, and Ola Berström, *The Job Security Councils in Sweden*. School of Business, Economics, and Law, Gothenburg University and Institute of Management of Innovation and Technology (Oct. 5, 2006).

Dobbs, Richard, and Anu Madgavkar, Dominic Barton, Eric Labaye, James Manyika, Charles Roxburgh, Susan Lund, and Siddarth Madhav, *The World at Work: Jobs, Pay, and Skills for 3.5 Billion People*, McKinsey & Co. (June 2012) http://www.mckinsey.com/insights/employment_and_growth/the_world_at_work

Ebbinghaus, Bernhard, *Reforming Early Retirement in Europe, Japan and the USA*. New York: Oxford University Press, 2006.

European Commission, *The 2012 Ageing Report: Economic and Budgetary Projections for the 27 EU Member States (2010–2060)*, Directorate-General for Economic and Financial Affairs of the European Commission, European Union, 2012. http://ec.europa.eu/economy_finance/publications/european_economy/2012/pdf/ee-2012-2_en.pdf (Accessed Jan. 8, 2014).

European Commission; CESifo Group Munich, "Pension Reforms: 67—or Higher—Is Becoming the New 65," *CESifo DICE Report*, April 2012.

Fishman, Ted C., *Shock of Gray: The Aging of the World's Population and How It Pits Young against Old, Child against Parent, Worker against Boss, Company against Rival, and Nation against Nation*. New York: Scribner, 2010.

Fouarge, Didier, and Trudie Schils, "The Effect of Early Retirement Incentives on the Training Participation of Older Workers," *LABOUR* 23 (Special Issue), 85–109, Fondazione Giacomo Brodolini and Blackwell Publishing Ltd. (2009).

Freedman, Marc, *The Big Shift: Navigating the New Stage Beyond Midlife*. New York: Public Affairs, 2011.

Freedman, Marc, *Encore: Finding Work That Matters in the Second Half of Life*. New York: Public Affairs, 2008, p. 9.

Freedman, Marc, *Prime Time: How Baby Boomers Will Revolutionize Retirement and Transform America*. New York: Public Affairs, 2002.

Fujita, Masahisa, "Economic Development Capitalizing on Brand Agriculture: Turning Development Strategy on Its Head," *Institute of Developing Economies*, Discussion Paper No. 76, November 2006.

http://www.ide.go.jp/English/Publish/Download/Dp/076.html

Fullerton, Howard N., Jr., "Labor Force Participation: 75 Years of Change, 1950–98 and 1998–2025," Bureau of Labor Statistics, *Monthly Labor News* (December 1999), p. 4. http://www.bls.gov/mlr/1999/12/art1full.pdf

GfK Custom Research North America, *Transitioning into Retirement: The MetLife Study of Baby Boomers at 65*. MetLife Mature Market Institute.

Goss, Stephen C., U.S. Social Security Administration Office of Retirement and Disability Report, "The Future Financial Status of the Social Security Program," *Social Security Bulletin*, Vol. 70, No. 3, 2010. http://www.ssa.gov/policy/docs/ssb/v70n3/v70n3p111.html

Gould. Elise, and David Cooper, *Financial Security of Elderly Americans at Risk*. The Economic Policy Institute (June 6, 2013). http://www.epi.org/publication/economic-security-elderly-americans-risk/ (Accessed Jan. 7, 2014).

Green, Steve, "Las Vegas Man Wins $1.868 Million in Employment Age, Retaliation Suit," *Las Vegas Sun*, March 18, 2012.

Gruber, Jonathan, and David A. Wise, "Social Security Programs and Retirement Around the World: Micro Estimation," NBER working paper 9407, National Bureau of Economic Research, Inc., 2002.

Guillemard, Anne Marie, *Aging and the Welfare-state Crisis*. Newark: University of Delaware, 2000.

Guillemard, Anne-Marie, *Les Défis du Vieillissement: Age, Emploi, Retraite, Perspectives Internationales*. Paris: Armand Colin, 2010.

Guillemard, Anne-Marie, and Dominique Argoud, "France: A Country with a Deep Early Exit Culture," in *Aging and the Transition to Retirement, a Comparative Analysis of European Welfare States*, Ed. Tony Maltby, Bert de Vroom, Maria-Luisa Mirabile, and Einer Overbye. Aldershot, UK: Ashgate, pp. 165–85.

Hall, Douglas T., *Careers in Organizations*. Dallas: Scott Foresman & Co., 1976.

Hall, Douglas T., et al., *The Career is Dead—Long Live the Career: A Relational Approach to Careers*. San Francisco: Jossey-Bass Publishers, 1996.

Harrington, Michael, *The Other America: Poverty in the United States*. New York: The Macmillan Company, 1962, p. 102.

Harrington, Laurie, and Maria Heidkamp, *The Aging Workforce: Challenges for the Health Care Industry Workforce*. National Technical Assistance and Research Leadership Center (NTAR), March 2013. http://www.heldrich.rutgers.edu/sites/default/files/content/NTAR_Issue_Brief_Aging_Workforce_Health_Care_Final.pdf

Heidkamp, Maria, "Older Workers, Rising Skill Requirements, and the Need for a Re-envisioning of the Public Workforce System," Council for Adult and Experiential Learning (CAEL), 2012. http://www.cael.org/pdfs/TMT_Reenvision_Public_Workforce_System (Accessed Jan. 9, 2014).

Ignelzi, R.J., "Ex-cop Enforces Change at Scripps Health," *San Diego Union-Tribune*, July 31, 2011. http://www.utsandiego.com/news/2011/Jul/31/ex-cop-enforces-change-growth-at-scripps-health/2/?#article-copy

Ilmarinen, Juhani, "An Essay on Longer Working Life," Retirement Commission, Swedish Ministry Health and Social Affairs (2013), p. 10 (Accessed Jan. 7, 2014).

Institute of Medicine of the National Academies, *Retooling for an Aging America: Building the Health Care Workforce*, April 11, 2008. http://www.iom.edu/Reports/2008/Retooling-for-an-aging-America-Building-the-Health-Care-Workforce.aspx

Japan Organization for Employment of the Elderly, Persons with Disabilities and Job Seekers, "Support for Promoting Employment of the Elderly." http://www.jeed.or.jp/english/support_for_emp_eld.html

Jepsen, Maria, David Foden, and Martin Hutsebaut, *Active Strategies for Older Workers in the European Union*. Brussels: European Trade Union Institute, 2002.

Johnson, Richard W., and Barbara Butrica, *Age Disparities in Unemployment and Reemployment During the Great Recession and Recovery*. Urban Institute (May 15, 2012) http://www.urban.org/retirement_policy/url.cfm?ID=412574 (Accessed Jan. 7, 2014).

Jolivet, Annie, *Employment and Labour Market Policies for an Ageing Workforce and Initiatives at the Workplace: National Overview Report: France*. Dublin: European Foundation for the Improvement of Living and Working Conditions, 2007, p. 5.

Jousten, Adain, and Mathieu Lefèbvre, Sergio Perelman, and Pierre Pestieau, IMF Working Paper, *The Effects of Early Retirement on Youth Unemployment: The Case of Belgium*. International Monetary Fund, 2008.

Kennedy, John F., *Special Message to the Congress on the Needs of the Nation's Senior Citizens*, February 21, 1963. http://www.presidency.ucsb.edu/ws/?pid=9572 (Accessed Jan. 7, 2014).

King, Dana E., Eric Matheson, Svetlana Chirina, Anoop Shankar, Jordan Broman-Fulks, "The Status of Baby Boomers' Health in the United States: The Healthiest Generation?" American Medical Association, published online, February 4, 2013. http://trends.psc.isr.umich.edu/pdf/pubs/baby-boomer-health-united-states-2013.pdf (Accessed Jan. 8, 2014).

Krugman, Paul, "Expanding Social Security," *New York Times*, November 21, 2013. http://www.nytimes.com/2013/11/22/opinion/krugman-expanding-social-security.html?module=Search&mabReward=relbias%3Ar

The Lancet, "Global Burden of Disease Study 2010" (Dec. 13, 2012). http://www.thelancet.com/themed/global-burden-of-disease (Accessed Oct. 29, 2013).

Ledebur, Larry, and Jill Taylor, "Restoring Prosperity Case Study, Akron, OH," Metropolitan Policy Program at Brookings (Washington, DC, Sept. 2008), p. 44. http://www.brookings.edu/research/papers/2008/09/17-akron-taylor-ledebur (Accessed Jan. 7, 2014)

Le Parisien, La petite phrase d'Ayrault relance la polémique, Le Parisien, October 30, 2012. http://www.leparisien.fr/politique/35-heures-la-petite-phrase-d-ayrault-relance-la-polemique-30-10-2012-2278117.php (Accessed June 15, 2014).

Lubrano, Alfred, "Steep Rise Seen in Deep Poverty among Elderly," *Philadelphia Inquirer* (Oct. 11, 2013).

Lynch, Caitrin, *Retirement on the Line: Age, Work, and Value in an American Factory*. Ithaca, NY: Cornell University Press, 2012.

Madrian, Brigitte, Olivia S. Mitchell, and Beth J. Soldo, *Redefining Retirement: How Will Boomers Fare?* Oxford: Oxford University Press, 2007.

Maestas, Nicole, "Cohort Differences in Retirement Expectations and Realizations," in *Redefining Retirement: How Will Boomers Fare?* Ed. Brigitte Madrian, Olivia S. Mitchell, and Beth J. Soldo, Oxford: Oxford University Press, 2007, pp. 13–35.

Maltby, Tony, Bert de Vroom, Maria-Luisa Mirabile, and Einer Overbye, *Ageing and the Transition to Retirement: A Comparative Analysis of European Welfare States*. Aldershot, UK: Ashgate, 2004.

Mason, Karen, "Composites Aboard High-Speed Trains," *Composites World*, December 2004. http://www.compositesworld.com/articles/composites-aboard-high-speed-trains.

Matos, Kenneth, and Ellen Galinsky, *2012 National Study of Employers*. Families and Work Institute, 2012, p. 36. http://familiesandwork.org/site/research/reports/NSE_2012.pdf

McHugh, David, Elaine Kurtenbach, and Paul Wiseman, "AP IMPACT: The World Braces for Retirement Crisis," *Associated Press*, December 29, 2013. http://bigstory.ap.org/article/unprepared-world-braces-retirement-crisis-0

Millar, Michael, "How Old Age Technology Could Help Stop a Demographic Time Bomb," *BBC News*, February 25, 2013. http://www.bbc.co.uk/news/business-21535772?print=true (Accessed Jan. 7, 2014)

Munnell, Alicia H., and April Yanyuan Wu, "Are Aging Baby Boomers Squeezing Young Workers Out of Jobs?" *Center for Retirement Research at Boston College*, October 2012, p. 5.

Munnell, Alicia H., and Steven A. Sass, *Working Longer: The Solution to the Retirement Income Challenge*. Washington, DC: Brookings Institution Press, 2008, pp. 121–130.

Myrdal, Gunnar, *Challenge to Affluence*. New York: Random House, 1963.

Mykletun, Reidar J., and Trude Furunes, "The Ageing Workforce Management Programme in Vattenfall AB Nordic, Sweden." *Older Workers in a Sustainable Society*, Ed. Richard Ennals and Robert H. Salomon, Frankfurt am Main: Peter Lang, 2011, pp. 93–105.

The National Bureau of Economic Research, *Social Security and Elderly Poverty*. (2004). http://www.nber.org/bah/summer04/w10466.html (Accessed Jan. 7, 2014).

The National Center for Education Statistics, *120 Years of American Education: A Statistical Portrait*. U.S. Department of Education, 1993, p. 66.

National Council on the Aging, *The Senior Community Service Employment Program: Its History and Evolution*. Report to the Chairman of the Select Committee on Aging, House of Representatives (December 1988).

The National Employment Law Project, *The Low-Wage Recovery and Growing Inequality*. August 2012.

National Institute of Population and Social Security Research, *Population Projections for Japan (January 2012): 2011 to 2060*. http://www.ipss.go.jp/site-ad/index_english/esuikei/ppfj2012.pdf

Öhlén, Mats, "Prime Minister Fredrik Reinfeldt Opens Up for Retirement Age at 75," *Stockholm News*, February 7, 2012. http://www.stockholmnews.com/more.aspx?NID=8385 (Accessed Jan. 7, 2014).

Organisation for Economic Co-operation and Development, OECD Better Life Index, http://www.oecdbetterlifeindex.org/countries/united-states/ (Accessed Jan. 7, 2014).

OECD, "An Overview of Growing Income Inequalities in OECD Countries: Main Findings." (2011). http://www.oecd.org/els/soc/49499779.pdf (Accessed Jan. 7, 2014).

OECD, "Statistics on Average Effective Age and Official Age of Retirement in OECD Countries." OECD, 2012.

OECD, "OECD Thematic Follow-up Review of Policies to Improve Labour Market Prospects for Older Workers, France." OECD, 2012.

PBS, "Manufacturer Vita Needle Finds Investment in Older Workers Turns a Big Profit," *PBS Newshour*, January 2, 2013.

Peters-Smith, Barbara, "Esselman to Lead Sarasota Institute for the Ages," *Herald Tribune*, April 26, 2012. http://www.heraldtribune.com/article/20120426/ARTICLE/120429652?p=1&tc=pg (Accessed Jan. 8, 2014).

Peters-Smith, Barbara, "Sarasota Institute on Aging Gets $25,000 Gift," *Herald Tribune*, July 26, 2011. http://www.heraldtribune.com/article/20110726/article/110729672#gsc.ab=0 (Accessed Jan. 8, 2014).

Powell, Cheryl, "Doctors to Take over Majority Ownership of Cuyahoga Falls Hospital This Month," *Akron Beacon Journal* (June 12, 2009).

Reaser, Joel M., William J. Rothwell, Diane Spokus, and Harvey L. Sterns, *Working Longer: New Strategies for Managing, Training, and Retaining Older Employees*. New York: AMACOM, 2008.

Retirement Commission, *Measures for Working Longer* (English Summary), Swedish Ministry Health and Social Affairs (April 9, 2013).

Rix, Sara, "Boomers—Will They Shun Retirement?" *Huffington Post*, June 20, 2013. http://www.huffingtonpost.com/sara-rix/retirement-work-longer_b_3442301.html

Roszak, Theodore, *The Making of an Elder Culture: Reflections on the Future of America's Most Audacious Generation*. Gabriola, BC: New Society, 2009.

Sarasota County Planning Services, "Sarasota County: How Are We Employed?" 2012. https://www.scgov.net/PlanningServices/Demographic%20Profiles/How20are%20we%20employed.pdf (Accessed Jan. 8, 2014).

Schlossberg, Nancy K., *Overwhelmed: Coping with Life's Ups and Downs*. Lanham, MD: Lexington Books, 1999.

Schlossberg, Nancy K., *Retire Smart, Retire Happy: Finding Your True Path in Life*. Washington, DC: American Psychological Association, September 1, 2003.

Schlossberg, Nancy K., *Revitalizing Retirement: Reshaping Your Identity, Relationships, and Purpose*. Washington, DC: American Psychological Association, January 1, 2009.

Schlossberg, Nancy K., "Transitions: Theory and Application." Paper presented to IAEVG NCDA Symposium in June 2004.

Schlossberg, Nancy K., *Transitions Through Life: How to Survive According to Nancy K. Schlossberg*. http://www.transitionsthroughlife.com/ (Accessed Jan. 8, 2014).

Schulz, James H., *The Economics of Aging*. Westport, CT: Auburn House, 2001.

Schulz, James H., and Robert H. Binstock, *Aging Nation: The Economics and Politics of Growing Older in America*. Westport, CT: Praeger, 2006.

Scriggs & Associates, LLC, and IronWolf Community Resources and RTI International, "Sarasota County Five Year Economic Development Strategic Plan: A Roadmap to a Robust and Agile Economy," Sarasota County, April 2009. http://static.edcsarasotacounty.com/docs/user/executivesummary.pdf (Accessed Jan. 8, 2014).

Sennett, Richard, *The Craftsman*. New Haven, CT: Yale University Press, 2008.

Sennett, Richard, *The Culture of the New Capitalism/Richard Sennett*. New Haven, CT: Yale University Press, 2006.

The Sloan Center on Aging and Work at Boston College, *Talent Pressures and the Aging Workforce: Responsive Action Steps for the Health Care & Social Assistance Sector* (June 2010, p. 31).

Sorrentino, Constance, "International Comparisons of Labor Force Participation, 1960–81," Monthly Labor Review, Bureau of Labor Statistics, February 1983, http://www.bls.gov/opub/mlr/1983/02/art3full.pdf

Terkel, Louis. *Working: People Talk about What They Do All Day and How They Feel about What They Do*. New York: Pantheon, 1974.

Thayer, Colette, "Protecting Older Workers against Discrimination Act (POWADA) Public Opinion Report," *AARP* (May 2012). The telephone survey was conducted for AARP by GS Strategy Group with a random sample of older registered voters.

Tompson, William, "France: The 2003 Pension Reform," in *The Political Economy of Reform: Lessons from Pensions, Product Markets and Labour Markets in Ten OECD Countries*. Paris: OECD Publishing, 2009, p. 8.

Towers Watson, "Italy: Major Social Security Pension Reform Introduces Austerity Measures—August 2012," Towers Watson, August 13, 2012.

Traphagan, John W., "Japan's Demographic Disaster," *The Diplomat*, February 3, 2012. http://thediplomat.com/2013/02/japans-demographic-disaster/

United Nations Population Fund, *Ageing in the Twenty-First Century: A Celebration and a Challenge, Executive Summary*, 2012, p. 4.

U.S. Department of Commerce, United States Census Bureau, "International Programs," http://www.census.gov/population/international/data/idb/region.php?N=%20Reslts%20&T=13&A=aggregate&RT=0&Y=2013&R=1&C= (Accessed Oct. 29, 2013).

U.S. Department of Health and Human Services, Health Resources and Services Administration, *The Registered Nurse Population: Findings from the 2008 National Sample Survey of Registered Nurses*, September 2010.

U.S. Equal Employment Opportunity Commission, "Charge Statistics FY 1997 Through FY 2012." http://eeoc.gov/eeoc/statistics/enforcement/charges.cfm (Accessed Jan. 9, 2014).

United States Government Accountability Office, *Unemployed Older Workers: Many Experience Challenges Regaining Employment and Face Reduced Retirement Security.* Report to the Chairman, Special Committee on Aging, U.S. Senate (April 2012). http://www.gao.gov/assets/600/590408.pdf (Accessed Jan. 7, 2014).

United States Senate, "Increasing Employment Opportunities for the Elderly, Hearings before the Subcommittee on Employment and Retirement Incomes of the Special Committee on Aging," U.S. Government Printing Office (Washington, DC, 1964). The hearings were held in Washington on December 19, 1963; Los Angeles on January 10, 1964; and San Francisco on January 13, 1964.

United States Senate Subcommittee on the Problems of the Aged and Aging, *The Aged and Aging in the United States: A National Problem*, 1960.

Index

Note: Page numbers in italics denote illustrations and figures.